Production
and Creativity
in Advertising

Pirelli's *Double Indemnity* TV commercial (created by Gerry Moira and John Aldred; Director: Marek Kanietska)

# Production and Creativity in Advertising

Robin B Evans

Pitman

**Pitman Publishing**
128 Long Acre London WC2E 9AN

© Robin B Evans 1988

First published in Great Britain 1988

**British Library Cataloguing in Publication Data**
Evans, Robin B.
　Production and creativity in advertising.
　1. Advertising
　I. Title
　659.1　　HF5821

ISBN 0-273-02728-X

All rights reserved; no part of this publication may be reproduced, stored in a retrieval system, or transmitted in any form or by any means, electronic, mechanical, photocopying, recording, or otherwise without either the prior written permission of the publishers or a licence permitting restricted copying in the United Kingdom issued by the Copyright Licensing Agency Ltd, 33–34 Alfred Place, London, WC1E 7DP. This book may not be lent, resold, hired out or otherwise disposed of by way of trade in any form of binding or cover other than that in which it is published, without the prior consent of the publishers.

Text set in eleven on fourteen point Sabon to a measure of 26 picas and printed on 90 gsm matt-coated cartridge. Cover printed on 240 gsm board and bound unsewn flush.

Typeset by Wyvern Typesetting Ltd, Bristol.
Printed and bound in Great Britain at the Bath Press, Avon.

# Contents

*Foreword* xi
*Preface* xiii
*Acknowledgements* xv

**Part one · Understanding Advertising**

1 The nature of advertising   1
   1.0  Pinning advertising down   1
       *Definition difficulties*
   1.1  Advertising expenditure   3
       *Where the money goes; how much is available*
   1.2  Advertising and sales   4
       *The objectives of advertising; its relationship with sales; why blamed for poor sales*
   1.3  Advertising and creativity   8
       *The ambivalence of the client; the meaning of creativity; advertising and art; creative awards*

2 Advertising theory   12
   2.0  What advertising must do   12
       *Critical review of models*
   2.1  Rosser Reeves and the USP   14
       *The classic USP formula explained*
   2.2  Critical comments   16
       *The circularity of Reeves' theory*
   2.3  Ogilvy and the brand image   18
       *Overview of Ogilvy's position*

2.4 Brand images and USPs compared   20
*How they mean the same thing*
2.5 Brand names   21
*The grammar of names; how naming fixes the product identity*

3 **The anatomy of persuasion**   24
3.0 Persuasive communication   24
*The myth of the distinction between informative and persuasive advertising*
3.1 Effective message approaches   26
*Self-persuasion; distraction; incompleteness; use of cognitive dissonance; inoculation; candour*
3.2 The role of the communicator   34
*How perception of the sender affects persuasiveness; use and abuse of endorsements; implicit endorsement by stereotypes*
3.3 The recipient   37
*The problem of effectively communicating to a mass*
3.4 The role of the medium   38
*How media affect persuasiveness; differences between TV and print; the 'hidden persuader' bogey; the creative potential and limitations of radio, cinema and posters*

**Part two · Creating and Producing a TV Commercial**

4 **The form of television and the TV ad**   45
4.0 The medium of television: creative characteristics   45
*Review of the main advantages and disadvantages*
4.1 Creative grammar: approaches, techniques and forms   48
*Attention-grabbing devices; the 'slice-of-life'; the announcer/presenter; pastiches and parodies of TV programmes and film genres; anachronism; testimonials; animals; music and song; 'table top'; vignettes*

5 **Prescribing the commercial**   59
5.0 The TV commercial – from idea to the screen: review of steps   59

5.1  Briefing and strategy  59
*Components of the creative strategy*
5.2  The script and storyboard  61
5.3  Script layout and technical terms  66
*The language of shots; main camera movement descriptions; transitions between shots and scenes; terms used*

6  **Pre-production and development**  75
6.0  The birth of the commercial: client approval  75
6.1  ITCA script clearance  77
*Vetting of commercials at the script/storyboard stage; evidence to support factual claims; use of substitute materials; approval of double head and final 35 mm print*
6.2  Pre-production: contracting the production company  78
*Basis on which the agency producer asks the production company to estimate; open and closed briefs; problems and practicalities*
6.3  Major factors affecting the budget  81
*Studio or location; art department; casting; music; shooting ratio; number of scenes/shots; opticals; special technical equipment; night shooting; animation; special effects*
6.4  The budget  87
*Production company estimates; items excluded; mark-ups; pros and cons of 'firm bids' and 'cost-plus-fixed-fee'*
6.5  Pre-production  90
*Issues for discussion and agreement; the role of the casting director; equity regulations; the reason for use fees and how they are structured*

7  **Understanding film and tape**  96
7.0  The grammar of film  96
*The illusion of motion; frame rates; speeded-up and slow motion; film formats: 35 mm and TV commercials; film stocks: reversal and negative; sensitivity to light; aspect ratio; how sound is recorded*

7.1 The grammar of video   106
*How a picture is displayed on TV; frame rates; colour TV; picture definition; the video camera; broadcast TV systems; how video recording works; tape formats and gauges; uses*

7.2 Comparisons of video and film   115
*Telecine transfer. Advantages and disadvantages of film and tape*

**8  Production**   120
  8.0  Live action   120
  8.1  Animation   123
  *Cartoons; computer animation and paintbox effects*

**9  Post-production**   128
  9.0  Film editing   128
  *The role of the editor; sequence of steps in editing: the raw material; viewing the rushes; the assembly; the rough cut; the fine cut; dubbing; master negative cut; colour grading and correcting; opticals; answer print; pre-transmission clearance; release prints; tape transfer*
  9.1  Videotape editing   137
  *Use of time code; off-line editing; generation loss*
  *Supers and special effects*
  *The wonders of Mirage*

## Part three · Into Print

**10  Creativity in print advertising**   143
  10.0  The creative teamwork   143
  10.1  Copywriting   144
  *Broad analogies; headlines and techniques for writing; subheads and body copy*
  10.2  Art direction   152
  *Roughs; photography*
  10.3  Appraisal of press ads   153
  *Salignac; the Parker Lady*

**11  The type world**   157
  11.0  Typography   157
  *Are there too many typefaces?*

11.1 The grammar of typography  158
*Classification of typefaces; anatomy of type; factors affecting legibility; reasons why legibility isn't sacrosanct*

11.2 Typesetting  170
*Hot metal; cold setting; photo-composition; electronic composition; headline setting; proofing*

12 **Printing processes**  175

12.0 Letterpress  175
*Principles and uses*

12.1 Lithography  178
*Principles and uses*

12.2 Gravure  181
*Principles and uses*

12.3 Screen printing  184
*Principles, advantages, disadvantages and uses*

13 **Reproducing pictures**  186

13.0 Halftones  186

13.1 Colour reproduction  191
*Principles of colour separation by film and electronic means*

13.2 Proofing  194
*Progressives; machine and dry proofs*

13.3 Colour correction  196
*Ways of achieving*

13.4 Machine press production: common faults  196
*Main causes of defective print*

*References and notes*  198
*Glossary*  206
*Bibliography*  215
*Index*  217

# Foreword

A man who is nothing but – goes an old Spanish proverb – is not even. The copywriter who is only a copywriter is not even a copywriter. Ditto the production executive, the producer, researcher.

Advertising is essentially a creative trade. At the heart is the business of getting an idea. Ideas are tenuous, fragile things. They begin often as half-thoughts. A few words, a scribble. They take shape. The birth may be painful but the immediate post-natal period can be hell.

If it's original how do you begin to judge it? If nobody's done it before how do you know it will work?

And what do we mean by 'work'? Work on the page. Work on the box.

*Can it be produced?*

Production is not some subsequent menial necessity but part of the total creative process.

Only by understanding what can be produced, only by understanding the disciplines, the possibilities and – probably most important of all – the constraints, can the creative person create productively.

By the same token, only by understanding what the creative person is trying to do – and what the ad is trying to do – can the production person produce creatively.

Advertising needs specialist skills. What it does not need are specialist mentalities. One of the major strengths of CAM is its broad spread of disciplines and its teaching of their relationship.

Robin Evans' book is a suitable textbook for CAM students because he understands these principles. Production, both print and television, are not only thoroughly explained but put into context.

The author quite rightly begins by helping the reader understand advertising. Indeed advertising itself is put into context. Advertising, despite all the showbiz glitz and ceremonies, after all is only a means to an end.

The scope of this book is comprehensive. Robin Evans is equally at home with repeat fees and advertising theories, high-band and low-band, squeegees and hot metal. The useful glossary will give you an indication of the ground he covers. The examples are many and mostly recent.

When disciplines seem to become more and more specialist it is refreshing to find a book which explains not only what happens but how it happens and why.

For the newcomer, for those who have forgotten all they ever knew, for the creative person who takes his or her job seriously . . . and, above all, for the CAM student, this book fills a gap in the market.

It certainly fills several gaps in my own knowledge.

*David Bernstein*
Chairman, The Creative Business

# Preface

This book has been written to explain the procedures and processes involved in making television commercials and print advertisements and to de-mystify the technical language and grammar used.

It is not a 'how to' practical manual of production.

While written primarily for students following professional advertising and marketing courses such as the CAM Certificate in Communication Studies and the Institute of Marketing's Certificate and Diploma, the book will be of value to students at art schools and to students taking mass communications and related courses at polytechnics and universities. In addition *Production and Creativity in Advertising* should be of use and interest to advertising, marketing and PR trainees as well as to people involved in the commercial communications industries and professions who, though not directly concerned with production and production-speak, would nevertheless benefit from familiarity with both.

As production costs – particularly of commercials – are wont to increase all the time, actual figures/prices have for the most part been left out.

The production of advertisements doesn't take place in a vacuum of technical considerations, of course. Like the proverbial tip of the iceberg, the end-product that is broadcast on TV or appears as a full-page in a magazine is the result of a great deal of marketing/advertising planning and creative stonewalling, sweat and ingenuity. This fact, coupled with the consideration that some of the intended readership is likely to be not wholly familiar with the nature and practice of advertising, has prompted the inclusion of, and provided the rationale for, Part One. This introductory section rehearses what advertising does and, in so doing, examines synoptically its relationship with marketing/sales, the role of creativity, the media and the key techniques of persuasion.

The core of the book, Part Two, covers the creation, origination and production of TV commercials.

Part Three deals with the creation, mechanics and technicalities of realizing print advertising.

September 1987                                              *Robin B Evans*

# Acknowledgements

The author is grateful to the following companies/bodies/people for their kind permission to reproduce the ads and other material in this book:

pp. 30, 64–65 Dr J B Evans; p. 31 Ogilvy & Mather; pp. 88–89 AFVPA, IPA & ISBA; p. 94 IPA; p. 147 Doyle Dane Bernbach and Volkswagen (UK) Ltd; pp. 159, 191 Esselte Letraset Ltd; pp. 162–168 The Monotype Corporation (excerpts from *The Monotype Letters*, origination and design: William Morgan FSIAD Assoc. IOP); p. 169 TBWA; p. 188 Paul Pinnock and David Fitzgerald & Co (for originating and producing screen work); pp. 189–190 Derek Williams and Schafline Ltd; frontispiece: Pirelli Ltd, McCormick-Publicis and Ridley Scott Associates; Plate 1 pp. 52–53: Pirelli Ltd and McCormick-Publicis; Plate 2 p. 125: Quantel; Plate 3 pp. 150–151: WCRS and BMW; Plate 4 p. 154: Hiram Walker International Ltd and Kirkwoods; Plate 5 p. 156: Collett, Dickenson Pearce & Partners Ltd.

The author is indebted to Danny Lawrence, Patrick Lau and Tony D'Annunzio for their technical advice on TV/video; to publishers Simon Lake and Eric Dalton for their patience and understanding when deadlines were continually elasticated; to editor David Carpenter for his painstaking care in 'sorting out' the manuscript. And, finally and everlastingly, to Brenda Cavendish and Dr J B and Stella Evans for their constant support and encouragement.

# Part one · Understanding advertising

# 1 · The nature of advertising

## 1.0 Pinning advertising down

Saint Augustine was once asked what time was. The good saint wryly replied: 'When I don't ask myself, I *know*'.

Few, if any, of us would disagree. And the difficulty of saying precisely what 'time' is is not unlike the difficulty of saying what advertising is. Just as 'time' is, obviously, to do with clocks, watches and the movement of planetary bodies and so on, so advertising, we all of us know, is about thirty-second commercials on television for Guinness; posters for the Social Democratic Party; radio commercials for DHL courier services, magazine ads for shampoos and newspaper ads for life insurance; cinema commercials for Gordon's Gin, for Levi's jeans. These are examples of the visible, high-profile part of advertising; the advertising that daily bombards, pesters or seduces us, with varying degrees of success or failure, to take notice of this or that product, to react or feel in this or that way.

We know, too, that advertising (a) is not undertaken by managements of marketing just for fun or to keep media owners solvent but to achieve prosperity in sales for the company's products or services; (b) has something to do with creativity and art yet is not 'art' in the core sense in which a painting by Rubens or an opera by Wagner is; (c) is principally involved in persuasion or advocacy even when apparently just giving us information; (d) typically uses mass communications channels and thus 'talks to' a mass audience, say, one million housewives or one hundred thousand business men; (e) uses media that are paid for, the identity of the advertiser being clear.

So far so good. But attempts to define advertising invariably end up by being too narrow or too wide. Usually too narrow. A definition that included all the elements (a) to (e) above looks very promising but is, alas, not entirely satisfactory: it rules out a number of very important activities that clearly can be referred to as 'advertising' if only in part. For example: a salesman – working door-to-door or visiting prospective industrial customers or whatever – is certainly advertising the products of the company he represents. Yet he is not talking to a mass audience; often he's just talking to an individual. His sales pitch may be wholly devoid of creativity or originality. The medium, the speech and body-language of the salesman, is paid for in a sense but it is a distinctly different one from paying for air time on TV or for spaces in newspapers.

A pack functions on one level as an advertisement. It informs us what the product is about, by description, by depiction or, in the case of transparent glass or plastic packaging materials, simply shows us the product. It proclaims the brand's image or personality. It functions on the supermarket shelf as 'the silent salesman'. Yet it doesn't use a paid-for mass medium like double-page spreads or thirty-second spots.

Again, Public Relations informs and advocates but, ethically and conceptually, is not 'free' advertising. Though if a motoring correspondent reviews a new car in a newspaper and says favourable or unfavourable things about the vehicle, he is, in effect, advertising the product.

Sales promotion activities, '10p off' flashed on the side of a pack of Persil, 'free glasses' displayed on posters in a garage forecourt – these surely constitute advertising. As do brochures for holiday companies and the gamut of sales literature, leaflets, catalogues, exhibitions. Indeed, all these activities are referred to generally as 'below-the-line' advertising. The division between 'above-the-line' and 'below-the-line' advertising is principally a practical, working one. Where the advertising agency receives commission from the media owner or contractor, normally fifteen per cent of the expenditure, the advertising is said to be 'above-the-line'; where the media involved don't pay commission, for leaflets or brochures, say, the advertising is described as 'below-the-line'.

The extended but nevertheless legitimate uses of 'advertising' are many and various. Though it would be convenient for the business of defining advertising to say that many of these uses are non-standard 'metaphorical' even. Convenient, yes; truthful in usage terms, no. Norman Mailer titles one of his books, *Advertisement for Myself*. We know what he means; it's Mailer selling Mailer with lots of pugnacious rhetoric! A person may be said to be advertising his life-style through the clothes he wears, the car he drives, the paper he reads, the drinks he drinks. A punk advertises his/her attitudes to society through clothing and hair style messages. And so on. However, most people would agree that these senses of 'advertising' along with the examples of advertising through packaging, PR and salesmen are really cousins at varying distances from 'above-the-line' and 'below-the-line' advertising.

The philosopher Ludwig Wittgenstein, despite being celebrated for obscurity and 'difficulty', came up with a wonderfully simple solution to the problem of pin-pointing the essence of something, i.e., saying what its common and peculiar properties are. There are, he says, no essences; rather there exist just a 'complicated network of similarities, overlapping and criss-crossing'[1]* like the resemblances that exist in a family. A brother shares some features with his sister, his sister shares some of those features with her cousins, and so on. But no member of the family has all the features of all the other members.

Using the analogy of 'family resemblances' the problem of defining advertising is dissolved. It's just a big, sprawling family. But we know what's in its genes.

The genes are deftly captured by J Walter Thompson chairman Jeremy Bulmore's definition: 'Advertising is any paid-for communication intended to inform and/or influence one or more people'. And by that of David Bernstein: 'Advertising is the origination and/or communication of ideas about products in order to motivate consumers towards purchase'.[2][3]

## 1.1 Advertising expenditure

According to figures published by The Advertising Association the money spent on 'above-the-line' advertising totalled around £3.8 billion in 1984, and climbed to £4.4 billion in 1985, around £1,376 million going into TV and around £2,801 into press. The 1985 TV expenditure breaks down into £1,190 million being

---

*For this and subsequent references, see References and Notes pp. 198–205.

spent on air time and £190 million paying for the production of commercials.

How much advertising money is potentially available is the source of considerable controversy. Some optimists within the industry argue – and very convincingly too – that advertising revenue will increase almost as a matter of course if the media available increase. One of the major arguments underlying the debate in the early part of 1986 on whether the BBC should accept advertising focused on whether there was sufficient advertising money both to 'bail out' the financially ailing BBC and also to maintain ITV company revenue. Or whether the overall increase in air time would result in a competitive reduction of rate cards, the TV advertising cake being cut smaller and smaller, leading to a lowering of quality in the programming put out by both the BBC and the ITV companies.

The concern about the limit of advertising pounds to spread around on broadcast TV becomes yet more urgent with the imminence of Direct Broadcasting by Satellite (DBS). On the other hand, the threat once posed to production values and programming quality by advertising revenues being siphoned into Cable TV in the UK would appear to have passed. With a mere 200,000 subscribers, give or take a few thousand, the cable medium would seem, despite all the hooha and bullishness surrounding its inception, to be a pretty big damp squib. But that's the price to be paid for: (a) one of the highest penetrations of video cassette recorders per household in the world, and (b) quality and excellence in broadcast TV programming.

## 1.2 Advertising and sales

Why do companies advertise? The stock reply is: to increase sales. This is the ideology behind the slogan: 'To sell you've got to tell'. Doubtless at the slogan level this sort of approach is harmless enough. And true enough too. To the extent that slogans, like clichés, contain useful and powerful truths, albeit blunted by wear. However, the relationship between advertising and sales needs to be unpacked with considerable caution.

One of the difficulties of talking about advertising is that it doesn't denote just one particular sort of activity. Rather it is a pluralistic enterprise; it means many things; and it is undertaken in order to achieve a wide variety of ends. These ends or objectives may at one extreme be highly remote from the point at which a purchase is made or purchase decision taken; at the other extreme the objectives may be very close to the point of sale.

Certainly we can say that the general aim or focus of advertising is to provide a positive help to sales. But the success of the advertising has to be measured in terms of whether it meets or falls short of (and if so by how much) the precise tasks it has been set to perform. So what can advertising do? The most common objectives of advertising are to:

(a) Provoke or motivate a prospect to find out more about a product or service, e.g., to phone for a brochure on *Winter Holidays in Austria*; to send off for literature on a car or photocopying machine.

(b) Create awareness. Of where to buy a product. Of what a product can do. Of the major benefits a product will bring to the user/buyer.

(c) Remind and reassure. That the brand is still the same, will deliver the same benefits. That the brand is a trustworthy and reliable servant.

(d) Induce preparedness to try. Here, very often, the content of the advertising is a particular sales promotion activity, e.g., an introductory offer – 25p off Rasputin vodka; 'Win a holiday in the Bahamas with Bacardi Rum'.

(e) Educate or convey information. Like details of a new share or stock offer in the *Financial Times*. Or like explaining to housewives the versatility of cheese or eggs.

(f) Project a new brand image; sustain a brand image; modify an existing brand image, e.g., that Kelloggs' cornflakes are the 'sunshine breakfast'; that Smirnoff vodka is an exciting, trendy and sophisticated drink.

(g) Project a corporate image. Of the Midland Bank as the 'listening' bank. Of Sony: where 'research makes the difference'. Of Bayer: whose products – from the discovery of Aspirin in 1899 to the most recent advances in crop protection – and know-how improve the quality of life.

(h) Bring about an immediate sale. Also known as 'selling off the page' and 'direct response advertising'. Like a full page in a Sunday colour supplement: headline '3-wave-band digital alarm clock radio only £10.95' with the bottom corner of the advertisement containing a coupon, the means to actually make the purchase.

Summarizing, we can say this: save in the special circumstances of (h) above, *advertising cannot in and of itself cause sales*. It can only help or contribute towards sales success. That this is so should be obvious if we look at advertising in the context of marketing.

The sales of a product are determined by the mix of marketing variables: the product, the price, the package, the public relations, the merchandising, the sales force, the distribution. No element in the mix taken in isolation, can be a unique determinant of sales. This is as true of packaging as it is of advertising. Rather, all the elements must pull together in combination (and in the right sequence). To borrow Bernstein's[2] highly apt analogy, a single mix element is like a thread. Alone it is pretty weak. But when intertwined with all the other threads it contributes to the force and strength of a rope. Threads cannot cause sales. Ropes can!

Conversely, if one thread suffers from weak spots or breaks or is poorly intertwined with other threads, the whole rope of sales will sag or fray or snap. The advertising can be flawless – right timing, right media, right copy and illustrations – but the sales turn out to be disappointing because, say, there is inadequate display of the product in-store or there is a bottleneck in physical distribution or even, worst of all, the product is one that people simply do not want.

Of course it may be that the entire deployment of the mix complex by marketing management is right but still the eventual sales are woefully below the target set because of unforeseen (and sometimes unforeseeable) and uncontrollable outside factors. Such factors often include: activity of competitors, changes of weather/climate, government legislation and controls (e.g., a credit squeeze will severely dent the sales of consumer durables such as motor cars and washing machines which are largely bought on hire-purchase).

When the sales performance of a product is buoyant, all the marketing variables tend to be democratically praised. However, when the sales figures are bad, there is a tendency to blame the advertising rather than, say, the effort of the sales force or the formulation and packaging of the product. Moreover, when the sales are positively disastrous, the agency responsible for the advertising campaign in question may even be fired. Why should this be so? Why should the relationship between advertising and sales be apparently understood in such a way that 'advertising causes sales' is invariably invoked when sales are poor?

One reason is that advertising, despite the best endeavours of all parties involved in its role – from planning it, budgeting for it, creating and executing it and so on – is not a perfectly understood activity. Indeed some people, experts and self-pronounced experts included, have gone as far as conceding, if not declaring, that no one knows how advertising works![4] (Though this declaration is probably partly a rhetorical one.) Put differently, we can say that advertising by its very nature is not a one hundred per cent science; what it does and how it does it always contains an ineliminably subjective – and thus unquantifiable – element. To the frustration of marketing management, and to the challenge of advertising practitioners, advertising is as much hunch and flair as science.

Other reasons are that:

(a) advertising typically constitutes one of the more expensive marketing activities. Thus it is only to be expected that management will question its contribution to the overall marketing offensive;

(b) at a corporate political level it is 'easier' to blame a marketing mix activity that has been undertaken by an outside party. And most advertising is done externally by advertising agencies, creative consultancies *et al.*;

(c) a lot of the work that advertising is commissioned to do is, by its very nature, not readily tractable to measurement in terms of its effectiveness. Or where amenable to measurement such measurement tends to be expensive to make if it is to have reasonable precision;

(d) much advertising is undertaken with a view to producing what are essentially intangible values such as brand or corporate images. Images are non-physical; they cannot be seen or touched; they are 'ghostly'. Unlike, say, new additions to the sales force or a new pack get-up design. Thus it is not unnatural that management is likely, when things are going badly, to be circumspect about the millions of pounds spent on the manufacturing of phantom images. Better to deploy some (or all) of the money in areas where the results can be seen, where the effects are more tangible, more readily measured. Knock ten pence off the price of a standard pack. Run a competition. Streamline the distribution network. Or panic and change the advertising. Or panic further and change the advertising agency.

(e) in some circumstances the client may look upon or invest in the advertising agency as a sort of 'magician'. Not to put too fine a point on it the ad agency's creative people may be seen as alchemists[5] with the power to transform a poorly performing brand into a successful one. Just as some brand advertising explicitly or implicitly taps into the consumer's belief that disproportionate benefits will, in a fantasy or mythical way, come about following purchase of the product[6] so the very advertisers themselves may believe that advertising agencies will be able to cast spells forged in creative fire. The trouble with this sort of magical thinking, or indeed any magical thinking, is that when results don't occur disillusion sets in rapidly. You try another magician, another agency. Or you change the spell and try a different creative approach, a different creative strategy.

## 1.3 Advertising and creativity

A great deal of argument rages about creativity in advertising. A lot of advertisers are downright suspicious of creativity, perhaps justifiably so. And a few advertising agency men are pretty cavalier in their attitude towards it. Nevertheless, what David Ogilvy[7] describes as the 'cult of creativity' continues.

To judge from the large number of creative awards in the advertising industry – awards for photography, illustration, typography, graphics, copywriting, music and so on – creativity is highly valued. And it is only proper that excellence in these areas be acknowledged and merited. But the nub of contention is: do these excellences make for 'good advertising'? From a client's point of view, 'good advertising' means, at the end of the day, advertising that helps to sell a product. Not aesthetic pictures, brilliant production values and coruscating copy. Though 'selling' and 'creativity' are far from being mutually exclusive.

The legendary ad man Rosser Reeves of the Ted Bates agency sums up the position of the advertiser. Taking an ebullient no-nonsense line with regard to creativity, Reeves says: 'Do you want fine writing? Do you want masterpieces? *Or do you want to see the goddamned sales curve stop moving down and start moving up?*'[8] Most clients want both. And why not?

Many advertisers appear to be locked in a curious ambivalence over creativity. On the one hand they court it, because a creative ad, whether in terms of ideas or their execution or both, is going to stand out, provoke interest, bring prestige and attention; on the other hand they are understandably wary: creativity can get out of control, become irrelevant, be an end in itself. And in times of recession, of squeezed advertising budgets, the caution of advertisers is likely to get the upper hand: clients tending to rein in creativity, to play safe, and opt for a more prosaic or even 'hard sell' approach. The ambivalence of advertisers is shown up pretty forcibly in a survey carried out by the Institute of Practitioners in Advertising (IPA) on what clients looked for in an ad agency. 'Creative ability' ranked as the second most important attribute. Yet the attribute 'wins a lot of creative awards' was held to be relatively unimportant. The upshot of this survey is either a severe indictment of the worth of creative awards or a testimony to the schizophrenia of advertisers or both.

The advertising agency Benton & Bowles[9] maintained: 'If it doesn't sell, it isn't creative'.[10] It's a smart way out of the impasse; it appears to solve the ambivalence; it's probably what the client wants to hear. But it's a bit of a cheat (or is it cheek!). And leads to some fairly odd logic. Rembrandt didn't sell much in his lifetime, therefore he wasn't creative! Doubtless, though, the assertion was coined as a slogan and thus permits a good dollop of rhetoric.

One of the principal talents of an ad agency is to innovate or originate (both terms virtually synonymous with create) a way to sell a product; there is a specific focus or objective to creativity in advertising. As such it is not very different from what a scientist does when he comes up imaginatively with a theory or model to explain a set of phenomena.[11] A 'good' scientific theory is a brand of explanation that gains acceptance by the scientific community, and is canonized as true. But explanations need to be sold. As Pat Sweeney observes: 'Psychoanalysis ... wasn't any more truthful than phrenology, it was simply marketed more efficiently. Freud was a great salesman'.[12]

Similarly, creative ideas and solutions in advertising rarely stand out with irresistible, spell-binding force. They have to be argued for, backed up by the full weight and skills of advocacy during presentation to the client. The selling of the ideas and their get-up to the client often draws on as much creative thought and flair as the creative solution itself. 'Good' creative advertising is innovative work that is accepted by the advertiser because he believes it's going to help sell his product. Thus the dictum of Benton & Bowles is rehabilitated. Moreover, final recognition of good creativity comes from its being praised by the advertising community as a whole.

It is impossible to talk about creativity without talking about 'art'. For Andy Warhol 'there is art that fills up space on walls and art that is business art'. But is there that much difference? The Warhol 'Coke' and Campbell's Soup silk screens that get on the walls of collectors and galleries largely get there by way of Warhol's 'business art'. For Warhol, the selling of the product, the hype, is effectively the art form. Turning to the history of art, there is an abundance of painters (Van Dyck, Rubens, Gainsborough, *et al.*,) who executed works uniquely in order to sell, i.e., to satisfy the client. Polarizing 'art' against 'selling' is predicated on purist romantic ideas of 'art for art's sake'. Furthermore most, if not all, art is endeavouring to sell something: a moral point of view (Picasso's 'Guernica'), the glories and power of the church (Michelangelo ceilings), piety and the need for suffering (Fra Angelico altar pieces), the value of a given aesthetic vision (Monet and the Impressionists) and so on.

Because creativity means so many different things, people tend to end up talking at cross-purposes. Advertising copy for Omo is never going to be 'creative' in the way that lines of a Shakespearean sonnet are. To make matters worse, the word or concept of 'creativity' has suffered from runaway inflation: everything and anything it seems can be described as creative. Ogilvy,[7] himself wonderfully and self-effacingly bemused by the proliferation and promiscuous use of the adjective, cites the case of a firm boasting a 'creative mail room'. Ogilvy prefers to say, you just have ideas, write copy, draw pictures, do layouts, take photographs, etc., and get on with the job. 'But I occasionally use the hideous word "creative" myself for lack of a better'.[7] Or again, 'creativity' is a 'high-falutin word for the work I have to do between now and Tuesday'.

The use of 'art' is ubiquitous in the agency world. Like 'creative' and Ogilvy's comment on the same, there is no useful alternative. Though when asked if what they do is art, ad men will invariably reply that it isn't. Frank Lowe, formerly at Collett Dickenson & Pearce and now heading his own agency Lowe Howard-Spink & Marschalk, asked by Germaine Greer on LWT's South Bank Show programme *The Art of the Ad* whether advertising is art, pondered for a moment and then said 'no, it wasn't'. Predictably Lowe's reason was that advertising is necessarily committed to selling a product. In the same programme Lester Bookbinder, the acclaimed stills photographer and TV commercials director, pronounced that what he did wasn't art because he 'was paid to make a positive statement about a product'.

The advertising industry is sometimes criticized for all the creative awards it gives out. Awards are a narcissistic indulgence, ad men patting each other on the back. Prize-winning ads do not necessarily have anything to do with shifting brands off shelves. The panels of judges are biased, are exclusively made up of agency people and clients. But most areas of human endeavour, particularly in the arts, have awards, honours, prizes. The Motion Picture Academy awards, the Booker Fiction Prize and so on. One seldom if ever hears the criticism that an Oscar-winning film was 'unworthy' because the box-office receipts were poor. Or that book-buying consumers should be represented on the Booker judging panel instead of novelists and literary critics. Or that there are too many film festivals.

Advertising creative awards are good publicity. They are good for morale and motivation of ad agency creatives. They give recognition to the teamwork involved in making a press ad or a TV commercial. And prestige and credit not only to the agency but the media owner and client too.

Some clients deserve a lot of credit. The advertising for Heineken and Benson & Hedges is probably the most celebrated and original of any in the last decade. Both have been lavished with creative awards over the years. But advertising that is innovative can rarely be research-led. Frank Lowe[13] recalls how the first drafts for Heineken's 'refreshes the parts other beers can't reach' campaign and for Benson & Hedges' surreal advertising were turned down flat when copy-tested. Consumers were baffled: it wasn't beer advertising; it wasn't cigarette advertising; the (proposed) ads were incomprehensible, well, at least as ads. It takes a courageous client to fly in the face of research, which of course Heineken and Gallahers Ltd did. And the rest, as they say, is history.

# 2 · Advertising theory

## 2.0 What advertising must do

Our environment is a mass and maze of visual, aural and other stimuli. Thousands of signals and messages shout, jostle, clamour and inveigle to get hold of our attention. No advertisement, whatever its ultimate objective, can hope to be successful unless it can stand out from the crowd of other advertisements, from the news stories, articles and features in the press, from the programmes on TV and radio. If it's going to have a chance of working, an ad has got to stop us in our tracks, momentarily deflecting us from our everyday social, leisure or business concerns, or forcing us to concentrate on one small area of those interests. Yet it isn't enough for an ad simply to grab our attention. It must make us want to read on, want to listen, want to watch. There is no point in just causing heads to swivel and stare. Like a streaker on a football ground or a high street punk with high-rise pink spiky hair.

Various models of the advertising process have been put forward: models of what advertising should or must do. According to Starch 'an ad to be successful must be seen; must be remembered; must be believed; must be acted upon'.

Another model, AIDA, an acronym for the stages through which the ad must take the prospect, posits four phases: Attention; Interest; Desire; Action. Russell Colley's DAGMAR[1] (Defining Advertising Goals for Measuring Advertising Results) lays down that all communications that aim at the ultimate objective of a sale must move the prospect through four levels of understanding: from unawareness to awareness – the prospect must first be aware of the existence of the brand or company; to comprehension – the prospect must arrive at an understanding of what the product is, what it can do for him/her; to conviction – the prospect must gain a mental disposition to want to buy the product; to action – finally the prospect is compelled to put his/her money down. Everett Rodgers' model prescribes six stages: from unawareness to awareness; to eliciting interest; to producing evaluation; to stimulating trial; and, lastly, to ensuring that product trial leads to repeat purchase that will harden into a habit, i.e., adoption of the product/brand.

Instructive as they are, these models are a bit oversimplified. They presuppose that an advertisement or advertising campaign has to work linearly. Research – and probably common sense – suggest that a lot of consumers do not reach decisions or behave in a logical way. They do not necessarily gather all the information they can relating to a product, then wait for their feelings or desires to surface and gel and then take some form of action. To put it differently, some people do not need to be taken through (1) cognitive steps, (2) conative steps, (3) behavioural steps. Some people are highly impulsive, quantum-leaping from minimal awareness of a product to actually buying it. Known as 'innovation-prone', these consumers don't really require 'conviction' to be produced by the advertising; they have already got the conviction. The fact that a product is new (hi-fi products are a good example) is sufficient to provoke purchase.

Different media constrain people to assimilate information and to react in different ways. While the form of the medium of print imposes a linear approach, the eye scanning left to right, moving from the top of the page to the bottom, in audio-visual media like TV and cinema the prospect's senses are forced to take in information in clusters, all at once rather than step-by-step.[2]

Underlying most of these models is the idea that the task of advertising is one of missionary conversion: making unaware non-buyers into purchasers. It is true in some cases. But the objectives of a lot of advertising are much narrower, much more specific. Like advertising aimed at reinforcing brand loyalty, at reminding and reassuring, at projecting brand or corporate images.

## 2.1 Rosser Reeves and the USP

Models of how advertising works (such as those outlined in Section 2.0) go some way to helping us understand what advertising does, but at the end of the day they are simply *models*. So what do the ad agency men have to say? Unfortunately they aren't a source of many actual *theories*. Rather they prefer to give tips and directions or to draw attention to sound principles incarnated in particular campaigns. Rosser Reeves, however, has the distinction of coming as close as anyone to a theory, to making advertising rulebound. As someone once put it, here was a man who reached the Holy Grail of advertising – though the snapshots he returned with are a bit blurred in parts.

According to Reeves in *Reality in Advertising*:[3] 'The consumer tends to remember just one thing from an ad – one strong claim or concept. ... Each ad must make a proposition to the consumer. The proposition must be so strong that it can move the mass millions, i.e., pull over customers to your product'.

This is the doctrine of the USP – Unique Selling Proposition or Point. Good advertising gives a product or brand a USP. And a successful USP will give a product a very long and prosperous consumer franchise. The worst sin an advertiser can commit, according to Reeves, is to change its USP-focused advertising. The really successful brands, and by implication the really successful advertising campaigns, are those that do not essentially change over the years, if not decades (Horlicks and Colgate are examples).

A crucial part of Reeves' theory is that the proposition or promise made by the advertisement must be one that the competition has not *so far* made. Genuine or substantive differences amongst brands are very rare. Where a unique product ingredient that delivers an easy-to-perceive and highly desirable benefit is developed, it is not long before the competitors are offering the ingredient-benefit. Fluoride ingredients in toothpaste are now offered by nearly all brands of toothpaste. Another example is Proctor & Gamble's Ariel: it has a USP with its biological washing concept/enzyme action but, given the state of R & D in the detergent world, it was not long before rival Lever Brothers produced their version of a biological detergent, Radiant. Thus most USPs come, and endure, from a brand or company establishing a benefit position for itself hitherto not claimed by competitors. The position becomes so strong and is so indelibly associated with the particular brand/company in the mind of the consumer that no competitor can wrest the benefit away and claim it for itself. Look at Volvo. Its USP is 'safety'. Any other motor-car manufacturer could have majored on this benefit. But Volvo positioned itself as synonymous with 'safety' first.

A premiss behind Reeves' theory is that the consumer thinks rationally. Doubtless this is another determinant of his view that advertising shouldn't be creative – creativity evoking appeals to, and associations with, emotions and feelings. Thus advertising should operate rationally too. A claim or benefit is made in the brand's advertising which is related to the prospect's needs, or his/her perceptions of those needs, and is then supported by reasons.

The consumer, then, is presented with the promise of a benefit. He/she will react by thinking: well, this is fine but why should, or why will, such a benefit take place? Promises aren't enough. In short, there is a credibility issue.

The 'safety' promise of Volvo could be supported in the body copy by reference to the gauge and calibre of the steel used in the body panels, to exacting quality control and testing procedures, etc. More recently Volvo advertising has amplified 'safety' into 'longevity': Volvos are built so strongly and sturdily they will still be on the road when other cars have been reduced to an ugly mound of decomposing, visceral rust!

Another example is Ajax. The promise is: Ajax will clean your sinks, baths and basins faster and more thoroughly than any comparable cleaning/scouring powder. Hackles of doubt and disbelief rise up in the mind of the housewife. A most desirable benefit to be sure. But why? How can this brand do this? Why, the housewife asks, should I believe what they say? Why should Ajax be tougher and quicker in its cleaning action?

Reasons, therefore, must be given. So following the promise of speed and thoroughness, the Ajax advertising goes on to say that Ajax contains bleach. Bleach is firmly associated in the mind of the housewife with cleaning power. And to support the USP of speed, Ajax is chemically formulated so that its slightly dull-white colour instantly changes to a crisp, vibrant blue on contact with water. Cosmetic as it is, the colour shift from white to blue demonstrates the speed of the brand's cleansing action.

From a sceptical point of view the unique promise-and-reasons format of Reeves surely gives rise to a considerable amount of pseudo advertising campaigns – pseudo in the sense that the advertising merely mimics Reeves' requirements. A good illustration is Mars. The long-running campaign ends with the sloganized promise: 'A Mars a day helps you work, rest and play'. And then the reason why: because it contains milk, glucose, etc., Mars ads have the grammatical form of a USP. But that's about it, the sceptic will argue. The ingredients given just aren't reasons. How on earth can they produce such totally different states – the working, resting and playing; it's just not logical. Worse, it's contradictory: if the glucose gives energy to work and play then it's going to frustrate resting. And so on.

But the majority audience to Mars advertising isn't for the most part this logical, at any rate not while being exposed to the advertising. It is enough that there is a vaguely credible connection between the promise and the reasons. In any event, the Mars slogan has effectively served to make the brand stand out distinctly from other chocolate confectionery products; the slogan has become part and parcel of the brand, a product 'plus'.

It is arguable that the connection between promises and reasons has more to do with myth than 'scientific validity'. Take PAL dog food with its brand name acronym containing the promise: Prolongs Active Life. The reason: because it contains marrowbone jelly. There may well be a highly technical explanation of how this ingredient helps man's best friend to live longer, though in all probability the evidence will turn out to be as controversial as, say, eating live Bulgarian yoghourt will increase longevity in man. But what is in point is that dog owners see their pet continually and habitually gnawing on bones to, among other things, reach the marrowbone jelly inside. The dog's behaviour says it all. Bone jelly *must* be good for dogs. We believe what we want to believe. The correlation between belief and desire is far greater than that between belief and evidence. Desires, wants and wishes are more important than reasons provided or couched in strict evidence terms.

## 2.2 Critical comments

Reeves' USP doctrine of advertising proved very successful with advertisers. Reeves' agency, Ted Bates, found itself well supplied with new clients.

For here was an advertising agency saying: This is the way

advertising works, should work and must work. Do advertising this way and your brands will become market winners. Advertising, at last, was law-bound.

But in reality the Reeves theory wasn't anything new. Products and brands had been marketed and advertised with USPs since the dawn of mass produced and packaged goods.

Advertising agencies are in a similar position to brands. Just as there may be fifty brands of toothpaste with no one brand having any real difference setting it apart from the others, until one brand makes a specific claim that no other brand had hitherto made, but could have made, so advertising agencies basically offer the same services: creation, planning, production and placing of ads. Any advertising agency could have distinguished itself, given itself an identity, by boldly proclaiming that its advertising was uniquely different because it produced USPs for products.

Thus Reeves' USP is itself a USP for Reeves' agency, Ted Bates.

Reeves' theory is wanting from the point of view of the contribution of *advertising* to a brand's identity. USP-based advertising may be a sufficient condition for a brand's identity, but it is not a necessary condition. A USP may be achieved through a distinctive and original pack design: a toothpaste packed in a floppy transparent tube; a lipstick in the shape of a 0.303 bullet. Or by a change in the physical 'get-up' of a brand: a liquid detergent standing out from powder-based ones; a cooking oil in an aerosol format (with the ready-made benefit of economy of use). Or by industrial design – through the shape, form, materials and colours of the casing for a TV set or hair-drier; through the ergonomics of an office chair or typewriter design. And in the world of fashion clothing moreover, the styling – the cut, colour and 'look' – is more or less constitutive of the USP. An advertising agency will, of course, communicate these distinguishing pack/style/design features. But the design-engineered USP of the product/brand (the trousers, dress, TV, toothpaste and so on) has, in all bluntness, little to do with the agency.

More telling still, Reeves' USP suffers from being circular. For Reeves says that what is important about advertising is that it does not get diverted by glamorous and artistic photographs and exquisitely honed copy. That it should keep its eye on the ball of making ads that lead to an improvement in sales. An advertisement, he avers, has to make a single unique proposition to the consumer. What must the proposition in the advertisement be? It must, says Reeves, be one that 'pulls over new customers to (the) product . . . that moves the mass millions'. This is tantamount to saying that successful advertising must be successful advertising! To qualify as a good USP, the USP must improve the sales figures.

Reeves' USP doctrine presupposes that the consumer behaves rationally. Research and common sense suggest that this is not so. To be sure, it is for the most part true that low interest repeat-purchase products, such as floor-polish, petrol, lavatory cleansers, are bought on rational grounds. Purchasers resent buying these sorts of products; they are boring but necessary. Accordingly purchases are governed in the main by the (professed) ability of brands in these areas to deliver benefits of economy, efficiency, safety, hygiene, etc. But other sorts of product largely become interesting, from a purchasing point of view, because they promise emotional satisfactions, such as pride, envy, vanity, self-esteem, self-transformation, love and affection and so on. Who, after all, buys a Porsche because of its fuel economy or safety? What rational grounds can there be for buying a tiny phial of French perfume for £35? Or for going on holiday to St Lucia in July? Even in the world of industrial buying behaviour, often characterized as *the* rational purchasing process, decisions are as often as not based on emotion (like the prestige of the supply company) as reason.

## 2.3 Ogilvy and the brand image

The primary job of advertising as David Ogilvy, along with Reeves, sees it is to give a brand an identity and individuation. But where Reeves comes down on the side of reason, Ogilvy by and large sides with emotion.

According to Ogilvy the task of advertising is to give a brand 'a first-class ticket through life'. The role of advertising is to invest the brand with a set of associations, favourable connotations or positive psychological overtones. For the most part, these associations are independent of, or external to, properties inherent in the product or its use.

Put differently, the brand image, the engineering of which is the main business of advertising, is a cluster of intangible attributes rather than real qualities: the brand image refers to the brand's 'chemistry' rather than what is literally in the pack, the 'chemicals'. Blind test American whisky: put Brand A in a milk bottle and

Brand B in a milk bottle. Ask the whisky drinker to tell the difference. He'll say they taste the same. Then 'give people a taste of Old Crow, and *tell* them it's Old Crow. Then give them another taste of Old Crow, *but tell them it's Jack Daniels*. Ask them which they prefer. They'll think the two drinks are quite different. *They are tasting images.*(4)

Let's look at a product such as cigarettes. What might make a brand different? Well, there might exist 'reasonable' distinguishing differences – such as where the tobacco was grown, how it was cured, how it tasted, etc. But many brands would be able to claim this pedigree. So Ogilvy says: accept that there are no – or precious few – differences in terms of physical properties pertaining to the brand. All the brands are more or less the same. What the advertising agency has to do, therefore, is to endow or invest the brand with highly distinctive associations. Associations that will carve out a distinct identity for it. And such associations must be geared to engage with the fantasies or aspirations of the target market.

What makes Marlboro Marlboro? Not the taste. Not, in fact, anything to do with intrinsic features of the product. What distinguishes Marlboro is the image. And it's an image that has been manufactured or engineered – a complex of rich associations of the mythical west ... maverick cowboys (cowboys that don't really exist other than in a fantasized or mythical context) ... freedom ... independence ... prairies ... macho. And more urban synthetic macho.

Everyone today perceives Marlboro in this way. That the macho never-never-land cowboy theme seems an essential part and parcel of what Marlboro is attests to the power of the advertising for the brand. It is chastening though to remember that Marlboro was originally targeted as a woman's cigarette. Philip Morris Inc. launched the brand in the late 1920s as a woman's cigarette; the tip was coloured red to disguise the smear left by the lipstick of the smoker (the red tip is of course a USP).

It must be said that Ogilvy, while for the main part apparently committed to the position that brands and products have no inherent factors to be talked about in advertising and so must be charged up in their advertising with 'image chemistry', is at the end of the day a great champion of sleuthing, of finding out facts about a product that can be incorporated in advertising. In short, Ogilvy's 'first-class ticket' for a product's quality can be, and has been, directly related to intrinsic product features. His classic advertising for Rolls-Royce is illustrative. The ad's headline runs: 'At 60 miles an hour the loudest noise in this new Rolls-Royce comes from the electric clock'. The headline says a lot without actually saying it. Starting with the 1958 Ford Mercury, quite a few limousine class cars have boasted of being 'library quiet'. But that's about it. Whereas Ogilvy deftly uses the loudest noise – the clock – to symbolize the Silver Shadow's 'patient attention to detail' and to communicate the product's engineering mastery.

## 2.4 Brand images and USPs compared

Confusingly enough, the different approaches of Reeves and Ogilvy turn out to be close. In the case of a USP the brand becomes identified in the mind of the consumer with a particular benefit; the brand evokes an association of the benefit. The association is of course an image. Thus the difference between a 'brand image' (such as Marlboro has) and a USP (such as Volvo's synonymity with safety) reduces to a difference of the degree of complexity of the associations. The image of Marlboro is a USP; it is what uniquely distinguishes it from, say, Peter Stuyvesant. Any brand of cigarette could have been invested with the image currency of the cowboy. Only Marlboro did it first. In sum, we can say that gaining brand identity via a USP involves a narrowly focused, concentrated identity, whereas gaining brand identity via a 'brand image' results in an identity that is diffuse, open-textured.

Nevertheless, it might well be claimed that USPs are still essentially different from 'brand images'. The basis, after all, of Reeves' position is that USPs are established by rational appeals. In contrast Ogilvy's 'brand image' approach by and large involves emotional appeals. But this contention does not hold up very well to scrutiny. Firstly, it is doubtful whether any advertising can work *uniquely* on the basis of rational appeals. At the risk of sophistry, even express and exclusive appeals to the 'economy' and 'savings' delivered by a particular brand can be seen implicitly to contain appeals to, say, pride, self-congratulation on being thrifty, shrewd, and so on. Secondly, it is often necessary when advertising the sort of product that consumers can't get excited about to supplement the rational benefit with an emotional trigger. Take Ajax: it has a USP of speed of cleaning matched by thoroughness of cleaning (from blue bleach power). But this promise doesn't carry enough motivation; it needs to be 'dramatized' in terms of what *is* interesting to the housewife. So an ad might show the housewife enjoying the time she's saved on household cleaning chores. She might be seen playing with her small children, reading them a story; or preparing a special dinner for her husband. Thanks to Ajax, as it were, she can be a better mother, a better wife. The brand is the hero.

Quite a lot of appeals in advertising are manifestly a mix of reason and emotion, of USP and 'brand image'. The American Express card is shown as an efficient tool, a problem solver: it eliminates hassles with currency changing and is never refused ('certainly, sir!'). Simultaneously these rational appeals are fused with emotional ones. Using American Express confers on the cardholder exclusivity and elitism. The Amex Man belongs to a privileged club whose members include the likes of Roger Daltry and champion golfer Ballesteros.

## 2.5 Brand names

Producing and maintaining a brand identity is one of the major objectives of advertising. However, the name given to a brand may determine in advance the USP that will individuate it: the name 'PAL' for a dog food contains the USP 'Prolongs Active Life', to be subsequently unpacked by the advertising. Also, with many names the sort of images to be woven round a brand, like a psychological aura, is to a large degree pre-set: the name prescribes the associations to be developed, shaped and enforced by the advertising. A vodka called Rasputin, for example, immediately conjures up images of Russia on the brink of revolution, of the 'mad monk', of power, sex, mystery and so on. A campaign to launch Rasputin would, from a creative point of view, be constrained to bring out and focus on one or more of these built-in associations.

Finding a strong and enduring brand name is a difficult business, one where creativity and marketing strategy come together. A good name will function as a shorthand for the personality or the personality potential of the product; it will 'position' the brand, i.e., how it is to be perceived and who will perceive it as such. A cosmetics range called Loren efficiently communicates 'graceful glamour' for the older, post 40-year-old woman; the reference to the Italian movie actress Sophia Loren summarizing a distinctive set of associations.[5]

Names denote, they are labels that pick out a thing or a quality. They also connote: they evoke associations. Swan picks out a species of bird; at the same time the word connotes majesty, grace, poise, cool arrogance and so on. Christening new products is fraught with difficulties: outstandingly, does the name have the desired connotations? It is a problem that becomes acutely severe in the case of naming a brand that is to be marketed overseas. A name or word may have favourable connotations in English but, literally or in translation, perhaps downright rude ones in French or Greek.

To minimize the risks of unwanted associations a brand name will often be made up. Thus: Omo, Exxon, Timotei. The hope is that the name will have a predominantly labelling function and will be as far as possible 'a blank', free to be invested with the required associations by packaging design, advertising and so on. But connotations are unavoidable: meaning emanates from the very sound or sense of the name – it 'feels' hard, soft, technical, aristocratic. Equally, meaning comes from the visual representation of a name: a name got up in a crate-box typeface will have a disposition to elicit one set of associations. Set the name in an olde Englishe tea shoppe typeface and a quite different mix of perceptions are likely to be generated.

Bernstein[6] draws the analogy between new-born babies and new brands. A baby starts life as a commodity product – six pounds of flesh and blood. A label is attached to it: 'John' picks it out. As he grows up, his personality develops. Now, the label 'John' refers to John the person; 'John' is a shorthand for his peculiar and distinctive mix of traits, qualities. Similarly a brand starts out as a commodity product: it is simply a beer or a detergent. It is christened Daz or Skol or whatever. The names imply some characteristics. These are midwifed, nursed, added to and tightened through the advertising, typographics and pack design. The packaging is equivalent to the clothes a person wears: both signal 'I am this sort of person' or 'This is the job I do'. Ernst Dichter described branding as 'the soul of the product'. The name is the soul. It is the most important and valuable property the parent company owns and is rightly guarded zealously.

An irony in branding is that some brands become too successful for their own good: the brand name becomes virtually synonymous with the general product from which it spent years and years fighting to be separate. Hoover is the classic victim. The brand means the generic product vacuum cleaner. It is even a verb: we speak of 'hoovering' the carpet but it may well be with a Morphy-Richards or an Electrolux. It is the price of fame for quite a few brands. Sellotape, Tipp-Ex, Kleenex, Tampax, Y Fronts, Videotape, Formica, Biro, Petrol and JCB earth shifters are just a few examples of brands that have suffered depersonalization and become generic products.

What makes for a good brand name? The name should (a) be registrable as a trade mark; (b) be easy to pronounce; (c) have good graphic and typographic potential;[7] (d) have appropriate meanings before advertising takes place and (e) communicate what the brand is all about – what its nature is, what it will do in terms of the benefit to be delivered.

# 3 · The anatomy of persuasion

## 3.0 Persuasive communication

The persuasive effectiveness of advertising depends on one or more of the following: *the message* (what is being said and how it's being said); *the communicator* (who says it); *the recipient* (the audience) and *the medium of communication*.

Before examining each of these in turn it is as well to look at a fairly widely held view that there is a distinction between advertising that is purely informative – providing information on how to use a product, where to buy it and so on – and advertising that is persuasive. Perhaps more widely held is the view of critics of advertising which maintains that advertising typically deals in half-truths (by, say, deliberate omission), blandishments, manipulations, propaganda even. By way of reaction to this, many defenders of advertising argue that advertising is simply providing a service to the consumer, giving much needed product awareness and explanation.

Firstly, let's see just how absurd the position of the critics of advertising is. In a free and open society it is extremely difficult, if not impossible, for companies to manipulate people into buying products or services that they really do not want. On a purely practical level, the budgets required to do this are way beyond those of even the biggest corporations; the financial and other power would have to be great enough to stifle the criticisms and protests of corporate competitors, consumer associations, journalistic and editorial comment and so on. Besides, advertising in the UK is subject to a comprehensive system of regulation and control:

TV and radio advertising by the Independent Broadcasting Authority, and all other advertising (print, posters, cinema) by the Advertising Standards Authority. Misleading and dishonest advertisements are proscribed; claims made for a product have to be capable of substantiation. In any event, product 'propaganda' is commercially counter-productive. You can con a person into buying a product once only. Experiencing that the product is different in its performance from how it was advertised, the consumer will refuse to buy not only that particular product again but also other products marketed by that company.

On the other hand, the defendants of advertising are guilty of elevating what is at best a half-truth into a whole truth. *Of course* a great deal of advertising is persuasive; it functions as an advocate for the brand, portraying it in the most favourable light. The advertiser will, like anyone else, present his 'best face'. If the product is very expensive or uneconomical, he may well not include these facts in his advertising; instead his advertising will, say, major on the exclusivity, prestige or elitism of the product.

So can advertising be purely informative? The short answer is: *no*. Messages purporting to convey pure information do not exist. This is because all presentation of facts or information is ineliminably selective. Ask two separate observers to describe an incident – such as a road traffic accident – and their accounts will differ. Selecting or editing the facts, giving prominence to some, playing down others, ignoring some entirely, occurs all the time. Notably we see it in news reporting in daily papers and on television.[1]

Information provision can be as persuasive as communication that is obviously persuasive. Perhaps a great deal more so. Communication that appears to be informative and objective is likely to be very effective as the recipient will be less vigilant, critical and circumspect.

A good example of the persuasiveness of information advertising can be found in the league table or comparative list advertising much favoured in recent times by car advertisers. The advertiser compares his car – call it Model X – with several others in the same broad category – say, small economy cars – with respect to certain features such as price, miles per gallon, standard extras like radios, etc. Model X invariably turns out to be the best on all scores. It all looks very convincing. Especially since such controversial facts as the number of miles to the gallon at different speeds are supplied by independent motoring bodies. But what if a particular feature has been omitted from the list of comparisons? Perhaps the X's warranty terms are not as good as those for one of the cars on the comparative table. Perhaps, even, a model of car has been completely left out of the list, a car which is cheaper and has greater fuel economy. Whether or not this sort of deliberate omission actually takes place in advertising is another matter. It is enough that it could do so. And it is enough to show that any clear distinction between 'information' and 'persuasion' advertising is a myth.

## 3.1 Effective message approaches

### (a) Self-persuasion

The philosopher Blaise Pascal summed it up in the seventeenth century: 'We are more easily persuaded, on the whole, by the reasons we ourselves discover than by those which are given to us by others'. In a sense this is a virtual definition of persuasion. The persuader makes us accept his reasons for doing something by getting us to believe they are our own. Foisting reasons on somebody is tantamount to a command. Though it is fond of using military metaphors like campaigns, tactics, strategies and so on, advertising can't order consumers about.

An explicit use of self-persuasion is letting the product speak for itself. Many advertisements conform to this approach. The advertiser says in effect: product A will do this or that; but don't take our word for it. Try the product yourself. Test drive our new jeep at your nearest dealer today. Sample the crisp dryness of Vino Rialto at selected off-licences.

A clever salesman, appreciating the prejudice towards his profession, will not attempt to sell. Rather he will endeavour to make the prospect think that he/she is an astute buyer.

### (b) Distraction

At first sight it seems paradoxical to say that an effective way to 'get a message through' is to distract the attention of the recipient. But what often tends to happen with advertising messages is that the prospect silently, and compulsively, argues with parts of the message that don't agree with his or her values and beliefs. At worst the prospect rejects the message from its very beginning because of hostile or distrusting attitudes to advertising as a whole. Thus if the message contains distractions, the resistance and arguments of the prospect are likely to be deflected, his or her antipathy suspended or dissolved, and so allow the message to 'come in'.

The dominant part of most press ads is the picture. It is what causes the reader, flipping through a magazine, to pause fleetingly. If it delivers the right momentum or 'hook', readers will skim, better still read, the copy. According to McLuhan[2] one of the strategic roles of copy in an ad is to distract from the insidious meanings in the picture. Copy – the printed word – is rational. We can argue with it; it is amenable to truth and falsity; we feel in control, able to question, accept or reject the claims made. Meanwhile, the potent or real work is being stealthily carried out by the graphics, photography, illustrations. With visual images we are poorly equipped to be logical, critical, discerning; the layers of meaning buried in pictorial images seduce and worm their way into our minds, often below the threshold of consciousness.[3]

Imitating editorial style is a device frequently used to good effect to overcome initial resistance to the fact that a page or doublepage is an advertisement. Many people, seeing that a page is manifestly an ad, will automatically 'switch off' and turn over. Editorial style ads, simulating the design, layout and typography of features and articles and usually involving full-bleed (the picture is spread to the edges of the page), can be very captivating. But a risk is that if the get-up of the ad is too distracting, passing itself off as editorial, the benefits gained will be cancelled out and worse. For the British Code of Advertising Practice prohibits ads that, looking too much like editorial, are liable to mislead: the advertiser will be bound to carry a warning at the top of the page – 'This is an advertisement' or 'Advertiser's Announcement'.

A lot of TV commercials gain attention, distract (from the message-sell) and get talked about by being entertaining. Being entertained is, after all, one of the main satisfactions to be had from watching TV. Commercials have to compete and hold their own against the programming if they are to avoid being zapped – a quicker and more ignominious fate than being 'page turned'. But while entertaining commercials compel watching and promote favourable attitudes, a danger is that the distraction will be counter-productive. The audience will recall the *advertising*, the knockabout comedians and the cavorting animals, but the *advertisement*, the 'window on the product', will be lost. The distraction has been dubbed the 'video vampire' effect. A classic example is the TV campaign featuring Leonard Rossiter, playing the irrepressible idiot, who unfailingly manages to cause a glass of drink to be slopped down the front of Joan Collins' immaculate dress. The tension is wonderful, the viewer riveted – waiting for the moment when the drink will spill. It is thirty seconds of viewing more star-studded and entertaining than you are likely to get in an evening in front of the telly. But brand name recalls for Cinzano, the slopped drink on Joan Collins' dress, were depressingly low. Worse still, some viewers thought the drink advertised was Martini!

Humour is well institutionalized in UK advertising. Like entertainment, which of course involves humour to a very large extent, humour serves to break down antipathies and suspicions, particularly with regard to selling and salesmanship. A joke cracked, a sharing of smiles, results in reality being temporarily suspended, a rapport being established between the advertiser and the audience. With his/her guard lowered, coupled with a disposition of goodwill, the prospect is open to the product message coming through. But does it? Humour, like any tool, can be used to good effect or it can bungle and bodge. Humour arising from funny or dramatic-comic situations on TV commercials tends to work well (think of John Cleese and Sony, or Lorraine Chase and Campari). In print advertising, humour, with its staple of the pun in the headline, tends to be less successful. All too often the pun is banal (so, 'Get in the Christmas spirit' for a brand of whisky) or the source of an 'ouch!'. Arguably, David Ogilvy's strictures on the use of humour in advertising – 'People don't buy from clowns' – and his subsequent relaxation of the same, stem from the different handling of humour on TV, largely witty and/or comic and pun-free, from its mostly word-play use in print media.[4]

Like humour, sex can be used for distractive purposes. But unless the product has a 'sex orientated' or romance theme or benefit, like a perfume or men's toiletry, the reference founders on irrelevance. It's one thing to feature a naked girl to advertise an exotic bath gel: the nudity is both functional and erotic, but quite another to show a scantily clad model in an ad for a range of photocopying machines. Though nudity and sex can, to be sure, get a campaign widely talked about.

## (c) Incompleteness

Incomplete, fragmented or puzzling messages are psychologically unsatisfactory, disturbing even. There is a deep-rooted desire to render such messages complete or whole or meaningful. (A large body of fairly academic theory based on *Gestalt* psychology is often invoked to explain this phenomenon.)

Resistance to the message is broken down as the prospect is constrained to join actively in its making, to become, as it were, a co-creator. Message closure, moreover, has the advantage of the message being better remembered – because the recipient has been *actively* involved.

Examples of messages demanding completion are teaser headlines and teaser sign-off slogans like Schweppes' 'Schh ... You know who'. Rival tonic water manufacturer Rawlings cheekily exploited Schweppes' teaser with the headline: 'We knew how before you know who'. (Rawlings' USP being that they were the first company to make tonic water.)

The use of absent products, brand names (Fig. 3.1) and pack shots cue participation, filling in the gaps of the identity of the product or advertiser. Silk Cut poster ads show a concrete cashing of the brand name: an expanse of gracefully rumpled purple silk which has been slit to expose below a layer of creamy-white silk material. The mandatory Government Health Warning is striped across the bottom of the ad, signifying that its subject is cigarettes. The purple and cream are distinctive of the livery colours on the Silk Cut pack. But beyond these colours there is nothing. It remains for the Silk Cut smoker to provide the brand name identity.

*The Financial Times*' 'No FT, no comment' campaign has used the missing identity strategy to good effect in its poster and other advertising; the idiosyncratic pink of the sign-off *'no comment'* provides the cue (Fig. 3.2).

Puzzles invite and demand participation. But the puzzle mustn't be too easy or too difficult. Striking a balance between the two isn't easy. When pitched at the right level, the prospect, solving the puzzle, will feel good: it is the satisfaction, the 'hit' of 'having got it'. This satisfaction, akin to that derived from solving crossword clues, disposes the prospect to a benign frame of mind and, as a consequence, to being receptive to subsequent claims, etc., being made on behalf of the product.

# Their master's choice

**Figure 3.1** Absence of the brand name/pack invites completion (The dogs are the trade mark of Black & White Scotch Whisky.)

# ABCDEGHI JKLMNOP QRSUVWX YZ ...no comment.

**Figure 3.2** A reminder ad with just the right level of puzzle

### (d) Use of cognitive dissonance

This is psychologists' jargon (after Leon Festinger) for the commonplace notion that we don't like being exposed to information or ideas that conflict with our established system of ideas, beliefs, values. We have, that is, a fundamental need to keep our beliefs and values *consistent*.

A message that does not agree (is cognitively dissonant) will cause us anxiety or discomfort. And we will do everything we can to eliminate it. Some advertising messages set up anxiety at the beginning and then quickly provide the means to reduce it, often by way of promising that certain benefits will accrue following purchase and use of the product.

Common emotional anxieties set up by ads are: loss of respect/ esteem/prestige/status; the threat of removal of affection from friends and family. In short these sorts of advertisement work by using fear appeals.

Ever-present dangers are of overkill: the threats are too great. The prospect's defence mechanisms come into action. The message is blocked off. For example: too much talk about death may well jeopardize the success of an ad for life insurance; a road safety campaign may backfire by dwelling too long or too graphically on what it's like to be the victim of a road accident. The dissonance overloads, short-circuiting the message from getting through.

The hazard of underkill is equally potent. If the fear of anxiety is too small the message will be ignored.

## (e) Inoculation

Attitudes are very hard – and so expensive – to change. Thus, much advertising seeks to reinforce existing attitudes, to make them resistant to change, more immune to outside pressures.

Typical applications of 'inoculation strategy' are 'knocking copy' – criticizing competing brands (though under UK advertising controls and regulations such criticisms must be capable of substantiation), and 'reassurance' advertising: telling the recipient what a great product he or she has bought, what a wonderful company he or she is dealing with.

## (f) Candour

If people openly and frankly admit to their faults and shortcomings, we are likely to believe what they subsequently say. Moreover to respect them for their forthright honesty.

Advertisements are wont to describe products as infallible; superlatives rule. So when an ad admits that the product isn't always flawless, or even insults the product, we are (a) disarmed by the candour, and (b) disposed to view favourably the other product claims made in the copy.

This candour approach was pioneered by Bill Bernbach (of Doyle, Dane Bernbach) in the 1960s. One of his classic ads, for the Volkswagen Beetle, carried the single headline: '*Lemon*'; lemon being US slang for something that's off-key, not quite right, sour (the movie actor Jack Lemmon, before becoming famous, was laughed out of Columbia Pictures' mogul Harry Cohn's office for his name). Never mind the intriguing and curiosity-provoking juxtaposition of the pack shot of the car and the bold word 'lemon' underneath, the ad, at the time, broke every rule. The product was, associated with a negative or pejorative adjective – 'lemon'. No advertiser had tainted his product in this way before. It was outrageously daring. How could a manufacturer say his product is, or might be, duff? Having admitted that it sometimes is, the onus is on the body copy to redeem the product, restore it to perfection. And to this end the VW 'lemon' body copy acquits itself masterfully. It goes on to explain how, occasionally, a VW Beetle like 'the lemon' illustrated, is flawed. The chrome strip on the glove compartment is blemished or whatever. But the team of inspectors at the plant in Germany is committed to pin-point and correct this and other defects. Just as it is dedicated to ensure the most exacting of standards on the shock absorbers, etc., and to see that the one of fifty VW's that rolls off the production line and doesn't perform to scratch never ends up in the showroom. As the copy concludes: 'We pick the lemons you get the plums'.

The candour approach is adopted and used to great effect by the car hire company, Avis. Its advertising makes a positive virtue out of humility. Thus: 'We're No. 2 ... We try harder'.

Being a small company isn't something to be apologetic about or to be hidden. It's to be flaunted. So, tyre manufacturer B F Goodrich runs the headline: 'We're the other guys ... remember'.

In a similar vein if the advertiser has a high priced product, he isn't coy about it. He comes straight out with it: yes, the price is silly, outrageous. When Parker launched a biro for women, price £9.95, the colour supplement ads shouted in the headline; 'A ridiculous alternative to the 10p ball pen'.

The honesty or 'honest-to-badness' approach commands respect. No less important, it produces salience and credibility. It treats the consumer as an intelligent being and enters into a pack of complicity with him/her. Gone is the divide or alienation between advertiser and audience. Instead they meet, in a 'let's-go-over-the-top-together' way (Bernbach's phrase).

## 3.2 The role of the communicator

Very often *who* says something is as important as *what* is being said. A favourable perception of the sender is vital to the effectiveness of the communication.

An historic example of this syndrome can be had from US presidential marketing. When Republican Richard Nixon was running for office, the Democrats mounted a massive campaign featuring a picture of Nixon with the headline: 'Would you buy a used car from this man?'. A second-hand car salesman is celebrated for his double-dealing, con tricks and shystering. And the reference to one of Nixon's albeit brief former occupations was overwhelmingly obvious; as was the implication: don't believe a word of what this man says he will do if he gets to the White House.

The influence of the communicator on the acceptance of, or receptivity to, a message has been called *the source effect* (after Theodore Levitt). The acceptance of a message is a function of the extent to which the source is perceived as being trustworthy, expert, authoritative.

If a manufacturer declares in his advertising that his product is wonderful, the chances are that a lot of consumers will view his claims with scepticism, benign or otherwise. Of course, the advertiser is going to trumpet the virtues of his product in suitable superlatives – the best, the most economical, the most safe. But if someone who is seen to be unconnected with the company and its products makes similar claims about the products, those claims, coming as they do from an impartial and objective source, are likely to be believed.

Motor-tyre manufacturer Goodyear has a type and specification of tyre, the Grand Prix-S, for which the claim is that it has formidable powers of road grip and thus leads to improved road safety. Do we believe the claim? Direct from Goodyear's people, the harsh answer is 'maybe' or 'probably not'. But when Goodyear's commercials and subsequent press advertising feature Sir Robert Mark, ex-commissioner of the Metropolitan Police, making the claim we *are* inclined to believe. Because Sir Robert Mark is perceived as being an expert and authority on road safety and, perhaps no less importantly, as a man of integrity. He is hardly likely to put his reputation on the block for the sake of a fee to appear in a commercial and say the right things. Should there be any lingering doubt in this regard, it is taken care of: Mark makes explicit that he wasn't prepared to endorse the tyre until Goodyear could prove its claims.

The use of impartial sources and the credibility they inspire or produce can be seen in PR. If a motoring correspondent for a national newspaper writes a favourable review of a new car, the merits of the car are more likely to be believed than if they were communicated from copy in a launch advertising campaign.

Expertise and appropriate experience of the communicator is essential for the message to be effective. Thus if Bjorn Borg endorses a brand of tennis rackets, Kevin Keegan a brand of football boots or Joan Collins a brand of cosmetic that promises the look of eternal youth, we are (a) let's face it, interested, and (b) disposed to respect and believe their judgements (even if, as we know, they have probably, through the financial wile and acumen of their business/management advisors, been in receipt of large fees).

But product endorsements by celebrities are sometimes used or featured in advertisements where the celebrity has at best only a cosmetic expertise, at worst, none at all. An example of the former is Sheraton Hotels' use of footballer Pele. 'It's been said,' so the copy runs, 'that I'm one of the most exciting soccer stars ever. Through practice and dedication I developed my own unique style, a winning style. And I admire others who have the dedication to develop a winning style of their own'. The Sheraton Hotel ad goes on: 'And like frequent guest Pele, we're sure it won't take you long to see how Sheraton wins on style'. 'Winning on style' is just far too generic. A case can be made out for 'winning on style' for just about *any* celebrity. And why should we believe Pele anyway?

Debonair movie actor David Niven used to appear front-on to camera plugging the merits of a brand of instant coffee. What possible or credible connection exists here? What does David Niven know about coffee? Charitably, perhaps quite a bit. But about instant coffee! Living in the south of France, a man of discriminating taste, a stereotype of smooth aristocratic upper-class Englishness. It just doesn't hold (though one can see the intention of the advertiser: to make instant coffee sophisticated).

More debilitating still than the absence of connection between the endorser and that which he/she is endorsing is the consumer's belief that the celebrity has been bought, handsomely paid to say fine things about the product.

The use of celebrities, if they don't have a distinct and specific relationship to the product they are advertising, tends to produce the 'vampire effect': they suck the life-blood of the product dry; the audience remembers the celebrity but not the product.

A 'source effect' is generated by the people who appear in ads (and sometimes they become a celebrity as a result, like Lorraine Chase in Campari). Whether featured or appearing incidentally – the macho male posing in the suit, the svelte and sophisticated woman standing near the eye-level oven in the setting of the custom-built kitchen range – the model is implicitly a spokesperson for the product. If he or she and the stereotype they instantiate produce likeable, trustworthy and/or admirable feelings, the images and copy in the ad are liable to be favourably received. On the other hand, a consumer may accept the claims made for, say, a brand of washing machine but dislike the sort of person represented by the model, the apparent owner and user of the product. 'She's not real'; 'She's just a model'; 'I don't believe she ever does her own washing'; 'I wouldn't get on with her if I met her'.

The purpose of using people in advertisements is often simply functional. They are a clothes peg for a shirt or a dress, they are a means to demonstrate the ease of operating a lawn mower or a vacuum cleaner. In this respect the presence of models is like that of a lot of props and settings. A cup-and-saucer in an ad for instant coffee can be purely functional. But it may have a metaphorical or symbolic role to play: to infect the brand with quality and good taste. A problem with the use of models, irrespective of the intentions behind their use, is that their metaphorical role tends to overwhelm their functional one. The risk of the prospect's being alienated by or not identifying sufficiently with the sort of person the model is or appears to be is an ever present one. But it's a risk that is, arguably, equally risky to avoid. Plain pack shots seldom involve enough. To a lesser degree, packs or products put into a particular setting or background don't either.

Companies function as 'source effects' too. It is one of the reasons why they spend large sums of money projecting corporate images. Once a company comes to be seen as reliable, reputable, possessing integrity and having specific areas of expertise and experience, its subsequent product advertising will stand a good chance of being believed. Imagine a new brand of paint by an unheard-of company, Smiths. Hard wearing, tough, the product advertising runs. Belief in the claims is likely to be at best, slender, at worst, non-existent. But what if the paint were made by ICI? Our perceptions would be very different: the background image of ICI, the product's parent, infects the claim made in the advertising.

## 3.3 The recipient

The recipient of advertising messages is a mass, the profile of the mass being described in demographic terms of age, sex, socio-economic class, area or region, and often refined by psychological type (e.g., rational, innovation-prone, sex-orientated, power-orientated, habit-bound). Manifestly, for communication to be effective, the composition of the audience has to be clearly defined and its salient features thoroughly understood. The business of demographic and psychographic definition of audiences belongs to media planning and consumer behaviour studies and thus falls outside the scope of this book.

It is desirable, nevertheless, to make a couple of points. The creator of the ad message is faced with a challenge: by virtue of the mass media used, his communication is directed to, say, six million housewives, yet in order to be effective the constructed message must strive to address not some mass entity but an individual – a Mrs Jones, a Mrs Robertson. No consumer sees herself (or himself) as a mass. To be treated as such depersonalizes, alienates. The copywriter and art director responsible for the ad should aim to talk to an individual while communicating to a mass. To this end they should imagine a real person at the other end of the ad and personalize the message accordingly. It's no easy task. And the bigger and more varied the audience is, the more arduous and challenging the task becomes. By way of contrast personal communication, such as direct selling, is easy. The salesman has the signal advantage of (a) talking to an individual and (b) having immediate feedback: he can change tack, explain more, answer doubts or criticisms as they come up.

If the audience is known or expected to be hostile, the writer and/or art director can, or should, start by sympathizing or even agreeing with its antipathies. Think of Mark Antony in *Julius Caesar*. He starts off by declaring 'I come to bury Caesar, not to praise him'. The crowd agrees; Brutus and the assassination squad agree, and leave moreover. But by the end of his speech Antony has adroitly effected a U-turn. Caesar is no longer a tyrant but a hero. A hero slain by Brutus and his conspirators. The crowd are in Antony's hands. In a TV age, Antony's persuasiveness would have been even more telling and effective (barring the fact that Brutus would, like any instigator of a coup, have gained control of the TV stations!).

## 3.4 The role of the medium

Media aren't transparent boxes through which the message passes unaltered. The formal characteristics of the medium necessarily shape the message being carried.[5]

Print media demand that the message be conveyed in a linear fashion because the eye scans the page left to right, top to bottom. A logical pattern, a cumulative flow is imposed on the copy. It's like a production line: bits of information being put together step-by-step to produce an end effect often summarized or recapitulated in a sign-off or slogan (so, 'Good food costs less at Sainsburys'). The end effect of the message can be examined: how was it arrived at? The reader can go back to the beginning and check the initial conditions, the propositions, and the way they have been developed.

Print advertising is 'consumed' privately. Television advertising on the other hand is largely taken in as a group or shared experience. Cinema advertising is essentially a collective experience. Print requires *active* involvement; TV can be — and often is — absorbed *passively*. Arguably this makes print advertising better remembered. Though on the whole it is less persuasive than television advertising. For on TV the message is locked in time; things happen all at once; there is neither the scope nor the inclination to trace back the development of an argument: the end impression rules supreme. More telling still, we don't know how to deal critically or rationally with emotionally charged music and meaning-laden images.

An ad is infected by the attitudes towards the particular medium in which it appears. TV is generally held to be a more trustworthy medium than print. Perhaps because moving pictures can't lie — or tell the truth for that matter!

The editorial or programme environment can exercise a powerful 'source effect'. An ad in *The Financial Times* will inevitably be imbued with that paper's prestige and authority. Again, an ad in *The Guardian* is more likely to be believed than if it appeared in *The Sun*, the editorial integrity of the former exceeding that of the latter. A TV commercial for Martini — glossy, glamorous, super-affluent — appearing at the end of a documentary on famine and poverty in a Third World country is likely to be received with distaste, at worst the values in the Martini world will be seen as obscene. But slot the Martini commercial into a break in a James

Bond movie: the fantasy and exotic scenarios of the ad are almost like an extension of the movie; the ad is favourably received.

Advertising messages are more effective when their style, tone and content agree with the way people typically use media. The gratifications delivered by television are largely to do with diversion and entertainment. Week in, week out, the programmes with the highest ratings figures are soap operas (*Dynasty, East Enders, et al.*), comedies, quiz and game shows. Thus commercials that entertain are likely to keep the audience.

Look at cinema box-office receipts. The top earning movies – *Raiders of the Lost Ark, Rocky, The Empire Strikes Back* etc., – deliver escapism, fantasy, romance. The audience is keyed up to expect satisfactions of these sorts. Cinema commercials that agree with this mood and expectation are likely to be effective. The audience doesn't want its nose rubbed into domestic reality. Nor is it favourably disposed to poverty-stricken or naff production values. Necessarily low-budget commercials for local advertisers – the take-away across the road – have a hard time of it. Derision, yawns, guffaws are all too often the response.

Radio, at least a lot of the time, is used for companionship. While doing chores in the house in the morning or while in the car on the way to and from work. Thus radio commercials that adopt an intimate, friendly and companion-like tone are, on the whole, likely to be the most effective.

## Subliminal use of media

The means used to convey the message affect its reception. So-called sub-threshold means are, at least in principle, capable of delivering the greatest persuasive effectiveness of all.

In the middle of a movie in the cinema or a programme on TV a split-second advertising message is flashed. It is so fleetingly quick that the mind of the consumer is unaware that it has been subjected to an advertisement. The stimulus of the ad message is below the threshold of consciousness, but it penetrates the consumer's subconscious mind. Put differently, this means of advertising is the logical upshot of the distraction strategy (Section 3.1(b)); the distraction is *absolute*: the audience isn't free to argue, to accept or reject.

Sub-threshold means are the 'brave new world' of the hidden persuaders,[6][7] where ad men and depth-motivation mandarins are made to look alarmingly like a clandestine CIA operation bent on total mind control. This means of advertising is illegal in the UK. Furthermore its value as an advertising tool is, according to the research done, extremely limited.

In one piece of research, a few frames of a pack shot of Coca-Cola were cut into a movie (for what it's worth the movie starred Kim Novak!). Sales of Coke following the film did not significantly increase. But sales of soft drinks as a whole showed a slight rise. This suggests that subliminal advertising triggers, at the subconscious level, general desires only – of thirst, hunger, etc. If the Coca-Cola company were to pay for subliminal 'blip spots' in theatrical films or on television it would in effect help the sales of competing brands, 7-Up, Pepsi and so on.

In practical terms, subliminal methods may be of deep and lasting interest to agencies like the CIA but to marketing managers of consumer products like Omo and Pepsi they are an illegal red herring![8]

## The features of media

From a creative point of view, the properties of media divide, broadly, into those relating to the formal characteristics and those stemming from contingent ones: the way the medium in question *happens* to be used, organized, controlled. If broadcast radio operated on a planet with intelligent life the inherent characteristics would be the same as radio services on the Earth: in both cases the messages would be locked in time, ephemeral, need repetition for acceptable memory scores to be achieved, lack colour and motion and so on. Whereas the organization of alien radio in terms of programming, scheduling, control of advertising (assuming it existed!) would undoubtedly be very different indeed. More mundanely, the contingent features of radio or any other medium will vary considerably from the UK to the Ukraine.

We've already looked at the way advertising can be made effective through harnessing the mental sets of the audience to various media. In the next section, Part Two, we consider in detail the advantages and disadvantages of the TV medium, and in Part Three overview the creative use of the press. Here, it is useful to review the main qualities of the other above-the-line media.

### Radio
That it can't *show*, its chief defect, is also the source of its strength.

For radio is a medium of the imagination: with the right music and effects sound-track, the listener's imagination can be appropriately stimulated. He or she can be cued to supply in their mind's eye their own pictures. Whereas on TV and in print these are almost always spelt out. It's like the difference between reading a novel and then, later, seeing the movie of it. In reading the book you create your own mind-images of the characters and the settings. In the film-of-the-book the images are necessarily cashed for you, often disappointingly.

Take a product like a destination country for a holiday – Cyprus, say. On TV and in the press various pictures are selected and shown: of a beach, a hotel, a landscape, of certain types of people enjoying these 'amenities'. But the world and the get-up of the benefits represented can be at variance with the dream images of the market. Whereas a radio commercial can both incite and allow the listeners' fantasy of what it's going to be like to roam freely, to create imaginatively that perfect holiday.

As with the use of all media, getting attention is prerequisite No. 1. This means being different, standing out, doing the exceptional. 'Hot' shouting is something of a tradition in radio commercials; so being cool, whispering even, is likely to bend ears. Or instead of using a slick, smooth singing voice use an immaculately appalling tone-deaf one. Like the eponymous Freddie Barrett, proprietor of a chain of off-licences, bellowing with all the sonority of a geriatric bull-frog suffering from chronic indigestion 'Come to Barretts . . . Yeah!'.

Production costs are low. There are no budget constraints on the scriptwriter. Virtually any world can be invoked with a few deftly chosen sound-track triggers.

Lead times are short. An ad can be produced, cleared for conformity with IBA regulations, and transmitted very quickly. Thus the medium lends itself to tactical use; to, say, exploitation of current events. When Big Ben stopped, Heineken was fast off the mark to capitalize, with radio ads about how the famous brew's equally famous refreshing properties were called for to restore the workings of the nation's clock.

The life of a TV commercial can be extended (the visual transfer phenomenon). The jingle or sound-track from the TV ad can be used, cueing the visuals of the commercial; the active co-creation of the listener making the message better remembered.

Sound can be used to fix the identity of brand. So, the distinctive 'fizz' of an Alka-Seltzer plopping into a glass of water. Or the 'snap, crackle, pop' sound of Rice Krispies. In short, audio logos can be as potent as visual ones.

In the car, in the garden: radio can be listened to anywhere. Its ambient nature makes it less susceptible to being zapped (TV) or flipped over (magazines and newspapers). It can also be intrusive. Someone lounging in the bath may not be thinking of health insurance or buying a second-hand car. The drawbacks of radio are:

Attention levels tend to be low; captivity poor. A lot of the time radio is *heard*, used as 'sound wallpaper', rather than *listened to*.

The want of vision makes it zero-limited in terms of pack awareness, recognition and product demonstration.

Complex or detailed copy points can't be conveyed. Response facilities, phone numbers and addresses to contact for further information and details, are difficult to get across.

Sales points need to be repeated many times. And the problem is, of course, to deliver the right number of repetitions: too many are prone to result in boredom or nuisance, too few in insufficient awareness.

### Cinema

Despite the fact that it accounts for less than one per cent of total advertising revenue, it remains a uniquely glamorous medium. If radio suffers from a poor image in terms of creative prestige, cinema enjoys a high cachet.

The audience is captive to an unrivalled degree; there is singular impact: darkened auditorium, big screen, lavish and high fidelity colour, motion and the resource of stereo sound. Ads tend to get good recall scores on the basis of a very small number of exposures.

Packages can be bought with a particular movie. Thus there is scope for creatively tying in with the theme and style of the programme. Hamlet ran a cinema campaign with *Star Wars* using clone R2D2 and C3PO robots puffing on the brand. When Australian comedian Paul Hogan, star of Fosters Lager TV commercials, graduated to the big time in his own movie vehicle *Crocodile Dundee* it was a ready-made coup for Fosters and agency Hedger Mitchell Stark to buy spots with the run of Hogan's personalized film.

## Posters

The sheer scale lends the medium impact potential (the standard sizes come in multiples of sheets: a 4-sheet is 60×40 inches, a 16-sheet 10ft×6ft 8in, a 48-sheet 10×20ft, a 96-sheet 10×40ft, with supersites going even bigger).

There is complete freedom and control over production (unlike press where the method of reproduction is fixed by that for the publication concerned). Apart from being able to use inks of striking visibility and saturation, 3-dimensional objects can be incorporated with arresting effect. Peugeot used a helicopter; Araldite glue, a car – with the line 'It also sticks handles to teapots'; Strongbow, a gigantic arrow.

Like the Araldite-stuck car, posters can generate publicity-attracting events. A small exotic-destination travel company created substantial editorial coverage by staging a 'living' poster in south-west London: a lissom, bikini-clad model posed in a hammock slung between two theatre palm trees. Traffic stopped, heads turned, press and broadcast media flocked.

Virtually anything can be pressed into service as an outdoor advertising medium. And the more ingenious, the more the attendant publicity. During the Brighton Festival several years ago Vladivar vodka hired a herd of cows in fields a short way outside the railway station. The animals were custom-fitted with plastic jackets emblazoned with the brand logo. Vladivar and milk!

Excepting the special 'consumption' conditions of cross-track underground and bus shelter sites where attention levels are wont to be high, posters have to deliver their payload, 'say it all', in a couple of seconds at best. Copy has to be pared to a minimum of slogans, brand names, strap-lines. Outdoor advertising is predominantly an art director's medium: striking and lethally impactful visuals constitute the currency.

Posters are prone to being torn, vandalized, adorned with graffiti. However, these liabilities can be teasingly and effectively turned to advantage. A multiple sclerosis campaign featured a picture of a woman sufferer's unclothed back, the length of her backbone being represented as a thin vertical-torn strip of the poster paper, a *trompe l'oeil* of defacement. Canada Dry ran a poster campaign 'Canada Dry rules OK', the headline being got up typographically to simulate red aerosol graffiti sprayed by a zealous football supporter.

**Part two · Creating and producing a TV commercial**

# 4 · The form of television and the TV ad

## 4.0 The medium of television: creative characteristics

We are not directly concerned with the media planner's perspective of the advantages and disadvantages of television, i.e., of the cost-effectiveness of using ITV and/or Channel 4 in delivering $x$ thousands of viewers of a particular sort—typically profiled in demographic terms of age, sex, socio-economic class and region. Nevertheless, the interest of the agency's media department overlaps with that of the creative department, the requirements of the two sometimes giving rise to conflict and compromise. The creative people—the writer and art director—may, for example, be of the persuasion that sixty-second length spots are necessary to communicate the complexity of the advertising message. The media people may demur because of the need for the campaign to clock up a given frequency of spots, the budget available only allowing for thirty-second spots.

The use of teaser TV commercials, known as 'top-and-tailing', requires the mutual understanding of creative and media departments. A TV teaser ad involves, say, a ten-second sequence at the beginning of a commercial break, the identity of the advertiser being absent, the product message being left tantalizingly and intriguingly open. The terminal spot in the break, say of twenty seconds' duration, completes the ad. Teasers have the virtue of involvement, of stimulating the audience to want to complete the fragmented message (see Section 3.1(c)). But the creative demand is expensive, requiring the media buyer to pay premiums in order to buy into specific positions, the first and the last spot in the break.

The creative potential of TV includes, principally:

(1) The evocation of experience. Involving colour, sound and motion, TV is a dynamic medium and can create or simulate the experience of using or owning a product.

(2) The demonstration of product benefits. It is a virtual cliché that TV is the most potent means to show the benefits of a product. And that showing is more persuasive than telling or saying. Indeed, it has been said that TV could have been invented, *qua* advertising medium, for the express purpose of product demonstration.

Benefits are seldom instantaneous; they require time in order to be realized. The TV medium allows for the manipulation of time, compressing it or expanding it. The virtues of a brand of floor-polish can be forcefully communicated by opening on a dirty, lustreless expansion of floor. The housewife starts to apply the polish. One hour of the real time of the housewife is shrunk into a few seconds of screen time. The floor is shown gleaming; the housewife pleased, proud or whatever.

(3) Exploitation of the viewer's mental set. In the way that a boxer can use the ropes of the ring for support and to bounce off, a commercial can make use of the environment of the programming: it can harness the prevailing interest and expectations of the audience for more comedy, for more fast-moving action drama, for more wild-life documentary and so on.

(4) The projection of powerful images. Of companies, and of brands and the people that use them – their life-styles, their characters and personalities.

(5) Triggering of emotion – nostalgia, sadness, tenderness, etc., music and sound effects often playing an important part.

(6) Animation and cartoons. The product and/or logo can be humanized. In cartoon form its personality can be dramatized and reinforced. Consumers represented in cartoon form have the virtue that they are less susceptible to causing alienation than if portrayed by actors/actresses (see Section 3.2). But they carry risks too. An animation-created housewife or businessman can appear

as simply unreal and so pre-empt involvement and identification.

The main drawbacks of TV are:

(1) The message is short-lived. After thirty seconds or whatever it has passed out of existence. So the message usually requires a lot of repetition. And repetition may be counter-productive, boring or irritating to the viewer. In particular over-repeating the brand name is wont to make the name less meaningful rather than more. It's the same if you say any word over and over again: it degenerates into strangeness or nonsense.

(2) The constraints of time. In thirty seconds, the most commonly used spot length, it is not possible to carry effectively more than one substantial proposition (this recalls Rosser Reeves' formula for a 'good ad' (see Section 2.1), though Reeves wasn't confining himself to TV advertising). Even if there is the budget available, longer spots shouldn't be adding copy points. A lot of copy points will just as easily be lost in a ninety-second commercial as a thirty-second one.

TV is poor or difficult to use for selling products directly off-the-screen: you can't put a physical coupon on the tube! Names and addresses and phone numbers for requesting brochures, lists of stockists, etc., are almost certainly going to be forgotten (though the use of Teledata 200-0200 and Oracle page numbers has to some extent overcome this problem).

(3) The production costs of commercials tend to be very high compared with those for print advertising. How much is spent on production is determined by the nature and objectives of the commercial and, of course, by the amount of money the client is prepared to spend. That aside, the effect of the commercial will often be conditioned by the production values of the programming (and the other commercials) surrounding it. A low budget ad consisting of a couple of talking coffee cups in a simple domestic setting may come over effectively in the middle of a TV quiz show. But slotted into a prestige drama series with feature film production values, such as *Brideshead*, it is going to look impoverished, dull, bland.

(4) The size of the commercial, and thus the detail it can convey, is contingent on the viewer's TV set. What looks great on a big twenty-four-inch TV may be lost on a viewer using an eight-inch portable.

A cinema film such as *Lawrence of Arabia* (with its spectacular long-shots like the famous one where Omar Sharif on a camel appears dot-like, blurred on the heat-and-sand-hazed desert horizon, and ever so slowly melds into a determinate yet still mysterious figure) is largely destroyed in impact and atmospheric terms when shown on TV. Few, if any, commercials have the money or time to feature these kind of scenes. But the point remains: commercials have to deliver and register as impactfully on an eight-inch screen as a forty-eight-inch one. In short, big impressionistic long shots are to be avoided. Product experience should be conveyed in close-up.

Commercials should be tested and appraised by the client, the agency and consumer panels under the conditions – including the worst ones – of real life, which may include not just midget-sized screens but also black-and-white (yes, there are still quite a few doing service as second sets).

(5) The reproduction of colour and detail on the average TV screen leaves a lot to be desired. In print media, the agency has a very large degree of control over how the colours will look, how a particular hue of red on a brand logo will reproduce as that precise hue over 1,000,000 copies of a publication. This sort of control is not possible on television. The colour balance and setting on the viewer's TV set determines the received colour. Domestically, TV colour is usually racked up, and the colour exaggerated.

(6) Statutory controls. What can be said or shown on a TV commercial is rigorously controlled by the Independent Broadcasting Authority in conjunction with the Independent Television Companies Association. All commercials have to be vetted prior to broadcast. Some products, notably cigarettes, betting shops and religious and political parties, are prohibited.

## 4.1 Creative grammar: approaches, techniques and forms

### (1) Use a 'grabber'

Because you can't keep an audience 'on hold' for long. If the commercial doesn't seize attention and interest in the first few seconds its chances of delivering its payload are seriously threatened.

What a commercial has to do is similar to that of a TV drama or series. To avoid the oblivion of channel switching both have to hook their audience — fast. Interest won't mount later on; it just spirals down. Only in the cinema, with its captive audience, can attention and interest have the luxury of being able to build-up slowly.[1]

Many TV drama series, particularly US imports and American influenced productions such as *Dempsey and Makepeace*, use a short action-packed sequence as the grabber before going into the main titles and credits. *Dynasty* combines the two: the protracted credits are in themselves a dramatic jigsaw.

Commercials can grab with a single strong image that intrigues or crystallizes a puzzle or problem. The Amstrad Personal Computer commercial starts with a dramatic low-angle shot of a towering steel-and-glass office building. An enigmatic object is jettisoned, or falls, from a window high up in the building. There is a sense of mystery, revealed moments later when, at street level, a typewriter crashes into a skip piled high with an Everest of obsolete typewriters.

The Pirelli P6 tyre commercial, *Double Indemnnity* (see the story-board on page 52–53), opens with the intrigue of a beautiful woman on the phone saying cryptically 'It's done . . . hurry . . .'. She can't put the receiver down fast enough as her husband appears, luggage in hand and bound for a business trip, at the top of the stairway in the elegant villa. Her goodbye embrace is just a shade too fond and forced . . . .

## (2) Be egregious

Stand out from the crowd of other commercials. With near-universal colour, be salient: use black-and-white. Courage's beer has used monochrome very effectively to convey nostalgia and tradition in beer drinking. And the refrain 'Gertcha!', from the 1920s pub-pianist, virtually entered the language of consumers. Aside from the nostalgia theme justification, the black-and-white production served to gain the commercial noticeability.

Don't use any pictures at all. Use just a rolling super (copy rolling on the screen). As the Alliance Building Society did, cleverly making a virtue of the pictureless commercial by saying that the savings on production are passed on to the investor in the form of better interest rates. Salience and relevance merge adroitly.

Use only half the screen, either vertically or horizontally. Or have a completely mute sound track. Or mix black-and-white and colour all through the ad – don't just use colour for the pack shot at the close of a monochrome commercial.

## (3) Slice-of-life

Show the product as it actually would be used in a real life situation, in an everyday context. A family, representative of the target audience, sitting down to a meal in which the product – a frozen food or ketchup, say, is featured. Oxo, Birds Eye and many packaged groceries use this approach.

Despite being low in creative flair and *élan*, this approach doesn't have to be mundane, corny, banal. To get it right is, arguably, one of the most demanding creative challenges. Properly handled it can be one of the most effective ways to communicate the benefits of a product.

The challenge is to show Mr and Mrs Average Target Consumer in a credible context. And if the 'slice-of-life' approach has something of a bad reputation it's largely because the situation represented and the dialogue is unnatural. The husband, the wife, the children being scripted to say things they wouldn't say in real life. At its worst, Mrs Roberts and her young son Johnny are made to act and speak like dummies, mouthing by ventriloquy, sales points from the advertiser. Again, housewives don't usually have passionate conversations at the stainless steel sink about the wonders of a particular brand of washing-up liquid.

## (4) The presenter/announcer

If you can't get it right using a 'slice-of-life', can't get convincing naturalism and realism, then don't try. Use a presenter.

Front-on camera, the actor or presenter delivers the sales message. Alternatively it comes over via a voice-over. This is the original of the TV commercial. And is virtually synonymous with 'hard sell'.

On the whole it tends to be counter-productive, the presenter being perceived as a spokesperson for the company advertising.

The effectiveness of this approach is, at the end of the day, down to the credibility and sincerity of the presenter. Sir Robert Mark championing the virtues of Grand Prix-S tyres produces conviction. A disc-jockey or generic TV personality fronting a detergent commercial doesn't.

There are some maverick presenters. Like the redoubtable Victor Kiam, the 'rags-to-riches' entrepreneur behind the Remington shaver. Kiam has made story-appeal from the fact that he was so impressed by the shaver that he bought the company. His highly personalized style and not inconsiderable chutzpah is the making of the Remington commercials fronted by him. You may not like him but he's difficult to ignore. It's hard to see a director of a detergent company doing the same for one of its brands.

## (5) Use a format of a TV show/programme

The staple of this approach is to use a quiz show format—like *Mastermind*. It's an excuse to mention the brand name over and over again. And in some instances to give the brand a tongue-in-cheek 'over-the-top' importance. Faced with an array of prizes, will the contestant opt for a holiday in the Bahamas or a packet of Brand X?

Then there's the parody of the antiques or art gallery documentary. The product hangs in a gilt frame on the walls or is displayed on a marble plinth. Stern-looking security guards are on duty. A connoisseur/expert waxes lyrically about the brand as though it were a masterpiece by Michelangelo.

## (6) Use a film genre

Lovingly or irreverently, the commercial apes the conventions of a type or style of movie.

The Milk Tray ads go all out to pastiche, and parody the conventions of the big-budget thrills-a-minute action film. The hero runs the gauntlet of enemy bullets, leaps across the top of moving rail cars, dives from buildings. In the face of outrageous danger and suspense the hero wins through. And delivers the Milk Tray. And, of course, he does it all because the lady loves Milk Tray.

The product is invested with a totally hyperbolic importance. In the spy-thriller genre, the product becomes the equivalent of the roll of microfilm that Soviet and CIA agents will stop at nothing to get hold of. In the 'bank job' or heist movie tradition the brand, often the 'secret' new product, turns out to be the quarry in the

**52  Creating and producing a TV commercial**

**Plate 1**
Finished storyboard for Pirelli's P6 'Double Indemnity' commercial. A tale of an adulterous wife, fixed brakes, attempted murder. And a 'torture test' for the product. It's gripping stuff.

**The form of television and the TV ad 53**

Plate 1 (*contd.*)

vaults of a bank. Benson and Hedges used a variation on this approach: after successfully stealing a cache of gold ingots, the character played by Spike Milligan remembers he's left a packet of cigarettes wedged into the alarm bell. Back he goes. And off goes, of course, the alarm. In the detective genre the product becomes the missing person the private eye is hired to track down, or the subject of a ransom demand.

The celebrated Holsten Pils commercials don't just 'tap into' movie conventions, they use actual footage from 1930s and 1940s black-and-white films. With consummate cleverness, original footage is cut into and married with new material featuring the comedian Griff Rhys-Jones so that the latter appears to be in a dramatic confrontation with James Cagney or Humphrey Bogart or Barbara Stanwyck. The technical verve and brilliance coupled with the compelling humour make it one of the most memorable, lovable and distinctive campaigns of the last few years.

Arty or 'difficult' continental firms can be effectively spoofed — particularly by making a surrealistic collision between the subtitles and the scene. For example an ardent and ever-so-earnest love scene being explained by subtitles of copy points about the product. Red Star, the express parcels service, did this with a scene from a Jean Renoir movie.

One of the most outstanding exceptions to the predominant spoof/send-up use of movie genre is Pirelli's *Double Indemnity* commercial. This ad adopts the style, tone and narrative idiom of its namesake, the Billy Wilder-directed 1944 picture. The commercial combines a powerful and effective message, staged around the theme of 'Gripping Stuff', with being a piece of pure cinema in the 'film noir' mould; it's like a two hour suspense-thriller compressed into a breathtaking sixty seconds.

## (7) Use anachronism

Have Julius Caesar nipping downtown to a fast-food hamburger joint. Genghis Khan putting his feet up after a hard day of butchery, relaxing with his favourite tipple.

British Telecom's call stimulation campaign 'It's for you-who!' made play of anachronistic situations. As did the Halifax Building Society with Count Dracula: to get across the message of its newly-introduced twenty-four-hour cash dispensers. The Count, surrounded by pesky flapping bats, steps out into the gothic night to get his cash out, complete with jokes about needing the wherewithal for a bite to eat.

One of the hazards of anachronism is that the humour doesn't on the whole bear repetition. On the other hand, judiciously chosen historical or fictional figures can deliver many of the benefits of using live celebrities and without involving fees!

### (8) Testimonials by people playing themselves

Mrs Williams, a champion dog breeder, talks to camera about the virtues of a brand of dog food, about how her pedigree canines will eat no other.

With the right 'Mrs Williams' and the right *cinema vérité* handling, this approach can be as refreshing as it is productive of credibility. The drawback is that few 'ordinary people' are that convincing in front of the camera. All too often they appear awkward. And, as a consequence of their self-consciousness, they tend to give the impression of delivering lines or making product points to order; the intention of sincerity just isn't enough. The risk of being unconvincing is greatest where the 'ordinary person' is seen as not having any *real* expertise, his/her testimonial appearing to be largely a matter of opinion: for example where 'Mrs Housewife' is called upon to pronounce on the merits of a washing-up liquid.

### (9) Animals

They can function as fertile analogies. They can symbolize power and strength (Esso's tiger, a loping logo replete with sleek potency and wildness); protection (a crab, with its 'custom-built' hard shell, as an analogy for the protection provided by an insurance company); survival (a chameleon for the corporate icon of a company committed to getting across its adaptability in changing circumstances); a humming bird (to focus on the pure nectar of Drambuie); wonder and amazement (Wimpey Construction used a flying snake in the jungle as an analogy for the incredibility and reality of some of its construction projects undertaken in far-away places).

Irresistible and seductive, animals can engage a wide spectrum of emotions. Isn't the animal featured just so lovely, soppy and cuddly? It'll eat your heart out; melt the coldest resistance. The J Walter Thompson agency has dubbed it, the 'Aaah!' factor. The agency's Andrex commercials testify. A Labrador puppy gambols across lawns, canal sides and elsewhere, trailing from its mouth, like naughty puppies will, a roll of Andrex toilet tissue. The 'soft, strong and very long' proposition is conveyed with singular effectiveness. The Labrador puppy is an integral part of the campaign. The dog is both a mnemonic and an emotional property. The advertising is loved and the product USP remembered.

Spend half an hour or so in a zoo: the predominant emotion is humour. It is no doubt partly the result of the 'pathetic fallacy' – animals doing or appearing to do things that humans do. Chimpanzee tea parties are guaranteed to make us laugh. As are the PG Tips commercials with 'talking' chimps. Not only are they funny but also memorable. And highly likeable too.

British Telecom's call stimulation campaign (from J Walter Thompson) uses a prodigious variety of animals on the telephone: elephants, camels, penguins and so on. The resultant mix of humour and affection play a telling part, dissolving our prejudice and resistance to paying for phone calls.

Commercials using animals, endearing and memorable as a lot of them are, come at a price. An animal used in production almost inevitably increases the time spent on shooting and so increases the costs of production. With a few exceptions (like Border collies), however domesticated and well-trained an animal is, it won't 'keep going through hoops' take after take. Wild animals – toads, magpies, foxes – are a producer's headache. Hence the saying: all animals are best stuffed!

Alternatively, show the 'zip fasteners' on the animal costume and make a virtue of it. Like Hofmeister's Jack-the-Lad bear, George. Or do a Disney and cartoon animate. Or special-effects build the creature – easier with frogs than bears!

## (10) Music and song

The power of music to incite, direct, mould and fix emotions is cliché-obvious. Music can make or break the product image and the affections attitudes and impressions that prevail.

'Old masters' are a fertile source. When all seems to have gone wrong – the 'sure-fire' racing tip that somehow failed – happiness comes, tongue-in-cheek with a Hamlet cigar. Bach's 'Air on a G String', wistful and laced with calm, provides just the right mood of consolation and redemption. The Dvorak 'going home' theme stimulates and upholsters the Northern nostalgia mood of the Hovis commercials. Rossini's *Figaro* is signal part of the making of the Fiat Strada commercial. The synonymity of Italy with opera overlays with the Italian-ness of Fiat. And the special electronic music effects added to Rossini by Vangelis, the *Chariots of Fire* composer, enhance and focus the theme of the campaign – the computer-designed and robot assembly of the Strada.

Pop music from the period when the target audience was emotionally impressionable in its teens can be very effective. Hit records from one's past turn a key in the lock of memory and sentiment. Thus advertising to 40-year-olds recommends using late 1950s material: Buddy Holly, Elvis Presley, *et al.*

Cosmetic resemblances between lyrics and titles and the product/product message are best avoided. So: Jerry Lee Lewis's 'Great Balls of Fire' being pressed into the service of Edam and becoming 'Great Balls of Cheese'. On the other hand a record/track can have a lyric or title that is ready-made for commercial use. Thus Manhattan Transfer's 'Chanson d'Amour' is a perfect alliterative fit for Lanson champagne.

A commercial music track can become a record hit in its own right, Coca-Cola's 'I'd Like to Teach the World to Sing' being the most famous example. Old pop hits can, through commercial fame with a younger audience, gain a whole new lease of life. The late Sam Cooke's 'Wonderful World', used in Bartle, Bogle and Hegarty's outstanding Levis 501 commercial, was re-released by Cooke's record company.[2]

Along with his pontifications about the irrelevance of humour, Ogilvy is renowned for his condemnation of singing in advertising. If you went into Selfridges to buy a saucepan and the sales assistant broke out into song you would, Ogilvy says, walk away. You don't buy from singers any more than from clowns.

The mistake Ogilvy makes is that advertising, though of course directed to selling goods, just isn't like personal selling in shops and showrooms. The singing of product virtues on TV (and on radio) is accepted just as it is in a musical. No one, after all, baulks at the want of realism or naturalism when Julie Andrews in *Mary Poppins* is one moment engaged in a conversation and the next erupting into song. It's part and parcel of the convention of genre. As it is with a lot of commercials. Like British Caledonian's ad featuring white-suited, top-hatted, cane-swirling businessmen prancing up and down in the airport, in the plane, chorussing

Caledonian Girls to the tune of the Beach Boys' 'Californian Girls'. However well-intentioned, Ogilvy's strictures on singing simply don't square with its prevalent use.

The grammar and language of the pop promo and video — fast-and-loose cutting; the bravura use of video special effects; random colours; anarchic and surreal mixes of animation, stock footage, graphics, computer-generated images and so on — have had a radical influence on commercials. A major effect of which has been the *primacy of music*: visual images being tailored to the music rather than music being added to underscore the pictures.

## (11) 'Table Top'

The brand/product performs on its own. A chocolate sauce drools lusciously and appetizingly over a cake with a slow balletic grace. The effect is like an 'old master' still-life but with the product moving, its contents/properties exquisitely and enticingly choreographed.

The product is often animated. A packet of biscuits unwraps itself. The biscuits start to dance up and down, perhaps bought to life with cartoon-style faces and arms and legs.

## (12) Vignettes

A quick succession of all manner of different people are shown as users or potential customers of the product. The British Gas flotation 'Tell Sid' campaign is a good example: an encyclopaedia of types of people — rockers, punks, body builders, housewives, businessmen, pensioners — are shown in rapid-fire succession. For whatever reason, share issue advertising has had something of a love affair with this approach (the TSB did it too).

# 5 · Prescribing the commercial

## 5.0 The TV commercial – from idea to the screen: review of steps

The broad sequence of steps is given in Fig. 5.1.

Some clients want to be actively involved and consulted in detail at each and every stage; others, after approving the script and story-board, will adopt a comparatively passive role throughout pre-production and post-production and will take very much a back seat during actual production. Much depends on the importance and nature of the campaign, the working relationship between client and agency as well as the production company and director involved. If the client has opted for, and is happy to pay for a League Division I director – a star – it will assume a low profile and non-interfering stance; it will let the director get on with it, trusting implicitly in his vision, skills, expertise and judgement throughout the development, production and completion of the commercial.

## 5.1 Briefing and strategy

An ad with an all-talking-and-dancing platoon of cartoon bears with an ironic music track and witty slogan at the end is the tip of the iceberg. Underlying it is a formidable structure of digested, processed and analysed marketing information and advertising planning.

In Section 1.2 we looked at some of the main roles assigned to advertising. The precise nature and scope of these are determined

# 60 Creating and producing a TV commercial

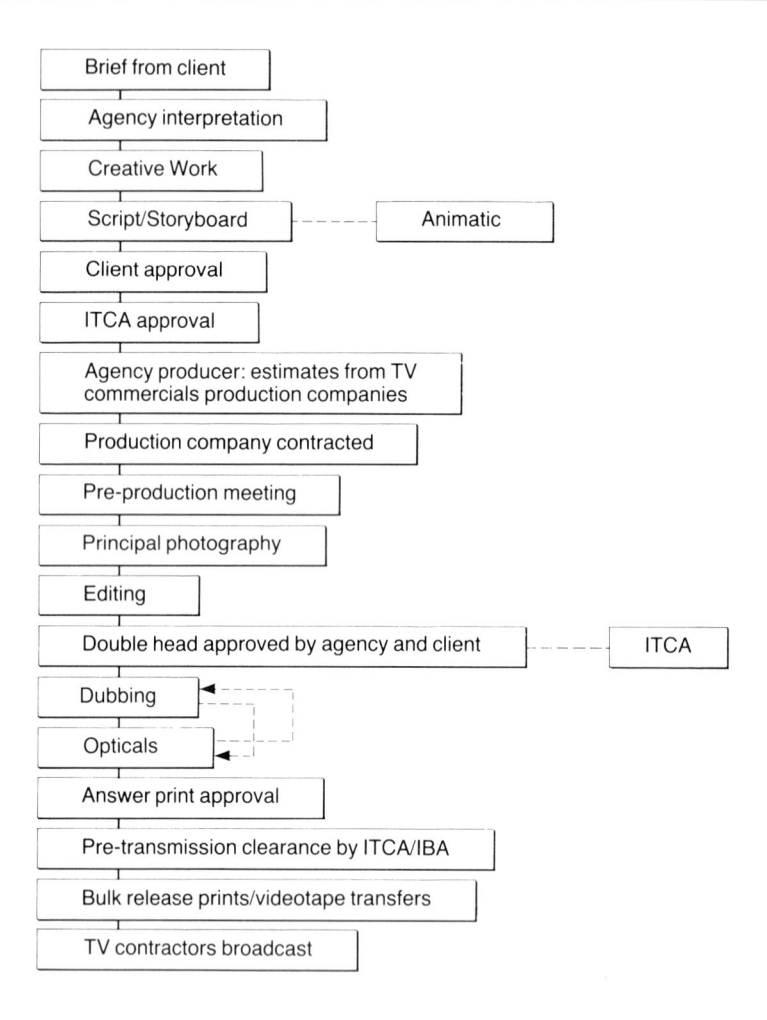

**Figure 5.1** Schematic evolution of a TV commercial

```
Brief from client
      │
Agency interpretation
      │
Creative Work
      │
Script/Storyboard ------ Animatic
      │
Client approval
      │
ITCA approval
      │
Agency producer: estimates from TV
commercials production companies
      │
Production company contracted
      │
Pre-production meeting
      │
Principal photography
      │
Editing
      │
Double head approved by agency and client ------ ITCA
      │
Dubbing
      │
Opticals
      │
Answer print approval
      │
Pre-transmission clearance by ITCA/IBA
      │
Bulk release prints/videotape transfers
      │
TV contractors broadcast
```

by the marketing objectives and strategies for the brand, product or service. The marketing perspective and the job given to advertising within it constitute the basis of the brief given to the agency by the client. The way to attain the advertising objectives — the advertising strategy — is set out in a plan jointly worked out by the client and the agency account management people, along with the media department and the creatives.

A sub-strategy of the marketing one, the advertising strategy consists of a mix of media and creative strategies that prescribe respectively the form and manner of deployment of the media and the overall approach to be adopted to the creative content and style. Though creative strategies will vary considerably regarding specificity, they will in one form or another set out the following:

(a) A statement of what the campaign is to achieve: the end reaction or impression to be realized;

(b) Who the advertising is to be directed at: the target audience, typically defined in terms of demographics – of age, socio-economic classification, gender (male/female/housewife), area (usually an ITV franchise one), and sometimes ownership or usership of products (say, car owners, credit card holders). The target may also be refined by psychographic considerations (e.g., consumers with a penchant for innovation);

(c) The principal and subsidiary benefits to be communicated to the target;

(d) The reasons why the benefits will accrue: the mix of emotional and rational appeals to be incorporated (say, economy and pride);

(e) The prevailing tone, manner and style of the advertising: is it to be light-hearted and funny, or frank and informative? Or whatever?

(f) The media to be used including envisaged spot lengths, positions in breaks, frequency and other media planning information.

The tersely summarized position for (c) and/or (d) and/or (e) is the creative platform – the thematic identity of the campaign.

The strategy provides the disciplinary framework for the creative process as well as the means for evaluating the resulting ideas and their development and execution by the agency account people. No less importantly it provides an agreed and common ground between the agency and the client so that when the agency makes its presentation, even if the client doesn't like the proposals (and, of course, it's his privilege to do so since he is footing the bill for the services), the agency can rationalize what it's done and the way it's done it.

## 5.2 The script and storyboard

Basically these perform the same job: they prescribe and envisage what the commercial will be like in order to plan production, obtain production estimates, gain the client's approval, and ensure at the start that the proposed commercial meets the statutory regulations on television advertising laid down by the IBA's Code

PRODUCT: BRAND X AUTOMATIC
TITLE: LIPSTICK ON YOUR COLLAR
LENGTH: 70 seconds

| VISION | SOUND |
|---|---|
| -Open on hallway. ANN, an attractive early thirties housewife, is about to go out. | 1½ seconds mute<br><br>Ann (shouting):<br>I'm off now darling - I'll see you later.<br><br>Peter (off):<br>Alright. |
| CUT TO | |
| -A study. As PETER hears the front door bang to he opens his briefcase.<br>PETER's POV: CU of shirt with collar covered in heavy lipstick smears.<br>CU: PETER | |
| FLASHBACK | |
| -A lounge bar. PETER on bar stool, engrossed in a newspaper. A sexy GIRL bears down towards him. As she plants a kiss on him he wheels round stunned. The GIRL draws away, flustering in embarassment. | Music over: ragtime piano<br><br>Girl:<br>Oh my God! I thought you were someone else.<br><br>Peter (stiff upper-lipped):<br>It's alright - really. |
| As the GIRL makes her exit PETER looks in the mirror to see lipstick smears on his shirt collar. | Fade music |
| RESUME | |
| -An up-market kitchen. PETER stuffing shirt into washing machine. Finding pack of Brand X all but empty. | |
| CUT TO | |
| -Exterior of supermarket. PETER clasping a pack of washing powder. | SFX: traffic/street |
| CUT TO | |
| -Kitchen. PETER ripping open pack of DASH. Pouring powder into washing machine. Turning it on. | SFX: washing machine gurgling |
| FAST MIX TO | |
| -Machine switching off; PETER opening the lid, delving in. | SFX: machine noises etc. |
| He whirls round in surprise as ANN, smiling, moves towards him. | Ann (off):<br>Darling!<br><br>Ann:<br>How sweet of you to start the washing...let me help you. |

**Figure 5.2** Typical script layout

**Figure 5.2** (*contd.*)

| VISION | SOUND |
|---|---|
| He backs off sheepishly as she retrieves the shirt from the machine and holds it up: the collar is still soiled with lipstick.<br>She snatches up the pack of DASH and waves it in front of him. | Ann: (icily)<br>But you know I only use Brand X. |
| CU: PETER, devastated. | Peter:<br>But...but..I can explain. |
| CU: ANN. | Ann: (in a take-off of a sales spiel)<br>It's the only washing powder to remove stubborn stains ('stubborn stains' is bled for all its double entendre worth). |
| CUT TO | |
| -Pack shot of Brand X.<br>Super: Brand X - The washing powder housewives can trust<br><br>Freeze frame 10 seconds. | FVO: Brand X - The washing powder housewives can trust |

of Advertising Standards and Practice. (Obviously it would be crazy to commit large sums of money to actually making an ad only to find that it is in breach of IBA regulations and so has to be re-shot or, worse, scrapped.)

The task of the copywriter and art director is to translate the strategy requirements into a sequence of compellingly watchable scenes or shots that implant in the mind of the consumer the desired impression, belief, conviction and/or propensity to act in a certain way. The creative chemistry needed to make this translation is not something that can be prescribed; there aren't rules for coming up with the 'big idea'. Arguably, ideas are easy to come by (Ogilvy dreams them!). But the real work and ingenuity, where perspiration takes over from inspiration, lies in cashing or exploring an idea, putting and weaving it into a dramatic or narrative context that forcefully communicates the product message. The test or check of any 'big idea' is: is it 'on strategy'? Does it deliver the right message, to the right people and in the right way?

If the commercial necessarily involves a lot of dialogue, the script will probably lead. On the other hand, if the commercial is predominantly visual and impressionistic, it is likely the storyboard will come first. The normal practice is for the agency to use

# 64 Creating and producing a TV commercial

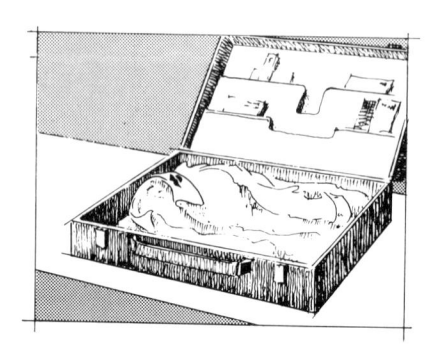

**Figure 5.3** Storyboard rough

**Prescribing the commercial** 65

**Figure 5.3** Storyboard rough (*contd.*)

both a script and a storyboard but occasionally a storyboard will suffice on its own.

Storyboards show the sequence of key shots/scenes. The roughs for these are done by the art director and, usually, the finished version by the visualizer or an outside art studio if a particular or specialized style of illustration is required. Sometimes single pictures in a 'flip chart' style are used for client presentation, often in conjunction with the proposed music track.

## 5.3 Script layout and technical terms

Scripts are laid out in two broad columns, vision on the left, sound on the right (Fig. 5.2).

The visual language of the script involves indicating how much of the subject or scene is to be taken in – the type of shot; the movement of the camera; and how the scenes/shots are to be connected. The function of the script is to convey what the commercial will be like, but it shouldn't pre-empt the role of the director, a major part of whose job is to decide precisely how the scenes or visuals are to be translated into camera language. Moreover, a barrage of detail about shot angles and camera positions makes the script difficult to follow (even though the storyboard (Fig. 5.3) will, or should, take care of this difficulty). The practice of feature film scripting is probably the best: shorts and angles are included when they are integral to the drama or to the sense of the story-line (usually this means close-ups and when what we see is from the point of view (POV) of a particular character).

### Shots

These are defined by how much of the subject fills the screen and range from an extreme close-up: a detail like an eye or a fingernail or part of a pack (the logo, say) to an extreme long shot: a figure a long way off in a landscape (Fig. 5.4).

An *establishing shot* (an 'establisher') is a loose term for a shot that gives a broad perspective showing or explaining to the audience where it is; it is also used for setting the mood and overall atmospheric impression. It is often indicated in a script by something like: 'Open on a nineteenth century colonial mansion surrounded by trees'. In soap operas such as *Dynasty*, establishing

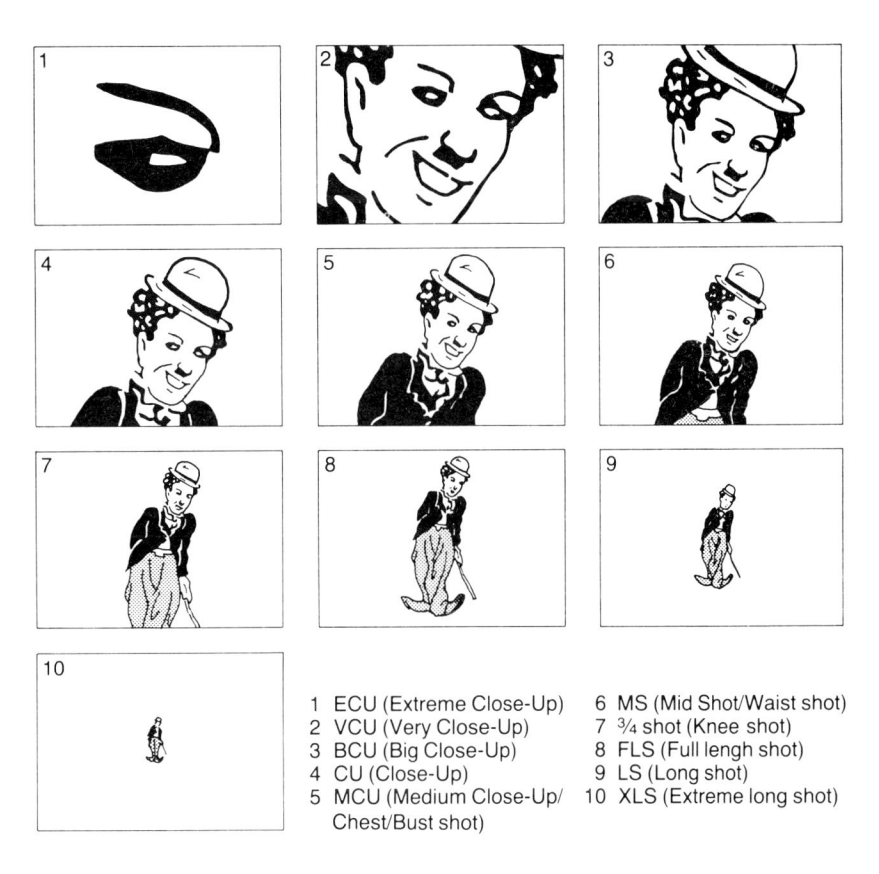

**Figure 5.4** Shot classification

1 ECU (Extreme Close-Up)
2 VCU (Very Close-Up)
3 BCU (Big Close-Up)
4 CU (Close-Up)
5 MCU (Medium Close-Up/Chest/Bust shot)
6 MS (Mid Shot/Waist shot)
7 ¾ shot (Knee shot)
8 FLS (Full lengh shot)
9 LS (Long shot)
10 XLS (Extreme long shot)

shots are, arguably, overdone: the excessive use of low-angle shots of the ColbyCo building, the Le Mirage restaurant/club, the apartment building where Joan Collins/Alexis lives and so on.

Other general shot instructions are: *wide-angle or cover shots* which prescribe a broad view of the action or scene; the *tight shot* which is roughly synonymous with a close-up (directors will tell the cameraman to 'go in tighter' on a particular detail or, if he goes too far, 'to pull out'), and the *2-shot* and *3-shot* which indicate the number of people in the shot when the subject is a group.

## Camera movement

There are two ways of moving closer to or further away from the subject: *tracking* and *zooming*. When tracking in or out, the camera is physically moved on a *dolly* or along a *track* (like a miniature railway line). When zooming in or out, the camera remains fixed and the subject is brought closer or remoter by optical means: by changing the focal length of the lens.

Dollies are used in the studio. The purpose-laid, dead-flat flooring allows for smooth, wobble-free movement of the camera mounted on the dolly. Movement is scripted as 'dolly left or right', 'dolly in or out'; left or right movement of the camera is also described as *crabbing*. On location filming, because of the unevenness of the ground, tracks have to be laid, or for complex camera movements sophisticated cranes and telehoists used.

Clearly, there are many filming situations where it is difficult or impossible to move the camera bodily, e.g., where crowds or physical obstacles prevent the camera from getting closer to the action, in news or sports coverage, in wildlife documentary, in commercials featuring animals or involving hazards such as explosions and fires. In these cases zooming is necessary. As it is when there is insufficient production time or money (which usually amounts to one and the same) to lay track or use dollies.

But aside from such determinants of the zoom, the director may choose to use it for purely aesthetic or dramatic reasons. Imagine a scene in which a character is looking frantically for, say, his keys. From a wide shot he sees a glint from under the sofa. With the character we zoom in to a big close-up of the lost keys.

The 'price' of the zoom is that it alters the perspective of the shot and the depth of field – the distance between the nearest and farthest object in sharp focus.[1] A zoom lens will range from a wide-angle, through to a normal lens and on to a telephoto one. Short-focus or wide-angle lenses, as their names implies, give a wide view. While they are extremely useful for shooting in confined spaces (like the interior of a car or a council house living room) to give a broad angle of view they exaggerate the distance between foreground and background. With close shots of people, the distortion (of hands, noses, feet) is distracting, or dramatic: a man pointing a pistol – the gun barrel will appear menacingly large and bloated, and an unnaturally long way off from his shoulder and face. Typical wide-angle lenses are 17.5 mm and 12.5 mm. A fish-eye lens is the widest, giving a 360-degree coverage of the subject along with grotesque distortion.

Normal lenses, typically 35 mm, give a naturalistic perspective approximating to that of the human eye.

Long or telephoto lenses, 50 mm and upwards, give a narrow angle of vision and compress the space between the foreground and the background, producing an unnatural flattening effect. But this shortening of the depth of field by a telephoto lens is often used for dramatic purposes to isolate the subject from his background: the close shot of the subject is in sharp focus, the people or scenery around him out of focus, producing a sense of isolation and detachment.

Prodigiously long lenses, which are virtual telescopes giving an angle of view of under one degree, are the stock-in-trade of wildlife film-makers (to zoom in close to a bird's nest atop a mountain crag) and show-biz *paparazzi* (to get a close, intimate shot of a star or royalty on a beach or wherever from quarter of a mile away).

Other camera movements are:

*Panning*: the camera remains fixed on its tripod head and is moved in an arc to the left or to the right. The pan follows action and maintains continuity. A woman comes out of a shop. The camera, on the opposite side of the street, pans with her as she walks along; as she stops, the camera stops. Checking her handbag, she panics and doubles back, the camera panning with her.

The *surveying pan*: with the subject the camera pans back and forth across a crowd. The camera stops and zooms to a close-up of a friend.

The *whip pan*: a delinquent throws a brick at a window. The camera fast pans in a visual blur with the brick's trajectory, going into focus at the moment of impact.

*Tilting*: the camera remains static and moves in an arc upwards or downwards (confusingly, also referred to as panning up and down).

*Craning*: the camera is bodily lifted in an arc, up or down.

*The hand-held camera*: the cameraman literally stands in the shoes of the subject. The camera bobs, crests, lurches from the point of view of a water skier, spray flying into the lens/our faces. Habituated as we are to smooth, stable camera movements, the hand-held camera can be strikingly and involvingly dramatic. Imagine a chase scene through woods: a girl is being pursued by a psychopath. The camera is hand-held with the girl: branches crash into us, the world stumbles, tilts and jerks violently; we fall down into the earth and leaves, stagger to our feet.[2]

### Transitions between shots/scenes

The scriptwriter is concerned, among other things, with the manipulation of time, usually compressing it but sometimes expanding it. A wedding service may take three-quarters of an hour in real time but may need to be compressed into ten seconds in screen time. In real time, a washing machine may take forty minutes to wash and spin dry a load; on screen this will need to be reduced to a few seconds. On the other hand a fleeting thought may be expanded into a screen reality lasting twenty seconds.

The classical way of shortening time in movies is to *fade* the scene out to black, then fade in the new scene. The fade is the equivalent of a new chapter in a novel. Sometimes when the time gap is ambiguously large or involves a radical change of location/place a *super* – short for superimposing words or a caption on the screen – is necessary, e.g., '1920', 'PARIS 1945'.

Getting through time by fading may have been fine in the 1940s and 1950s but it slows the pace down unacceptably for modern audiences. Commercials haven't got the time; nor can they afford a second or so of blank screen (which is likely to be costing the advertiser thousands of pounds).

Typically in TV ads time is compressed through *dissolves*: the moment the old scene/shot starts to fade the new scene is faded in; mid-way, both old and new scene/shot will be on screen simultaneously. Video people tend to talk of *mixing* or mixes rather than dissolves.

Many primitive 'special effects' sequences resort to using a series of cross-fades or dissolves. In vintage lycanthrope movies the metamorphosis of the hapless man into a werewolf is inexpensively achieved through a sequence of rapid dissolves: the subject getting progressively hairier and more wolf-like with each dissolve.

When the dissolves are speeded up to the point where they aren't separately discernible the process is synonymous with time-lapse filming. A bulb sprouting, shooting up, the bud filling out, the flower bursting open. Or a cake in an oven: rising, getting brown.

Another device for shortening time is the *wipe*. The old shot is shunted off the screen by the new one. The direction of the shunting may be horizontal (left to right), vertical (up or down), diagonal. Or the new shot may emerge from the old one by way of a square, circle, diamond, ellipse or other geometrical shape starting in the centre of the frame of the old shot. The new shot is 'pulled out' in the form of a square, say, and then rapidly fills the screen. Conventionally, travelling scenes like car journeys are compressed through a sequence of horizontal wipes.

With video effects generators the wipe function, exiting old shots or parts of shots and entering new ones, can be performed in a dazzling variety of ways: tumbles, spins, reveals, conceals, rolling page turns, image explosions. A portion of the old image can be manipulated to introduce a new one: take a pack shot of canned fruit – the label appears to tear itself open or to part like a theatre curtain to reveal a cascade of pineapples, strawberries or whatever.

Collectively known as *opticals*, wipes, fades, dissolves, etc., don't have to be used. Indeed, it is often argued that it is preferable to avoid them as they tend to have a cluttering effect; worse, that they draw attention to the medium, signalling in effect: 'this is a movie' or 'this is a commercial'. The excessive or promiscuous use of video generated effects has come in for a lot of criticism, the most commonly heard complaint being that the effects either obscure a good creative idea or disguise the fact that there isn't a solid idea on which to build and develop in the first place.

Imagine a dinner scene in a restaurant. A young couple looking at the menu. Instead of dissolving to the man paying the bill we cut away to a different place, a different action. The girl's mother at home wondering where her daughter's got to. Then cut back to the restaurant; the couple are now putting on their coats, about to leave. As a device for getting through time the cut away is very effective. But while workable in TV and film drama it can't be used all too frequently in TV commercials as, given the necessary simplicity of many of the scripts, there just isn't any parallel action to cut away to.

How might we get the couple through their dinner without dissolving or cutting outside to some synchronous action? We could use conventions that signal time has passed. Clocks and watches are hammered by cliché and burdened by slowness. But there are standbys such as the bottle of wine. The camera goes in close on the full bottle of wine and loses focus; quickly refocusing, the bottle is seen to be empty. The next shot reveals the man paying the bill.

If the purpose of the scenario is to provide a setting to advertise, say, a brand of liqueur, we could cut from the couple starting their dinner to a waiter at the bar pouring out two glasses of the liqueur. Here, the cut-away is integral because it gives a natural or realistic context to show the brand in close-up – bottles of liqueur seldom if ever being brought to the table.

The most versatile time-shrinking device is the *buffer shot*. An executive is at home getting up, in the middle of shaving, say. We want to get him into his office – fast. We could cut to an establishing shot of a concrete-and-glass office building and then to an interior of the executive dictating or in a meeting or whatever. Or we could cut from a close shot of an electric razor to a shot of lift doors sliding open, the man stepping out, suited and carrying a briefcase. Or we could cut from a bathroom interior to a close-up of a phone ringing: the camera pulling back to reveal the executive in his office as he stretches forward to take the call. The essence of the buffer shot is any shot, however fleeting, that does not contain the subject.

## The audio script

As we've seen, all instructions for sound appear in the script in a column on the right-hand side of the page.

The prescriptions for sound will include synchronous sound, i.e., that recorded during the shooting of the commercial: dialogue, sound effects; and sounds that will have to be recorded during post production – music, voice-overs, atmosphere tracks and sound effects.

The main abbreviations used are: VO, MVO, FVO (for voice-over, male voice-over, female voice-over). A voice-over, as its name implies, is an off-screen voice, a narrator or commentator. Frequently the VO is used at the end of commercials to underscore the super of the slogan or final sales message. The final frame of the Carlsberg commercials consists of a pack shot and the super: 'Probably the best lager in the world' and, coincident with it, the resonant bass voice of Orson Welles intoning 'Probably the best lager in the world'. With the passing on of probably the deepest voice in the voice-over world, James Coburn's larynx now booms the slogan.

Voice-overs are used to 'go inside' a character's head, to externalize his/her thoughts and feelings. The camera goes in close on the character's face; we hear his/her thought. A perfume commercial might feature a beautiful girl in a French chateau. She's sitting at an antique dressing table finishing her make-up. We hear, over, her thoughts, dreamy and wistful.[3]

Sound effects are indicated by SFX or just FX, e.g., SFX birds singing; FX car tyres squealing. There is, admittedly, some confusion here, as in feature film scripts SFXs are used to denote special visual effects whilst AFXs denote audio effects.

## The script and ITCA technical requirements

Commercials' scripts specify at the beginning: one second or one and a half seconds mute. This is because the sound track (S/T) on film is in advance of the picture to which it refers by about one second. 'In all cases, irrespective of length, the running time of the sound-track should be less than that of the picture by at least one and a half seconds, starting not earlier than one second after picture start and finishing not less than half a second before the end of the picture.... A minimum one second mute section ensures no loss of sound when films are joined at the start of picture content.'[4]

For commercials submitted on videotape the ITCA requires that 'the running time of the sound should be less than that of the picture by at least one second, starting not earlier than half a second after picture start and finishing not later than half a second before the end of the picture'.[5]

Unlike the opening mute section which conventionally is indicated in the script, the ITCA requirement for the close of the visual part – that there should be a mute over-run of the final picture by at least ten seconds – is normally only included when a freeze-frame is required for dramatic reasons, e.g., to halt in mid-air a group of children jumping for joy. 'In cases where (freezing the action) is not possible, the over-run should consist of repeat printing of the last frame of the commercial which may have to be transmitted by the Programme Companies according to the needs of the service.'[6] To make up the precise number of seconds for a commercial break, the final commercial may have to be extended for an extra few seconds. We've all seen a still picture effect at the end of a break going on with awkward and unnatural silence, second after second.

The restrictions imposed by the above on the scriptwriter are slight but nevertheless need watching, i.e., don't crack off with dialogue or sound effects. And have a logo or slogan at the end. That half second of silence could be costing a couple of thousand pounds! (Though it's hard to imagine any script being acceptable to a client without some form of closing slogan or brand name super.)

# 6 · Pre-production and development

**6.0 The birth of the commercial: client approval**

The writer and art director have come up with a proposal – or a series of proposals – for the commercial after approval and perhaps some revising here and there by the creative director. The script(s) and storyboard(s) then have to go through 'a marketing mill': they have to be sold to the agency account management team. The account executive will analyse and assess the script from a marketing perspective, from the brand's objectives, from a client's likely point of view.

How sound is the basic concept/idea? How effective is the execution or get-up of the idea? Overall, how rigorously 'on strategy' is the envisaged commercial?

The account executive may approve the script as it stands. Or he may reject it outright. And then it's back to the drawing board for the creatives. Or, more usually, he will view it like the curate's egg. Great in some parts, wanting in others. He will discuss ways to improve it, suggest how it could be tightened, made more effective.

With his understanding of the client's marketing and advertising objectives and, not to be underestimated, what 'makes him tick' as a person, the account executive will be able to advise the creative team on the best way to sell the commercial to the client.

Client presentation is the big day: adrenalin and nerves rule. A great script can be lost if the presentation is maladroitly handled. Stunningly good ideas rarely sell themselves. Cynics will aver that what counts isn't what you do but the way you do it. You don't have to be a cynic, just a realist! For, arguably, the crux of creativity in commercials (and advertising in other media) lies in the persuasive art of getting the client to see eye to eye with your ideas and proposals.

Before or after client presentation – it depends on the circumstances – consumer research is undertaken. What is obvious or likeable to an agency creative or executive or brand manager, may not be so to a C2 beer drinker or a northern housewife.

If the creative approach is radical, it is pretty likely that research with a panel of representative consumers will be largely negative or at best inconclusive. Frank Lowe[1],[2] has made the point that innovative advertising can seldom be research-led in the way that product benefits or product formulation can. If it is, you end up with the sort of advertising that went before. Lowe cites the campaign for Heineken, now lauded and canonized as a classic but at the time of its inception, rule-breakingly revolutionary. Lager drinkers said the proposed Heineken ads didn't make sense, they weren't proper beer advertising. One of the most outstanding advertising campaigns in the last twenty years would, if consumer research had been adhered to, never have seen the light of day. The credit for it doing so must go to the bold and pioneering stance of the client as much as to the creative brilliance of the agency, Collet Dickenson & Pearce.

Sometimes the client may be unconvinced – especially if visually naive – and the consumer puzzled or diffident because the storyboard by itself doesn't evoke a sufficient impression in their respective minds' eyes of what the eventual commercial will look like. To make the ideas in the storyboard more telling, more easy to grasp imaginatively, the agency will develop the storyboard into an *animatic*. Usually augmented by music, it consists of a series of rough drawings or illustrations that animate in the formal manner of a cartoon the scenes and shots. Sometimes, too, an audio tape providing a dramatic or narrative commentary on what's happening will be compiled and played over the animatic or the storyboard.

An alternative to producing an animatic, and usually done on grounds of keeping costs down, is to make a series of still photographs of the key scenes and then show them to the client as a slide/tape presentation.

However, for some commercials, animatics or slide/tape presentations are a waste of money as the impact of the proposed commercial is uniquely bound up with the production values resulting from shooting in a particular – often exotic – location, the use of elaborate models, the use of special effects wizardry.

## 6.1 ITCA script clearance

Commercials on UK television must conform with the statutory regulations of the IBA Code of Advertising Standards and Practice. The code is operated in a preventative rather than a prosecutive way: all commercials are vetted prior to transmission by the IBA and the ITCA.[3]

To avoid squandering large sums of money (and large amounts of time) on making a commercial that then turns out to be in breach of the code, commercials are examined at the script stage by the ITCA's Copy Clearance Committee which acts in close cooperation and agreement with the IBA. If revisions to the script are required, the ITCA will discuss with the agency the nature and manner of such amendments that will make the script acceptable.

Factual claims made in a script must be accompanied by evidence from, say, technical, clinical or scientific tests. And for some products (deodorants, underwear, lavatory cleaners), because the visual treatment is likely to be critical, the agency is required to submit a storyboard.

Most scripts are cleared within a few days. Those involving complex, controversial, scientific or technical claims take longer, perhaps several weeks, as the scripts have to be referred to specialist panels and consultants for detailed consideration. If there is a genuine urgency and the proposed commercial does not contain anything contentious, clearance can be obtained within a matter of hours.

Where visual treatments are at a premium it is prudent for the agency to send a roughcut[4] of the commercial to the ITCA for its approval or advice. The roughcut is in the form of a double-head, i.e., the sound and the picture are separate; for once combined, alterations are not possible or expensive.

Can demonstrations be faked? Can substitute materials be used? Like the fabled use of mashed potato for ice cream? The short answer is that substitute materials are permissible provided they do not give a misleading impression of the product or its performance. Thus to demonstrate the high sheen produced by a brand of floor polish it would not be permissible to cover the floor with plate glass. On the other hand it is in order to use painted wood for a chocolate bar because given the conditions of heat from studio lights 'a normal shot would not do justice to the product'. But the 'final visuals (must be beyond all doubt a perfectly accurate representation of the product and its performance as the public would find it'. 'Whenever necessary ITCA will obtain a sample of the product to compare with visuals. Agencies are advised to see that production units are very carefully briefed.'[5]

When the commercial has been completed it is necessary for a 35 mm print (or videotape transfer) to be submitted to the ITCA for approval. Via a closed-circuit link the commercial is also viewed by the IBA for its approval of the final version of the advertisement.

Representatives from the sixteen independent TV companies will also view it, so that they will be in a position to ensure that the scheduling of the commercial on their respective stations will conform to IBA regulations, e.g., that an ad featuring a well-known actor isn't booked to be transmitted in a break sandwiched in a programme featuring that actor (the IBA code proscribing any suggestion or implication of sponsorship: programmes and advertising breaks having to be seen as clearly distinct and separate).

## 6.2 Pre-production: contracting the production company

Once the script is approved by the client and the ITCA, the agency TV producer comes on to the scene. He (or she) has the overall responsibility for translating the script into a 35 mm (or one-inch videotape) moving picture. He understands the business of advertising, the technical and practical aspects of making a commercial and has wide experience of the production and facilities companies. He needs, too, to be possessed of considerable powers of diplomatic tact. He has, in the words of David Abbott, 'to be something of a jack of all trades and master of them all'.

The agency producer will not have been directly exposed to the fire and wrangling of the creative process, to the selling of the commercial's concepts, ideas and script execution both to the agency account management team and to the client. He will thus be looking at the script and storyboard with a fresh perspective and with objectivity. He will first need to satisfy himself that the scenes/shots/dialogue/music in the script can in fact be realized within the thirty seconds (or whatever) time span of the commercial.

The next step is for the agency producer to obtain estimates from a number of TV commercials production companies.[6] Basically these consist of several producers and directors; they rarely own the physical means of production – studios, lighting, sound equipment, editing facilities; these are rented by the company as needed.

The agency producer will select production companies on the basis of their showreels (a compilation of the commercials they've done either as a 'house' or for one of the directors on their books), past experience of working with a particular producer or, invariably the most deciding factor, because of a director attached to the production company (there are virtually no freelance directors). The choice of the production team/unit is, clearly, critical. As John Hegarty, creative director at Bartle, Bogle and Hegarty says: 'TV advertising is particularly tricky because it's less controllable ... the leap from a good script to a good commercial is intangible, the one doesn't necessarily lead to the other.'[7]

The style, look and 'feel' of the commercial is determined by the director. The agency producer and agency creatives (and occasionally even the client) will be convinced at the outset that a certain few directors are going to be 'right' for the commercial in question. There may be a preferred choice for a particular director if a distinctive, idiosyncratic even, treatment and handling of the script's theme, dialogue and/or visual style is sought after. A particular director may be renowned for working sensitively and effectively with children, for handling humorous themes and situations with skill and consummate timing, for mastery of mood and impressionistic visuals, for expertise in directing narrative, for diplomatic handling of 'difficult' celebrities, for a pop/video promo look, for animation and so on.

Occasionally a 'star' director will be the first choice. Stars, of course, cost the proverbial arm and a leg (some cost an artificial limb factory!). On rare occasions a flier will be taken on a director with an illustrious profile in feature films or TV drama who is new to commercials (Fellini was contracted to do a commercial).[8] But such inspired innovations are likely to be the source of sleepless nights for the agency producer. At the end of the day he is responsible for the final print that is sent to the TV companies and that is acceptable to the client.

Though the agency producer and the art director/writer creative team will have their ideas about the locations and so on, the production companies asked to submit estimates will usually be given an open brief: it is left to them to work out from the script (and storyboard) how to realize the commercial.

A script may call for exteriors and interiors of a fairy-tale medieval castle. One production company might predicate its estimate on a model for the exteriors and constructing and dressing interiors in the studio. Another might decide, following a series of preliminary location reconnaissances, to shoot the entire commercial on location in Scotland. A third company might elect, in the interests of achieving absolute authenticity, to go for an overseas location – to a romantic fifteenth-century chateau in the Loire Valley in France or a 'mad king' Ludwig of Bavaria castle overlooking a lake in southern Germany.

In order to prepare an actual *budget* the production company will need to discuss the script with the agency people to iron out interpretations. Perhaps, even, the script can be improved without altering its essentials. Obviously it helps if the production company producer has a fairly good idea of how much money the client is prepared to spend. Invariably not enough!

Where competitive quotes are needed, the agency will give the production company a closed brief: all the variables – the locations, sets, number of days of shooting and so on – will be rigorously specified.

As with estimates for most things, the cheapest is seldom the best. You get what you pay for. As J Walter Thompson TV administration head Michael Warhurst says: 'Every script has its price. If a client wants a spectacular production he will have to pay for it. You cannot cut corners if you want creative excellence.'[9] Don White, former creative director at McCann-Erickson, underlines the point: 'Of course production costs can be cut. There is always a cheaper director, a cheaper lighting cameraman, cheaper actors, cheaper voiceovers. And usually that's how your finished commercial will look. Cheaper.'[10]

Misunderstanding and ill-will in some areas surround the whole business of production estimates. Costing commercials remain a source of some friction between production companies and agencies. Escalating costs are responsible for agencies accusing production companies of extravagance. But the difference between extravagance and high production values and creativity is a grey area of striking the right balance.

Production companies have a reasonable grouse which some agencies recognize. 'In an ideal world', says Nicky Webster at Foot Cone and Belding, 'agencies would not talk to production companies until they have a serious script. In my view, a serious script is one that has been approved by the client, researched, and approved by the ITCA.... There are too many agencies which waste everybody's time by talking to a production company the moment a script is written. This should not happen. The agency producer should be able to gauge a broad area of costing, but until the creative team and producer sit down with the directors, a serious budget cannot be obtained, because the final cost of the commercial relates directly to the director's interpretation of the script. As we all know, this can vary tremendously.'[11]

The practice of some agencies asking production companies to quote on commercials for which client and ITCA clearance hasn't been obtained has prompted some production company producers to start talking about payment for quotations. Directors Studio producer Jim Baker has suggested a one per cent fee.[11]

## 6.3 Major factors affecting the budget

### (1) Studio or location

Which is cheaper? The newcomer is inclined to say 'studio'. But it all depends on the sort of interiors and exteriors required. If the script calls for a pub interior it will be cheaper to find a pub 'off-the-peg' and hire it for a day or a couple of days than to build a saloon bar in a studio, furnish it and set dress it.

The more elaborate the interior the more imperative it becomes to find a location. For period interiors, locations are virtually essential.

A studio build only becomes an economic proposition if you want a starkly simple present-day set, preferably for two days or more. But even a contemporary C2 living room or kitchen will probably be cheaper to do on location than in the studio; it will probably look better too. Though the problem is to find one that is large enough to house a crew, actors and sprawl of equipment. It's best, too, if the location is empty.

On the other hand, using a studio has the advantage that nearly all the facilities – catering, dressing and make-up rooms, power – are on tap. (Studio hire is either done as a package, which may include all lights and equipment, or as a '4-wall deal' – the production company rents just the bare stage.) Moreover, when using a studio you don't pay the crew until they arrive. On location, even if it's a house bang next door to the studio, you pay travelling expenses (and almost everyone takes taxis!).

The commonplace myth of the expense of location shoots is based on foreign locations. And here the myth dissolves into stark reality. Budgets climb into Everest-steepness. A two-day shoot in Australia will effectively take a week. Getting out there, a jet-lag rest day, getting back. Air fares for an entire crew, cast and support production personnel, air freight and hotel expenses and so on. The cost becomes awesome, but worth it if special production values and backdrops are vital, such as perfect blue skies and exotic scenery; or if the brand on the breakfast table or wherever needs the TV-mediated chemistry of dream imagery; or if the personality of the brand is inherently connected with a foreign setting (Bounty bars and the West Indies).

## (2) Art department

Any producer will warn: this is the area to watch. Very carefully. Costs can creep up to an alarmingly high level. These include: set design, construction and striking (all frighteningly labour-intensive); hire of properties (always far greater when it comes to it); special packs (wooden chocolate bars and so on); model making; special effects; costumes and wigs.

## (3) Casting

Celebrities of course are going to load the budget heavily. And mega-stars will be astronomic.

The daily rate for jobbing actors and actresses is a relatively small part of the overall costs – unless you've got a cast of 50 and they all need to be attired in seventeenth-century costumes, tail coats, wigs, the full regalia.

The real cost of thespians comes after the commercial is transmitted. They are paid 'use' fees based on the number of times the commercial goes out. The use (or 'repeat' fee) is a cumulative percentage of the actor's basic studio fee (see pages 93–94).

True to the cliché about them (and animals), children can be a problem. Babes-in-arms apart, the younger they are the more of a headache they're likely to be. They tire easily – and understandably – after a lot of takes. A director might succumb to open exasperation with an actor for continually doing something wrong but to do so with a child can end in more than temporary tears. Employing children is subject to strict regulations on hours worked and rest periods. You can't go into overtime. Overall, using children is likely to increase the shooting schedule and in consequence the budget.

## (4) Music

This is in many ways as variable a cost element as casting. There is virtually no recorded music worth using that is in public domain (i.e., free). The composer or lyricist may have been dead for fifty years but the performance will be protected by copyright unless the recording was made in the 1930s or earlier. And there can be few occasions when the authentic crackles and noise of a shellac seventy-eight r.p.m. are required. If a vintage recording has been electronically washed and digitally brushed-up then the rights to it will have to be negotiated. As will the use of modern performances of classical music; so while Vivaldi's *Four Seasons* score is free, Neville Mariner's conducted performance with the Academy of St Martin-in-the-Fields is a copyright product.

An ageing rock 'n' roller and/or his record company and/or the music publishing company concerned may be delighted to sell the rights to a hit from the late 1950s to a pet food corporation for a few thousand pounds. At the other extreme, rights to a track from the Stones or Bob Dylan are likely to prove very hefty.

Some music can't be bought to sell products. 'Every man has his price' – but not Bruce Springsteen who reportedly turned down flat an offer of $12 million from Chrysler to use one of his songs in a major campaign. Paul McCartney, too, has steadfastly declined to sell rights to his and the Beatles' work. Though computer company Hewlett-Packard (in the UK) and Lincoln-Mercury (in the US) managed to pull off coups by acquiring the music and lyric rights to, respectively, 'We can work it out' and 'Help!' and then using sound-alikes to record the material.

McCartney's antipathy to Beatles' tracks being used in commercials effectively ended when, in 1985, Michael Jackson outbid him for the rights to some 250 Beatles songs. Jackson evidently doesn't see the music as 'sacred': in 1987 he sold 'Revolution' to Nike-Air for a year's use. Out in the States, the commercials for the famous training shoes are the first time ever that Lennon and McCartney's voices/playing can be heard in the service of product selling. Nostalgists and purists are outraged, whilst Nike and its ad agency are justifiably chuffed. (Beatles music won't, however, be entirely up for grabs: Jackson has declared that if he *really* loves a song, his company won't sell at any price. Two numbers purportedly 'not for sale' are 'Eleanor Rigby' and 'Fool on the Hill'.)

When 'off-the-peg' recorded music is not suitable or not available, music will be commissioned from scratch. Here, by and large, you pay for the 'name' of the composer, his track record or special expertise. Especially if he's a highly successful jingles writer. Or you cut costs, and back your judgement, with a hungry new composer. Even then, costs can be large if the score is of a sort that requires a full symphony orchestra to perform it rather than a single synthesizer, which may well be played by the composer himself.

## (5) Shooting ratio

The shooting ratio is a broad determinant of how long the filming of the scenes and shots in the script is estimated to take. It refers to the average number of takes for each shot. Thus a ratio of 10:1 allows for ten takes for each shot. From these one take is 'bought' and goes forward into the assembly or edit of the commercial.

The adage 'time is money' applies in any field. But in filming, when you're paying for an entire crew, for equipment and facilities, for a location hire or for a studio rent, time really is money. And how!

A take can be fouled for a whole variety of reasons. The actor may fluff his lines – though it's pretty unusual in shooting a commercial as the actor has very few lines to deliver compared to TV drama or film features. Most likely is that he (or she) fails to say the lines in the way the director requires. Or that his (her) facial expression and body movements aren't right.

When the performers are animals, even if allegedly well-trained domestic ones, getting a satisfactory take can prove to be a nightmare. So it's prudent to allow for a very high shooting ratio. It may be predicted to be so high that it would be cheaper to have the art department commission animal simulated models or animatronic effects.

Takes may be ruined, too, by any number of technical problems or malfunctions: loss of focus, 'dirt' on the sound track, a cable or light in shot, etc. Or unwanted sound – an airplane going over.

Though minor compared to the time and labour costs, the shooting ratio is a determinant of stock costs. A 10:1 ratio means effectively that for every ten feet of film exposed just one foot, gross, is going to be used on screen. (Though if shooting on videotape the burden on the budget is slight as (a) the cost of tape is negligible compared to celluloid and (b) tape can be wiped and re-used.)

## (6) The number of scenes/shots

Each new shot takes about an hour to set up, to move the camera, change the lighting, rehearse, etc. Each new scene will take longer still, requiring major changes of lighting, rigging, technical blocking, performer rehearsal.

## (7) Opticals

A lot of dissolves, wipes and other shot transition effects, as well as intricate and complex titles and captions, whether done by the film labs or, as is more commonplace today, by video post-production will load the budget.

Opticals charges can be a source of frustration and grievance for production company producers. As Meno Ziessen says: 'Some agency producers and creatives who have shown remarkable restraint in pre-production and shooting, become quite uncontrollable in post-production.'[12] Inside a highly sophisticated and/or state-of-the-art video post-production facility house, where costs can run up to hundreds of pounds per hour, the panoply of effects wizardry can sometimes prove irresistible.

## (8) Special technical equipment

For complex tracking shots, for crane and telehoist shots, for underwater shooting, for aerial filming from a helicopter, for shooting inside a moving car with a 'steadicam' camera mount, for complex camera grips and mounts necessary for filming the outside of a car on the move, for special lighting effects, etc.

## (9) Night shooting

Some night scenes don't have to be shot – and usually aren't – at night. Interiors, like a conventionally-lit living room with curtains drawn, are almost always filmed in the day: shot 'day-for-night'.

It's feasible (well, just about) to shoot some exteriors day-for-night by stopping down the lens, i.e., reducing the amount of light reaching the lens (which technically translates into increasing the f-stop number) so that daylight looks like, say, a grey dusk or gloomy night.[13]

Where conventional point light sources are called for – exteriors with street lamps and shop/café neon signs, car headlights cutting through the darkness of a country road, a character finding his way through the darkness with the play of a torch beam – day-for-night expedients and simulations won't work because it's impossible to simulate the intense stark contrasts between the light source and the surrounding darkness (if you switch on your car headlights during the day they will be puny to the point of being unnoticeable).

'Night-for-night' shooting is expensive as the entire production unit is paid at overtime rates.

## (10) Animation

Always highly time-consuming: weeks and weeks, if not months. If combined with live action (an all-dancing-and-singing pack cavorting on a breakfast table at which are seated Mr and Mrs C2 and children) costs escalate fairly alarmingly.

## (11) Special effects

For, say, flying sequences as in the British Airways 'Superman' pastiches. It's a vague term – but arguably better for being so – that may overlap with (a) art department materials and labour costs – chairs specially built to collapse for a wacky comedy commercial; models of buildings designed to explode; properties for stunt work – simulated brick walls through which a car is to be driven, and (b) video facilities post-production costs – colouring a product in a black-and-white commercial as in the *Financial Times* commercials.

## 6.4 The budget

The production company producer will submit an estimate (Fig. 6.1) to the agency producer using the standard AFVPA (Advertising Film and Video Producers Association) budget forms. Added to the total cost of the items is a percentage mark-up. This can vary considerably but is quite often around thirty to thirty-five per cent. Extraordinary items such as special effects, special builds and foreign location transportation are subject to a lower mark-up, typically between fifteen and twenty per cent.

If there is an item in the budget that is very unpredictable, say the use of latex-modelled jumping frogs, the company will protect itself by building the cost into the budget as a contingency or by excluding it, leaving the cost to be accounted for by the advertising agency.

If the production company has got its figures wrong and the shoot goes over budget, the overage is borne by it and so eats into its mark-up. Thus an unrealistically drawn up budget or a run of bad luck during shooting could result in the company making very little, or, worst of all, doing the job at a loss. On the other hand, it may be that the company has over-budgeted and so brought the commercial in below the estimated figure. Some clients insist on an independent audit to see whether the production company has made profits in excess of its mark-up. If so, the benefit of any excess on the actual cost of the production is reaped by the client. With ever-escalating costs and the ubiquitous demand for 'value for money', client-originated audits are likely to become fairly widespread. However, the costs of auditing are likely to outweigh any savings except in cases where there is a lot of padding in the budget or where by dint of superb efficiency the production company succeeds in making the commercial for a great deal less than the estimated cost.

The production company budget does not include the costs of fees to artistes and their repeat fees, stills photography (which the agency will use for trade publicity and perhaps for reproduction in poster and press media), music, voice-overs, artwork and packs

# Creating and producing a TV commercial

**Standard Breakdown of Film/Video Production Estimate**
Approved by AFVPA/IPA/ISBA

SUMMARY OF ESTIMATED COSTS

| Page | | | | | | |
|---|---|---|---|---|---|---|
| 1 | **A** | Pre-Production | | | | |
| 1 | **B** | Recce | | | | |
| 1 | **C** | Casting & Cast | | | | |
| 2 | **D** | Production Salaries | | | | |
| 2 | **E** | Unit Salaries | | | | |
| 3 | **F** | Electrical Unit | | | | |
| 3 | **G** | Camera Equipment | | | | |
| 4 | **H** | Art Department | a) | Personnel | | |
| 4 | | | b) | Costs | | |
| 5 | **I** | Studio Costs | a) | Labour | | |
| 5 | | | b) | Costs | | |
| 6 | **J** | Location Costs | | | | |
| 7 | **K** | Stock, Negative & Processing | | | | |
| 8 | **L** | Editing, Optical & Film Finish | | | | |
| 9 | **M** | Editing, Optical & Video Finish | | | | |
| 10 | **N** | Insurance | | | | |
| 10 | **O** | Sundries | Sub Total | | | |
| | | Annex A – Animation Production | ° ☐ | | | |
| | | Annex B – Video Shoot | ° ☐ | | | |
| | | | Mark Up % | | | |
| | | | Sub Total | | | |
| | | | * Mark Up % | | | |
| | | | Sub Total | | | |
| | | | * Mark Up % | | | |
| | | | Total Production Est. | | | |
| | | | Weather Day | | | |

\* Costs subject to special mark-up
° Tick if included

**Figure 6.1** Production estimate: main headings

and weather insurance. Various other items will be included or excluded after prior agreement between the advertising agency and the production company as to which of them will be responsible for what (Fig. 6.2).

The agency prepares a total estimate for making the commercial which is then submitted to the client. It will consist of: (a) the production company's figures (plus mark-up), (b) the cost of all the items excluded and (c) the agency's mark-up, typically fifteen to twenty per cent.

The above method of budgeting, known as the 'firm bid' or

## Standard Breakdown of Film/Video Production Estimate
Approved by AFVPA/IPA/ISBA

| Client: | Prod Co: |
|---|---|
| Product: | Director: |
| Titles 1: | Producer: |
| 2: | Prod Co Job No: |
| 3: | Shoot Film/Tape |
| 4: | Post Prod Film/Tape: |
| No & Length: | Air Date: |
| Agency: | Sales Conference Date: |
| Agency Job No: | |
| Producer/Agency Authorised Rep: | |
| Creatives: | |
| Agency Brief(s) Received: | |

BASIS OF ESTIMATE

| INC | EX | | INC | EX | |
|---|---|---|---|---|---|
| | | 1. Location Recce | | | 23. Artiste Insurance |
| | | 2. Casting Director | | | i) Personal Accident |
| | | 3. Video Casting | | | ii) Non-Appearance Fee |
| | | 4. Artistes Tests · Fees | | | 24. Weather Insurance |
| | | 5. Artistes Fees · Featured (BSF) | | | 25. Rushes Only |
| | | 6. Artistes Fees · Extras | | | 26. Directors Cut |
| | | 7. Artistes Fees · Stand-Ins | | | 27. To D/H without opticals |
| | | 8. Artistes Fees · Stunts | | | 28. To D/H with film opticals |
| | | 9. Artistes Fees · Voice Overs | | | 29. Complete to A/P |
| | | 10. Child Audition Fees | | | 30. Reprints for VTR Transmission |
| | | 11. Child Artistes Fees | | | 31. TXFR and Playout Facilities |
| | | 12. Chaperone Fees | | | 32. G Spools Safety Copies |
| | | 13. Hand Artiste | | | 33. CRI |
| | | 14. Animals and Handlers | | | 34. Neg. Insurance |
| | | 15. Provision of Wardrobe | | | 35. Recording · No of Hours |
| | | 16. Home Economist | | | 36. Dubbing · No of Hours |
| | | 17. Special Personnel | | | 37. Umatic/VHS txfrs No |
| | | 18. Artwork/Packs | | | 38. Original Music and Recording |
| | | 19. Special Props | | | 39. Singers Session Fees |
| | | 20. Stills | | | 40. Library Music Search |
| | | 21. Travel/Agency ........ Client | | | 41. Sound Fx |
| | | Artistes ........ (Number of) | | | 42. Music Licence |
| | | 22. Hotel/Agency ........ Client | | | 43. |
| | | Artistes ........ (Number of) | | | 44. |

| COMMENTS: | | NO | DAYS |
|---|---|---|---|
| | Recce | | |
| | Travel | | |
| | Location Prep | | |
| | Location Shoot | | |
| | Location Strike | | |
| | Studio Build | | |
| | Studio Prep/Light | | |
| | Studio Shoot | | |
| | Studio Strike | | |
| | Rest Days | | |

BUDGET TOTAL: £          WEATHER FIGURE: £

This estimate is subject to:
1) A.F.V.P.A., I.P.A. and I.S.B.A. approved procedures.
2) Shooting commencing within the following dates
   ..................................................

Signed: 

Dated: 

For the Production Company

**Figure 6.2** Items for inclusion/exclusion in the production estimate

'fixed bid', is the most common. Occasionally a 'cost-plus-fixed-fee' system is used. The production company receives a set fee, based on an agreed mark-up on its budget, which remains the same whether the production goes over or comes in under budget. The benefits to the client are: (a) in the event of the latter it doesn't pay the savings made to the production company, (b) the system eliminates or inhibits padding of the production estimate. The drawbacks are: if the commercial exceeds the budget the client pays for the overage; secondly, the practice of the system necessarily requires an audit which, as we've seen, may cancel out any financial advantage.[14]

From the production company's point of view the 'fixed fee' is preferable when the production involves considerable risky or unquantifiable elements. This of course is why the company, if it's making a 'firm bid' for the job, will endeavour to insulate itself against financial exposure from 'unpredictables' by 'rounding out' the estimate.

## 6.5 Pre-production

At one or more pre-production meetings the agency people (the agency TV producer, the writer, the art director, the account executive), the production company people (the producer, the director, the freelance production designer – confusingly also known as an art director) and representatives from the advertiser will get together and discuss and exchange ideas about all the strategic and specific factors bearing on the realization of the commercial. It goes without saying that meticulous planning along with advance agreement between all parties concerned prior to shooting is absolutely vital.

On the agenda will be:

(a) the schedule: lead times and dates for the building of sets, for preparations and set-ups, for travel to locations, for editing and post-production;

(b) the designs for the sets, the properties and style of the set dressing, special properties (like packs);

(c) the style of the lighting and the overall 'look';

(d) artwork and titles;

(e) how, shot by shot, camera movement by camera movement, the director envisages photographing the commercial (the production designer will, after detailed briefing from the director, have created a series of illustrations showing each of the planned shots and camera angles);

(f) music;

(g) casting and wardrobe;

(h) opticals and post-production;

(i) other matters.

Where the commercial calls for a demonstration, say, how a sauce mix pours over a plate of meat and vegetables, it may be necessary to run a test sequence with the director, the lighting cameraman and a home economist. Costs can be kept down by running the test footage demo on videotape.

## Casting

For some commercials the casting may have been effectively decided as early as the script stage. A celebrity or 'name' actor or actress may have been an integral part of the script from the dawn of its creation. The script may have been written from the outset with a John Cleese or other in mind.

Some of the larger advertising agencies have a resident casting director but casting is mostly done by freelance casting directors (most of whom are women) chosen by the production company.

The director, who will have discussed in detail the imaginary CV's of the character with the agency creatives, calls a casting director with a brief: the product, the shooting dates, the number of characters, what types they are – age, class, looks, whether any special skills are required – can ride a horse, a motorbike, drive a car, swim, tap dance, sing and so on, and the broad range of fees on offer (say, £150 to £200 per day).

The casting director is then sent a detailed brief together with a script. To obviate any misunderstanding she will call the director with some representative names: she's thinking of a John X and Sarah Y as possibles for the husband and wife, and a Billy Z as their ten-year-old son.

Armed with her 'little black book' and tapping into her experience of actors and actresses from past commercials, from TV, theatre and movies, she will then get in touch with the artistes' agents. Some of the actors may be unavailable. Others, very occasionally, may reject the prospect of doing the commercial because the daily rate is too low. And every now and again you come across an actor who won't do commercials for certain products (like cigars) on moral grounds. Or because the actor doesn't want to be associated with an ad for, say, a lavatory cleanser, particularly if it's a hard-sell front-on camera sort.

Some actors' agents can be remiss: failing to establish the availability of their client on the shooting days, inadequately briefing their client on the nature of the part and on what to wear for the casting, and, most seriously, failing to check whether their client has done a commercial for a competing product in recent years.

So-called 'character' parts – an Alf Garnett type, an ageing wrestler, an old biddy – are relatively easy to place. As are parts for models: for a mane of sensuously swirling hair for a shampoo ad, for a pair of luscious lips to enfold a glass of drink. The most difficult, because the most subjective, are to cast Mr and Mrs Average for a breakfast cereal, or a suited businessman for a charge card or photocopier commercial.

Ideally, the casting director will produce around six to ten candidates for each part. On the whole it is better for the director to see a small number of performers, giving them about fifteen minutes each to read through the script, than to deal with thirty people, banging them through at three-minute intervals.

At the production company offices or one of the increasing number of casting facility suites, the actors and actresses will rehearse the script in front of a video camera. The director will be looking for not just credibility and sincerity in respect of the part but also the right chemistry between the actors. During the script read-through and rehearsal, useful little additions and embellishments can sometimes spontaneously surface: a word or two in the dialogue, a gesture here, a nuance there.

The director will decide on whom he wants to use. And if there's not a great deal to choose between A, B or C, he will, being human (and practical) opt for the performers he instinctively feels will be the easiest and the most fun to work with. The final decision on casting rests with the client. Except where a star director is being used. In that case the director's judgement will be respected by client and agency alike.

## Union requirements and use fees

Offers to perform in a TV commercial are normally restricted to performers who are members of the actors' union, Equity. The main exceptions are: (a) the engagement of people who are playing themselves, i.e., a dog-breeder doing a testimonial-type commercial for a brand of dog food or an expert/authority like Sir Robert Mark appearing in Goodyear's Grand Prix-S tyre commercials, pronouncing on the safety benefit of the said tyres; (b) models; (c) 'body-dubbing' artistes – like hand artistes used in, say, washing-up liquid commercials that involve a close shot of a pair of hands; (d) instrumental musicians; (e) certain extras and 'walk-ons' – people appearing incidentally in background/crowd scenes; (f) commercials made abroad and subsequently shown on UK TV.

When a commercial is transmitted more than once, the Equity member actors and actresses have to be paid use/repeat fees. These fees are not royalties (in the sense in which an author receives an agreed percentage across the number of sales of his book) but a compensation for subsequent loss of earnings.

If an actor does an ad for, say, Rolo he won't be considered for a commercial for any other brand of confectionery. If the commercial is shown a great many times the actor is likely to become known as 'the man in the Rolo ad' which, in practical terms, tends to limit the number of other commercials in all product categories that he's going to be put up for. The actress used in the Woolwich Building Society commercials, shown repeatedly over many years, is typecast: she *is* the Woolwich girl. Accordingly, her chances of doing other TV commercial work are virtually zero.

The typecast phenomenon doesn't appear to affect celebrities, well, some of them. John Cleese is probably the best example. Doing his outrageous, manic 'silly twit' character, Cleese has appeared in commercials for many different products, from Sony video recorders to Compaq computers, with great success. Indeed, so prevalent is his appearance in different commercials that it has led a number of commentators waggishly to suggest that there should be featured in the many awards for TV advertising a special category for 'best use of John Cleese'!

Repeat fees (Fig. 6.3) are based on the performer's Basic Studio Fee (BSF) for which there is a minimum Equity-agreed rate. If the commercial is transmitted on ITV in all areas the actor/actress is paid repeat fees as follows: Block One (between two and eleven showings) – 405 per cent of the BSF; Block Two (between twelve and twenty-one showings) – 405 per cent of the BSF; Block Three (twenty-two to thirty-one showings) – 255 per cent of the BSF. By Block Nine the rate reduces to 105 per cent and continues at this level for all subsequent blocks of ten transmissions.

## Guide to the cumulative percentage of a performer's BSF payable in use fees

**ITV**

(Effective for contracts entered into on or after 13th January 1986)

| No. of transmissions | | 2-11 | 12-21 | 22-31 | 32-41 | 42-51 | 52-61 | 62-71 | 72-81 | 82-91 | 92-101 | 102-111 | 112-21 | 122-31 | 132-41 | 142-51 | 152-61 | 162-71 | 172-81 | 182-91 | 192-201 | 202-11 | 212-21 | 222-31 | 232-41 | 242-51 |
|---|---|---|---|---|---|---|---|---|---|---|---|---|---|---|---|---|---|---|---|---|---|---|---|---|---|---|
| Block numbers | | 1 | 2 | 3 | 4 | 5 | 6 | 7 | 8 | 9 | 10 | 11 | 12 | 13 | 14 | 15 | 16 | 17 | 18 | 19 | 20 | 21 | 22 | 23 | 24 | 25 |
| | Area class | % | % | % | % | % | % | % | % | % | % | % | % | % | % | % | % | % | % | % | % | % | % | % | % | % |
| London | (A) | 80 | 160 | 210 | 260 | 285 | 310 | 335 | 360 | 380 | 400 | 420 | 440 | 460 | 480 | 500 | 520 | 540 | 560 | 580 | 600 | 620 | 640 | 660 | 680 | 700 |
| Midlands | (B) | 60 | 120 | 160 | 200 | 220 | 240 | 260 | 280 | 295 | 310 | 325 | 340 | 355 | 370 | 385 | 400 | 415 | 430 | 445 | 460 | 475 | 490 | 505 | 520 | 535 |
| Lancashire | (C) | 45 | 90 | 120 | 150 | 165 | 180 | 195 | 210 | 220 | 230 | 240 | 250 | 260 | 270 | 280 | 290 | 300 | 310 | 320 | 330 | 340 | 350 | 360 | 370 | 380 |
| Yorkshire | (C) | 45 | 90 | 120 | 150 | 165 | 180 | 195 | 210 | 220 | 230 | 240 | 250 | 260 | 270 | 280 | 290 | 300 | 310 | 320 | 330 | 340 | 350 | 360 | 370 | 380 |
| Tyne Tees | (D) | 25 | 50 | 65 | 80 | 90 | 100 | 110 | 120 | 125 | 130 | 135 | 140 | 145 | 150 | 155 | 160 | 165 | 170 | 175 | 180 | 185 | 190 | 195 | 200 | 205 |
| Central Scotland | (D) | 25 | 50 | 65 | 80 | 90 | 100 | 110 | 120 | 125 | 130 | 135 | 140 | 145 | 150 | 155 | 160 | 165 | 170 | 175 | 180 | 185 | 190 | 195 | 200 | 205 |
| Wales | (D) | 25 | 50 | 65 | 80 | 90 | 100 | 110 | 120 | 125 | 130 | 135 | 140 | 145 | 150 | 155 | 160 | 165 | 170 | 175 | 180 | 185 | 190 | 195 | 200 | 205 |
| South | (D) | 25 | 50 | 65 | 80 | 90 | 100 | 110 | 120 | 125 | 130 | 135 | 140 | 145 | 150 | 155 | 160 | 165 | 170 | 175 | 180 | 185 | 190 | 195 | 200 | 205 |
| Anglia | (D) | 25 | 50 | 65 | 80 | 90 | 100 | 110 | 120 | 125 | 130 | 135 | 140 | 145 | 150 | 155 | 160 | 165 | 170 | 175 | 180 | 185 | 190 | 195 | 200 | 205 |
| S W England | (E) | 10 | 20 | 26 | 32 | 37 | 42 | 47 | 52 | 57 | 62 | 67 | 72 | 77 | 82 | 87 | 92 | 97 | 102 | 107 | 112 | 117 | 122 | 127 | 132 | 137 |
| Ulster | (E) | 10 | 20 | 26 | 32 | 37 | 42 | 47 | 52 | 57 | 62 | 67 | 72 | 77 | 82 | 87 | 92 | 97 | 102 | 107 | 112 | 117 | 122 | 127 | 132 | 137 |
| Border | (E) | 10 | 20 | 26 | 32 | 37 | 42 | 47 | 52 | 57 | 62 | 67 | 72 | 77 | 82 | 87 | 92 | 97 | 102 | 107 | 112 | 117 | 122 | 127 | 132 | 137 |
| N E Scotland | (E) | 10 | 20 | 26 | 32 | 37 | 42 | 47 | 52 | 57 | 62 | 67 | 72 | 77 | 82 | 87 | 92 | 97 | 102 | 107 | 112 | 117 | 122 | 127 | 132 | 137 |
| Channel | (E) | 10 | 20 | 26 | 32 | 37 | 42 | 47 | 52 | 57 | 62 | 67 | 72 | 77 | 82 | 87 | 92 | 97 | 102 | 107 | 112 | 117 | 122 | 127 | 132 | 137 |
| NETWORK | | 405 | 810 | 1065 | 1320 | 1470 | 1620 | 1770 | 1920 | 2025 | 2130 | 2235 | 2340 | 2445 | 2550 | 2655 | 2760 | 2865 | 2970 | 3075 | 3180 | 3285 | 3390 | 3495 | 3600 | 3705 |

**Read these tables as follows:** A performer, appearing in a commercial transmitted 50 times on ITV, Central Scotland, shall receive use fees equivalent to not less than 90% of his negotiated basic studio fee.

**Note 1.** These are cumulative percentages. For the rates applying to individual blocks, see the tables in section (5) of the *Form of Engagement for Performers in Television Commercials*, revised January 1986.

**Note 2.** Use fees are to be calculated on the basis of the following minimum levels of basic studio/session fee: Visual performers – £85, Voice-overs – £51, Out-of-vision singers – £45, or such minimum sum as may subsequently be advised.

**Note 3.** In the event of a commercial being screened for the first time on each of a second or third channel (channels for this purpose are defined as ITV, Channel Four and TV-am), performers will receive, together with the appropriate use fees for the first block of such showings, an additional payment of 100% of their BSF. (Except for commercials shown in not more than two D or E areas on Channel Four, where this additional payment will be 50% of the BSF.)

**Note 4.** Where commercials for *only* ITV or *only* Channel Four are to be screened in a single D or E area performers will receive a non-refundable advance payment against use fees equivalent to 50% of the BSF.

**Note 5.** For UK cable/satellite use fee payments, see Clause 11 of the 1986 IPA/AFVPA/Equity Agreement.

Institute of Practitioners in Advertising
44 Belgrave Square London SW1X 8QS. Tel: 01-235 7020 Telex: 918352.

© IPA February 1986

**Figure 6.3** Equity performer's repeat fees (*Courtesy*: Institute of Practitioners in Advertising)

Lower rates are payable when the ad is shown in particular ITV areas, which are broken down into five classes (A, B, C, D and E), corresponding to the relative size of the ITV area concerned in terms of its percentage of the network. Thus the London area with over twenty per cent of the network's potential audience ranks as Class A; at the other extreme Border TV with one per cent of the potential viewership ranks as Class E.

Channel 4 use fees (over which there was a heated and protracted dispute between Equity and the Advertisers/Advertising Agencies prior to and during the launch of the fourth channel in the autumn of 1983, resulting in several months of largely blank screens during commercial breaks)[15] are slightly over half of those for ITV.

The basic studio fee (BSF) on which repeats are predicated is, as its name implies, the fee for the day's shooting. On a BSF of £175 an actor engaged on a three-day shoot will receive £525 (less, of course, his agent's commission and VAT) but his repeat fee will be based on £175. Sometimes an agent may be able to increase his client's daily fee but it is unlikely that the advertising agency will budge from its BSF figures.

Where 'name' performers and celebrities are being used they will be contracted on a 'buy out' basis (a celebrity's demand for a daily fee of £X,000 would prove financially punitive if subject to the normal repeat fee percentages). The star and his/her representative will, after a lot of delicate negotiations, agree on a fee for the day or however long the shoot is scheduled to take which allows the commercial to be shown any number of times on TV in the UK. Showing of the ad overseas will be subject to separate 'buy out' arrangements.

For a jobbing performer on a BSF, overseas use of the commercial in which he/she appears is subject to a 'buy out'. There are minimum rates for the 'buy out', agreed between Equity and the IPA, which relate to the number of TV sets in the territory concerned (e.g., if the ad is to be shown in a country with over ten million TV sets – excluding the USA – the performer will receive a minimum of 300 per cent of the BSF).[16]

# 7 · Understanding film and tape

## 7.0 The grammar of film

### The illusion of motion and frame rates

A still photograph picture is obtained by gathering light, via a lens, from the subject: the pattern of light defining the subject then acts on a light-sensitive emulsion coated on to a strip of acetate to produce a negative (and inverted) image of the subject.

Motion-picture photography, an optical/mechanical/chemical process, is effected by exposing a series of still images – frames – in quick-fire succession. In the movie camera an electrically driven system transports the film past the lens: a claw engages with the sprocket holes punched into the edge(s) of the film stock pulling the succession of frames down past the lens so that one moment a frame of film is exposed, a fraction of a second later the shutter blanks out the light as the next frame is advanced into position in front of the lens, then the shutter comes up and the next frame of film, held still for a fraction of a second, is exposed. And so on.

When the series of frames is projected, the illusion of motion is achieved. The eye, because of the phenomenon known as 'persistence of vision' or 'retinal retention', is unable to distinguish the separate images and merges them into a continuous motion.

The rate at which the frames are passed through the projection gate – the position where the frame is exposed to the light beam in the projector – must exceed a certain frequency for the eye to be deceived seamlessly. If the projection speed of so many frames per second is too low, the eye (or rather the perceptual system of the brain) will perceive the series of frames as a staccato chain, one image jerkily following another.

The internationally agreed speed for the projection of sound film is twenty-four frames per second (fps). This standard is arbitrary – it could have been, say, twenty-two or twenty-six fps, so long as the rate is fast enough to 'fool' the eye.

Slow-motion sequences/effects are used fairly frequently in commercials, mostly for emphatic or dramatic purposes. Milk glugging with lazy mellifluity into a glass, then rearing up the sides with slow balletic grace, then globules of glistening white dancing in languid suspension (the descriptive prose has to be dramatic-poetic too!); stunt scenes – people falling from or through windows, cars crashing. To achieve slow motion it is necessary to shoot at a higher speed than the projection rate; the higher the speed of filming, the slower the motion.

To speed motion up requires shooting at a speed slower than the projection speed. In feature films, action sequences such as car chases are sometimes realized in this way. The vehicles appear to be screeching and squealing around hairpin bends with breathtaking danger (the effect being heightened by being shot from the point of view of the driver(s) and by a lot of rapid inter-cutting) whereas in fact the cars are travelling at a relatively modest speed.

Typically, commercials use speeded-up motion for its humorous effect. A commercial for instant Horlicks is set in a generic aerobics/gymnastics class. A Strauss waltz, speeded up, provides the punishing work-out tempo. Svelte, leotarded girls skip, and pull and push Nautilus weights in an agonizingly jerky fast frenzy. As the music gradually and mercifully stretches out to its natural tempo the girls slow up. We cut to a pack shot of Horlicks, the lid unfastens itself, a visible hiss of relief escaping. Ditto the girls as we cut back to them. Phew!

Commercials also reach into our experience of silent movies: where the characters move about as if they've been wound up on massive doses of amphetamines. In point of fact, though we think of silent films as being largely synonymous with hilarious breakneck jerky motion, the film audiences at the time (before the advent of the talkies in the late 1920s) would have had a rather different experience of Charlie Chaplin, the Keystone Cops and others. For silent pictures were shot at sixteen fps and projected at that rate: the movement of the actors was naturalistic. But when a silent film shot at sixteen fps is shown on a modern projector

**98   Creating and producing a TV commercial**

running at twenty-four fps the movement is of course speeded up to frenetic levels. Occasionally specialist film societies and institutes screen silent films on projectors running at sixteen fps. Alternatively, to show a silent movie in a manner approximating to how it would have been seen at the time requires *stretch-printing*: this is an optical printer process done by the labs and involves printing alternate frames twice. Thus treated, a silent film can be projected at twenty-four fps without resulting in unnatural speeding up of the motion.

For reasons which will be explained in Section 7.1, the frame rate for television (in the UK) is twenty-five. Thus when a commercial is being originated on film for TV broadcast it is necessary to shoot with a camera having a motor speed of twenty-five

35mm film: speed – 16 frames per foot
Cinema projection rate: 24 frames per second; TV frame replacement rate: 25 every second
Time shrinkage: material filmed at 24 fps and shown on TV – approximately 4 per cent

| Time | Feet/frames used at Cinema rate | Feet/frames used at TV rate | Frame Difference | Time loss on TV |
|---|---|---|---|---|
| 1 second | 1 foot/8 frames | 1 foot/9 frames | 1 | 0.04 seconds |
| 10 seconds | 15 feet | 15 feet/10 frames | 10 | 0.4 seconds |
| 30 seconds | 45 feet | 46 feet/14 frames | 30 | 1.2 seconds |
| 60 seconds | 90 feet | 93 feet/12 frames | 60 | 2.4 seconds |
| 30 minutes | 2700 feet | 2812 feet/8 frames | 1800 | 72 seconds |
| 60 minutes | 5400 feet | 5625 feet | 3600 | 144 seconds |
| 120 minutes | 10800 feet | 11250 feet | 7200 | 288 seconds |

**Figure 7.1**   Running times and footage

fps. Otherwise the commercial will be slightly shortened. Though the speeding up by one frame per second will not be noticeable to the viewer, i.e., there will be no perceptible quickening of the motion, losing a frame every second results in losing thirty frames – a bit more than a second – over the duration of a thirty second commercial.[1] In practice, though, this wouldn't happen. Suppose the commercial was, extraordinarily, originated at film speed. Then either it would be stretch-printed or, when telecined for transmission (see Section 7.2), the last frame would be repeated thirty times over, producing the impression of a still image – a freeze frame. But both expedients are, clearly, a waste of precious air time: in the lost one and quarter seconds the advertiser, at some point during the course of the commercial, could have had another three words of dialogue/voice-over or another quick cut.

## Film formats

The principal formats in use today are 70 mm, 35 mm, 16 mm and 8 mm. The wider the gauge is, the bigger the image area is and so the better the quality and definition of the picture. The image area can be increased by either reducing the size of the edge perforations (the sprocket holes) or, in the case of 16 mm and 8mm, having these down one side of the film only (Fig. 7.2).

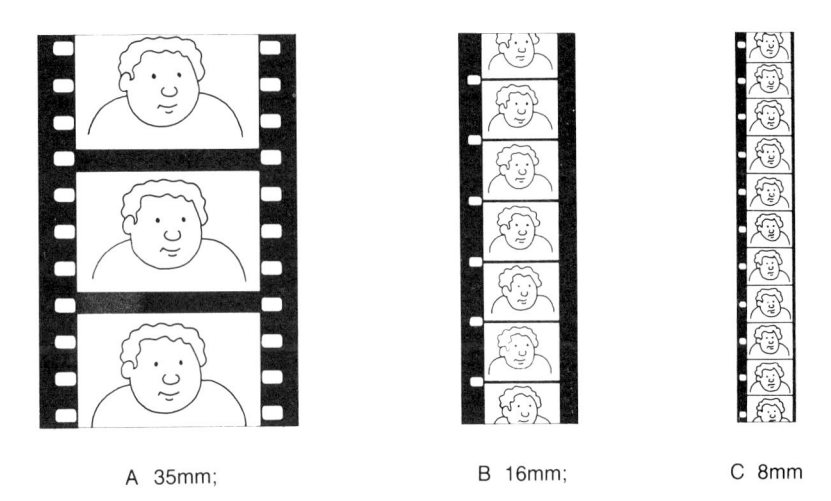

Figure 7.2  Film gauges       A  35mm;        B  16mm;        C  8mm

The size and spacing of the sprocket holes is different for each gauge. On 16 mm stock each frame is spaced by two sprocket holes; on 35 mm there are four holes to each frame. Because of the variations in the image size of the frames in different gauges, the amount of footage per second varies too.

The superior image quality obtained from large format stock has to be reconciled with cost. As the gauge increases the costs of the stock itself, of processing/printing and other lab charges, of the hire of cameras and lenses, rises steeply. It rarely pays to shoot on narrow gauge stock and blow-up to a higher gauge. 16 mm footage blown up to 35 mm for cinema projection is usually not very satisfactory as any inherent imperfections in the original will be magnified.

70 mm, because of its inordinately high costs, is confined to big-budget epic movie-making. 35 mm is the standard for feature films and is virtually universal for film origination of TV commercials in

the UK. Documentaries as well as what's left of industrial and corporate film production using celluloid (videotape largely having taken over) use 16 mm as does nearly all location filming for TV plays, series and serials. The image quality of 8 mm is so poor that it's only suitable for home movie use, and this use has all but vanished, overtaken by the cheapness and other advantages of video.

The argument arises that if 16 mm is adequate for location filming of programmes for TV broadcast (*The Professionals*, for instance, is shot on 16 mm) and, moreover, is often used in the USA and elsewhere to originate commercials, why aren't commercials in the UK shot on 16 mm too? Another argument is that the quality of the picture can only be as good as the weakest link in the chain. A hi-fi audio system provides an analogy. You can have a very expensive turntable, pick-up arm and amplifier. But if fed through a pair of tin-pot cheapo loudspeakers the quality of the sound produced will only be as good as their limited reproduction capabilities. Thus the quality and sophistication of the system prior to the speakers is effectively a waste of technical excellence and money. And so it is with television. The image sharpness and colour authenticity produced by the average domestic TV set just doesn't, and cannot, do justice to the high picture quality input from the 35 mm print (or videotape transfer) submitted to the TV station for onward transmission. The average viewer, furthermore, can't tell the difference between a programme or a commercial made on 16 mm and one made on 35 mm or indeed one made on videotape.

It has to be conceded that these arguments appear pretty telling. They are, however, largely specious. What is produced from grotty loudspeakers *will* sound better if the equipment supplying them is of a high quality. Accordingly, precisely because of the degradation of the image (and the sound) on a domestic TV it is imperative that the picture source is of the highest possible quality to start with. Secondly, a TV commercial can be, and often is, subjected to a scrutiny that no TV-filmed programme is: it is liable to be looked at many times over whereas an episode of *The Professionals* or whatever will be seen only once. Thirdly, the TV campaign may need to be supported by press advertising: a frame or frames may need to be cut out and used for print reproduction, to which end a 16 mm frame will be inadequate for enlargement purposes. Fourthly, the range of film stocks and the range of editing, lab processing and printing facilities for 35 mm vastly exceeds that for 16 mm. Lastly, in the UK the TV commercials industry prides itself on maintaining the highest possible production values. A commercial may of course be made for cinema showing as well as TV, in which case 35 mm is essential.

## Film stocks

Light sensitive salts – silver halides – are bound together by gelatine or a similar agent and coated as an emulsion on to a transparent film base. Light from the subject reacts with the silver crystals in proportion to its intensity. In colour film the emulsion is made up of a series of layers which are respectively sensitive to the primary colours of light: red, blue and green, mixtures of these producing all other colours.

Film stocks come in two broad categories: reversal and negative. Reversal film produces a positive image on the original camera film. The tones, from black through a succession of incrementally lightening greys to white, are recorded as natural, as are the colours. Negative film produces tones and colours that are the opposite to those in the subject: white appears as black and vice versa, and colours likewise appear as their opposites: green is rendered as magenta, red as cyan, blue as yellow (see also, Section 13.1).

The respective merits and drawbacks of negative and reversal film are rather technical and lie outside the scope of this book. However, at the risk of being over-simplistic, negative film gives the commercials film-maker the greatest degree of flexibility and control.

The chemical make-up of the film emulsion varies according to its sensitivity to light. Described as the 'speed' of the stock, the light sensitivity of film is measured by its ASA – American Standards Association – rating. The higher the ASA rating, the faster is the film, i.e. the greater is its sensitivity to light. Stocks designed for shooting under normal light conditions can be forced or uprated to compensate for low light levels by increasing the aperture (the f-stop number), a diaphragm which governs the amount of light reaching the lens.[2] But the more a stock is forced, the more 'noise' or unwanted grain there is on the image.

Filming a commercial for a brand of liqueur where the script calls for an end-of-dinner party setting lit solely by a candelabra in the centre of a table would require using a very fast stock. As would shooting a very slow-motion sequence on location in the available light of a winter's day. The slower the motion required, the greater the number of frames to be exposed each second, and so the higher the ASA rating of the film stock to be used.

## Aspect ratio (Fig. 7.3)

This refers to the horizontal and vertical proportions of the presented picture. When television was introduced it adopted (and continues to use) the then prevalent cinema screen proportions of 4:3 or 1.33:1 (four units wide and three units high). Cinema presentation today uses a picture shape that is much wider than

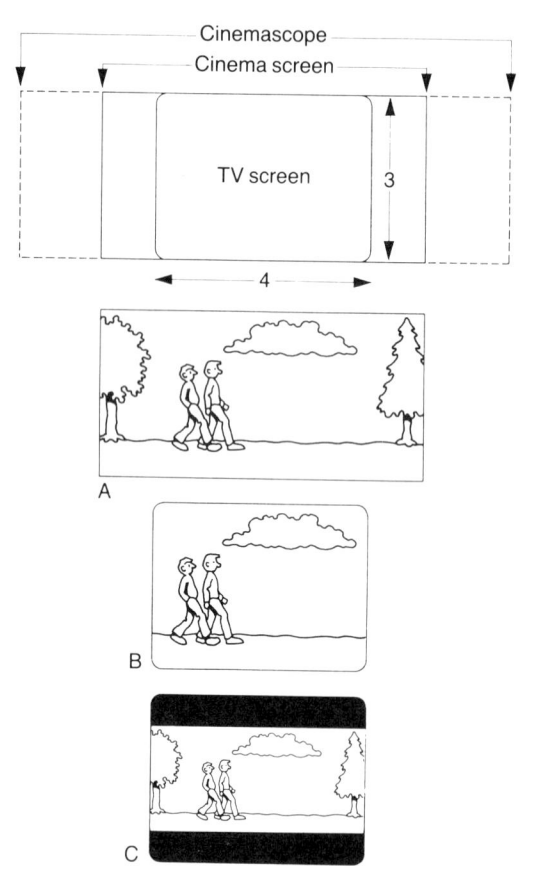

A  Wide screen film picture (Panavision)
B  Film screen picture fitted to TV screen
   Proportions at the expense of the width of the original
C  Original film screen proportions retained

**Figure 7.3**   Aspect ratio

that of TV. Films shot in Panavision have an aspect ratio of 1.65:1.

When a movie shot in a wider format that TV's 4:3 is shown on TV, the picture must be altered to fit the shape of the screen. To retain the full height of the screen, the original width of the picture has to be sacrificed. Alternatively to preserve the full width of the original picture necessitates losing the height of the image on the TV screen and results in broad stripes of black at the top and bottom. As TV audiences won't tolerate the latter, broadcast made-for-cinema movies have their width cropped at either side so that the whole TV screen is filled. However, for legal reasons the title and credits sequences at the start of the film are transmitted in the original cinema screen dimensions.[3]

A picture unadjusted to the TV screen proportions has come to mean 'this-is-a-feature-film'. In their love affair with the cinema and quest to find new devices to arrest the viewer's attention, TV commercials have not only parodied and pastiched the genres and styles of movies (see Section 4.1 (6)) but also the conventions of their presentation on TV. At least a couple of commercials have wittily used cinema screen proportions on TV – the images sandwiched between fat horizontal bands of black.

## Film sound (Fig. 7.4)

In film production the sound is recorded magnetically. The process is the same as recording sound on a domestic audio cassette. Electrical impulses representing the varying pressures of the sound waves reaching the microphone are encoded on to a coating of ferrous oxide or similar magnetically sensitive chemical deposit.

During shooting, the dialogue and sound effects, the synchronous (sync) sound, can be recorded directly on to a magnetic track striped along one side of the raw film stock in the camera. However, this method of sound recording, known variously as the single system or commag (combined magnetic) is now defunct as it doesn't permit subsequent editing of the footage without loss of sync. In a camera equipped for sound-on-film shooting the sound head is physically distanced from the picture gate (on 16 mm it is 28 frames ahead of the picture frame to which it refers, on 35 mm it is ahead or behind by 28 frames) so that the sound and corresponding frame are displaced by just over one second. Thus cutting the picture will cut the sound at the wrong

## 104 Creating and producing a TV commercial

Separate sound recording:

Sync pulse

Cable or radio link locking camera and tape recorder in sync.

Tape recorder

Microphone

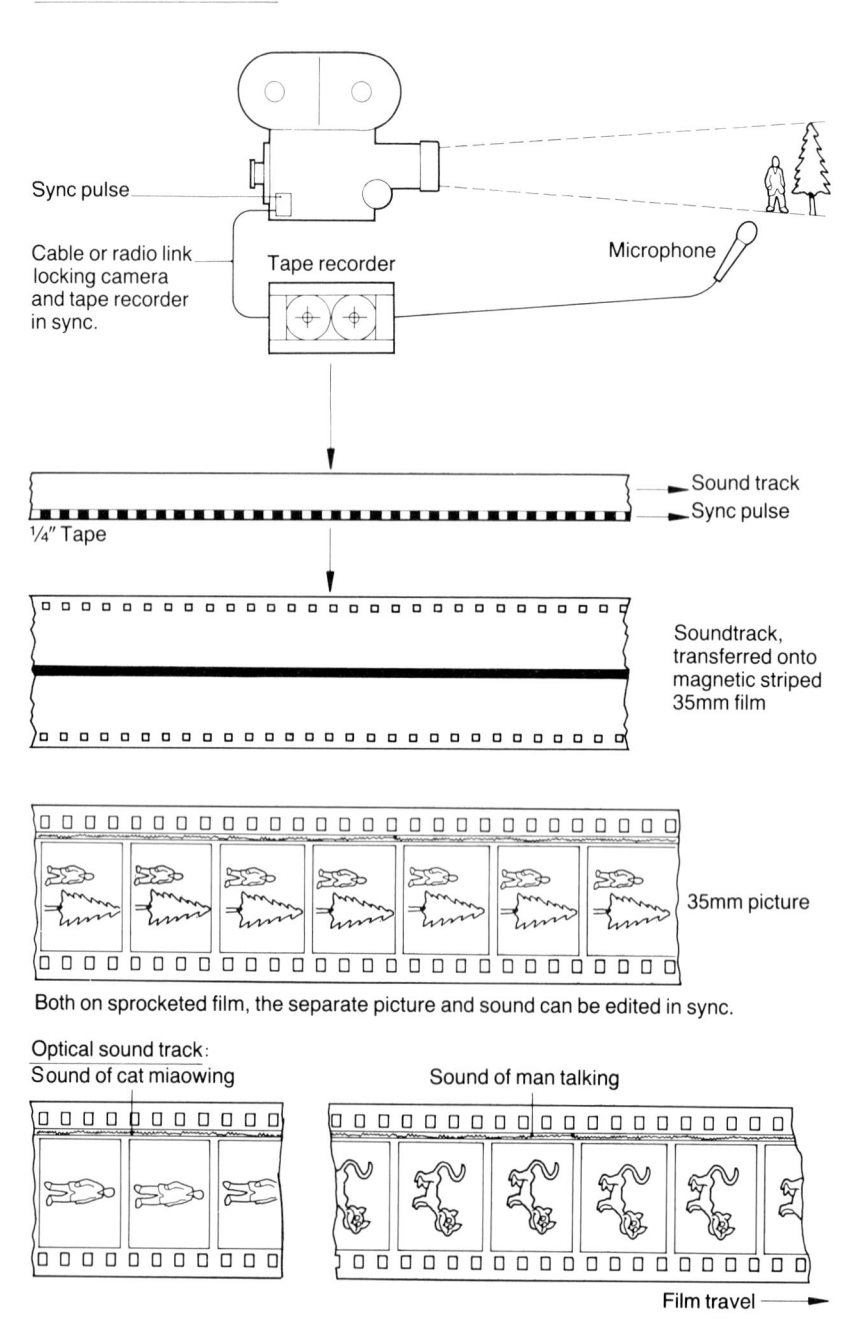

¼" Tape

Sound track
Sync pulse

Soundtrack, transferred onto magnetic striped 35mm film

35mm picture

Both on sprocketed film, the separate picture and sound can be edited in sync.

Optical sound track:
Sound of cat miaowing

Sound of man talking

Film travel ⟶

**Figure 7.4** Film sound

On a combined optical print the sound is ahead of the picture by 20 frames (on 35mm). On 16mm the sound is ahead by 26 frames point, resulting in 'lip flap' – the movements of the performer's lips don't coincide with the words he's saying – or absurd non-synchronization of sound effects: we hear a door banging to, and then a second later we see the action of the door slamming shut.

It is standard for the sound to be recorded separately from the picture on a quarter-inch open-reel recorder (Nagra recorders being the industry standard). Because the tape is liable to stretch and because of slight variations in the speed of the motors transporting the tape and the film, synchronization between the frames of film exposed in the camera and the dialogue or other sound being recorded is going to be lost. It is not enough simply to start the camera and the recorder at the same time. To ensure accurate synchronization the camera and tape recorder are locked together by a sync-pulse generator. Where cable connections between the two are hampering, the sync-pulse can be delivered to both by means of a radio link.

Recording on separate quarter-inch tape (sepmag) allows complete flexibility in cutting with preservation of sync until, finally, the sound and picture are married together on one strip of film at the end of the editing process.

The separate system also produces a much better quality of sound, sound fidelity being a function of the width of the tape and its speed – seven and a half inches per second being the norm.

Film sound can be represented by photographical means. After the picture has been cut in tandem with the separate magnetic sound and any other sound (such as music and voice-overs) added, the labs record the mixed magnetic sound-track along one of the edges of the edited film in the form of an optical print. The optically encoded sound-track, a narrow band of variable area or variable density, is subsequently 'read' by an exciter lamp in the film projector and converted into audio.

Release prints of commercials for cinema showing have optical tracks (comopts) as do commercials delivered on film to the TV companies. Exceptionally, some TV companies may accept commag (combined picture and magnetic sound) prints.[4] On an optical track the sound is in front of the picture frame by 20 frames on 35 mm and by 26 frames on 16 mm.

## 7.1 The grammar of video

### How television works

Just as a movie camera is basically a film projector in reverse, so a video camera is in principle a TV set in reverse. At the heart of both a video camera and TV set is a cathode-ray tube (CRT) which translates electronic impulses into light values (on TV) or converts the varying intensities of light emanating from the subject into electronic signals (video cameras). Since we're all familiar with TV it will be easier to start by looking at how, in its basic essentials, a picture is displayed on a TV screen.

In a TV, from the base of the tube is emitted a stream of electrons. This is focused, rather like a beam of light, and directed to the inside of the screen. As the beam of electrons impinges on the phosphor or chemically similar coating, it causes it to glow. The glow varies with the intensity of the charge of the electrons: a big charge causes a very bright dot on the screen, a small charge a very dim dot.

The electron beam traces a pattern of dots across the screen (Fig. 7.5). The varying degrees of lightness and darkness of the dots

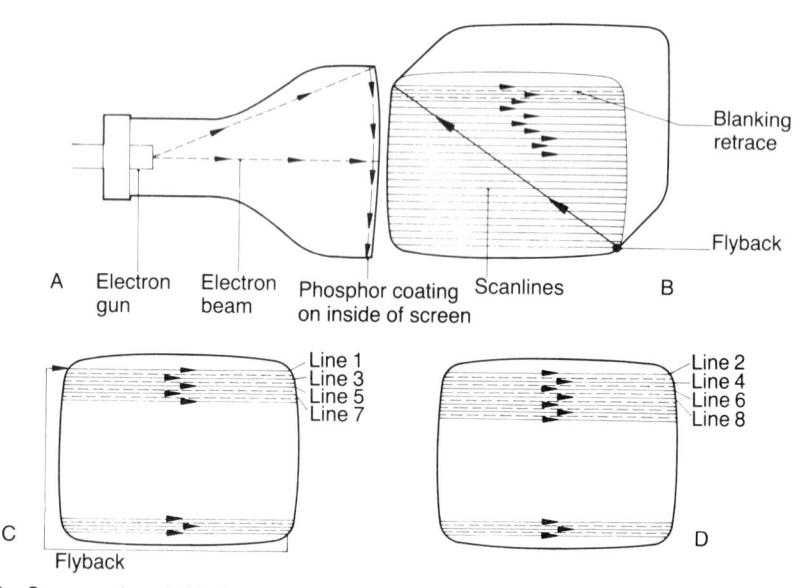

**Figure 7.5** How TV works

A  Cross section of TV tube
B  Front aspect of TV tube
C  One field: odd lines scanned from 1 to 625
D  One field: even lines scanned from 2 to 624
   Meshing of odd and even lines, known as 2:1 interlace scanning, produces one frame.
   In a second on TV there are 50 fields, 25 frames.

correspond to the fluctuating intensities of the original picture signal. Starting at the top left-hand corner the beam 'writes' a line of dots across the screen. At the end of the line the circuitry momentarily shuts off the picture signal and causes the beam – the scanning spot – to whip back to the left. It then traces a second line, then a third, until the whole screen has been scanned with 625 extremely close parallel lines. The scanning spot is now at the bottom right-hand corner of the screen: at this point the circuitry causes the beam to fly back to the top left-hand corner of the screen and then to trace across it with a second pattern of 625 zigzagging lines, then a third pattern and so on.

Each pattern of 625 scan lines constitutes the picture *frame* of television. Since it takes one twenty-fifth of a second to trace the 625 line image there are twenty-five frames per second on TV. However, because the twenty-five successively replaced patterns/frames are liable to cause a flicker effect the screen is actually scanned fifty times each second. It works like this: the scanning spot first traces the odd numbered lines (one, three, five, seven, nine, eleven, etc.), then it flies back to the top left of the screen and traces the even numbered lines (two, four, six, eight, ten, twelve, etc.). The complete pattern made up of odd- or even-numbered lines is known as a *field*. Thus there are two fields to a frame. To put it differently, TV has a frame frequency of twenty-five and a field frequency of fifty.

If the above has been a source of some mental indigestion, the analogy of reading text should allay the discomfort. Think of the scanning spot as your eyes reading a page of print like the one you are reading now. Your eye enters the text at the top left-hand corner, travels quickly, left-to-right, across the first line of print. When it reaches the end it effectively 'blanks off', flying back and then dropping down to the second line of words. You read a second line, shut off, and sweep back to read a third line. When your eye has reached the end of the last line of text in the page, you turn over and scan the next page. Think of the book you're reading as having 625 lines of text on each page. And that every time you turn a page you are passing to a new frame. Only TV's got the edge on you: it turns pages a great deal faster: twenty-five of them every second!

## Colour TV

In a colour television the electronic coding of the original image is split up into its component red, green and blue values. In the tube there are three scanning spots carrying respectively the red, green and blue signals. The scanning spots converge through a fine mesh of tiny holes or slits placed just in front of the inside of the screen and then, diverging slightly, strike the coating on its surface, causing the hundreds of thousands of clusters of red, green and blue sensitive dots to glow with varying intensities. The eye merges the rapid-fire succession of the varying proportions of the three colours, reading them as a range of colours corresponding to those present in the original image.

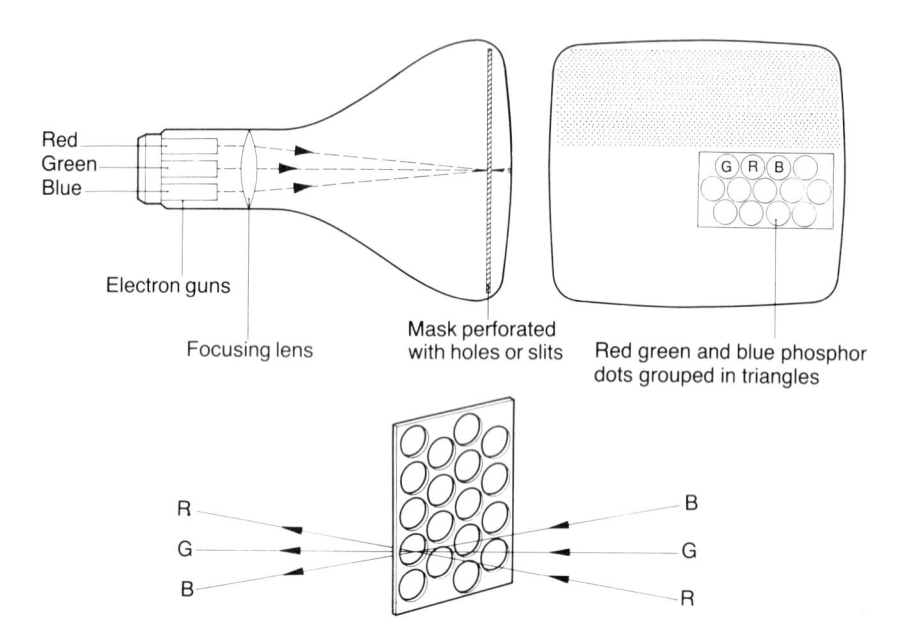

**Figure 7.6** Colour TV tube

## The definition of the TV image

The number of lines making up a TV picture is a limit to the sharpness of the image that can be displayed. The more lines there are, the greater the picture definition. Domestic TV sets, the presentation medium of commercials, are restricted by the amount of detail in an image that they can discriminate or resolve from broadcast reception. You can see the resolution capabilities of your TV set by looking at the Electronic Test Pattern which is transmitted, on and off, during the morning. The test card shows, among other information of concern to engineers, strips of resolution gratings that run from one hundred lines through to six hundred. The four-hundred-line grating patch is likely to be fuzzy, the detail of the separate lines lost in a shimmer. It is for this reason that presenters and performers on TV are not allowed to wear clothing with finelined patterns: herringbone suits, thin striped shirts, etc., for on screen this type of clothing is liable to appear as a dizzying strobe.

## The video camera

The video camera works on the opposite principle to that of the TV receiver. At the front of the camera the lens, which often is of the same sort as that in a movie camera, gathers light information from the subject. This then impinges on to a metallic coating on the front of the camera tube: the fluctuations of light intensity striking it are converted into variations of electrical charge which in turn affect the electron beam scanning the surface of the tube

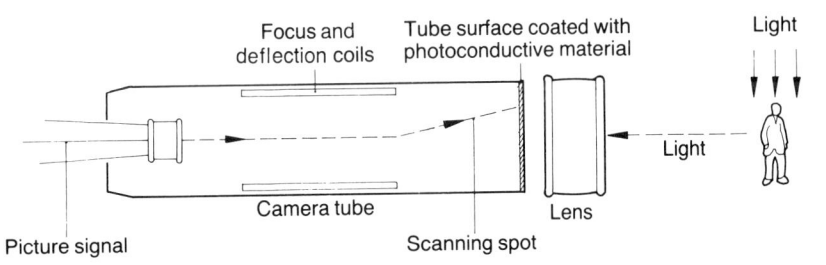

**Figure 7.7** Video-camera tube

and subsequently result in a corresponding picture signal. This signal, routed through the line of circuitry to the scanning spots at the base of the TV picture tube, is reconstituted as a pattern of dots of varying degrees of light/dark and colour on the surface of the TV screen/monitor.

## Broadcast TV systems

There are three systems in operation throughout the world. They differ in respect of (a) the number of close parallel lines providing the grid for the image, (b) the number of frames/fields per second and (c) the way in which the colour is encoded and decoded.

The reasons underlying the different systems of TV broadcasting are complex and need not for the most part concern us.

However, it is in point to explain why there are twenty-five frames per second on TV in Britain and thirty of them in the USA. We saw (in Section 7.0) that the speed of frame projection in the cinema is arbitrary. But on TV it's a different story. The number of frames is determined by the alternating cycle of the household mains current. In the UK the electricity mains frequency is fifty cycles a second (fifty hertz/Hz); this frequency is the reference to which the TV or video camera is locked, i.e., the fifty cycles a second alternating mains current provides a pulse that results in fifty fields of odd and even scan lines a second or twenty-five frames a second (odd and even scan lines being meshed together). In the USA the mains frequency, which is sixty cycles a second, determines the number of fields and frames on TV there, sixty and thirty respectively.

| System | No. of Frames | No. of Lines | Main Countries |
|---|---|---|---|
| PAL (Phase Alternating Line) | 25 | 625 | Great Britain, Germany |
| NTSC (National Television System Committee) | 30 | 525 | USA, Taiwan, Japan |
| SECAM (Séquentiel Couleur à Mémoire) | 25 | 625 | France |

**Figure 7.8** Broadcast TV systems

If you receive a video cassette recording of a programme broadcast in the USA and then play it back through a VCR (video cassette recorder) in the UK, the action will be slowed down by five frames every second. The colour will look fairly weird too.

### How video recording works

The output of the video camera is a coloured picture encoded as a pattern of electrical impulses. In the video recorder these are reproduced by an electromagnet, the video head across which the tape is passing, as a pattern of magnetic pulses which magnetize the thousands and thousands of tiny iron particles on the surface of the tape. The magnetic pattern on the particles thus created represents the picture. The video record head is described as 'writing' a magnetic code on the tape; the replay head as 'reading' it. In principle very simple; in practice very complicated!

The manner in which transfer of the picture signal from the video head to the magnetically sensitive coating on the tape takes place is basically the same as what happens when you scatter iron filings on to a piece of paper and then move a magnet underneath it: the randomly spilled bits of iron become alert, changing into an ordered pattern that corresponds to the strength of the magnetic field from the magnet passing beneath the paper.

Though essentially the same as sound recording on tape, video recording is, technically, a great deal more difficult to achieve. That this is so can be appreciated from the fact that sound recording on magnetic tape was practicable as long ago as the beginning of the century whereas video recording, even in its crudest versions, didn't develop until the 1950s. Before then all broadcast TV went out live; repeating a commercial meant doing it all over again with the inevitability of, at best, a slightly different performance each time.

The problem in recording pictures magnetically is this: the amount of information that needs to be encoded on the tape is vastly greater than that required for sound. To illustrate why necessitates being technical – again! It boils down to frequency range. While audio needs a limited frequency range to be encoded, from thirty cycles up to 20,000 cycles a second, i.e., from the deepest bass rumble up to the highest pitched whistle, video needs a prodigiously wide range, from 0 to 4,000,000 cycles a second or more. The spectrum of frequencies that can be recorded with realistic faithfulness is a function of the amount of tape passing across the video head and so depends on (a) the width of the tape and (b) the speed with which it is transported. In the 1950s video recorders used either unmanageably wide tape running at slow speeds or narrow tape running at uncomfortably high speeds (eighty feet a second was one standard!).

The Ampex Corporation, who incidentally gave tape the brand name of 'videotape' which is now of course a generic, was responsible for coming up with an ingenious solution of how to combine slow tape-transport speeds with relatively narrow gauges of tape. Its engineers devised a system that used four heads that moved rapidly up and down perpendicular to the tape which was simultaneously passing across all of them. Known as *quadruplex* or *quad*, this system was a breakthrough, and was rapidly adopted by all the major network TV studios.

The moving head and moving tape principle was subsequently developed into a system known as *helical scan recording*. Pioneered by Toshiba and JVC, the system uses a rotating drum,

## 112 Creating and producing a TV commercial

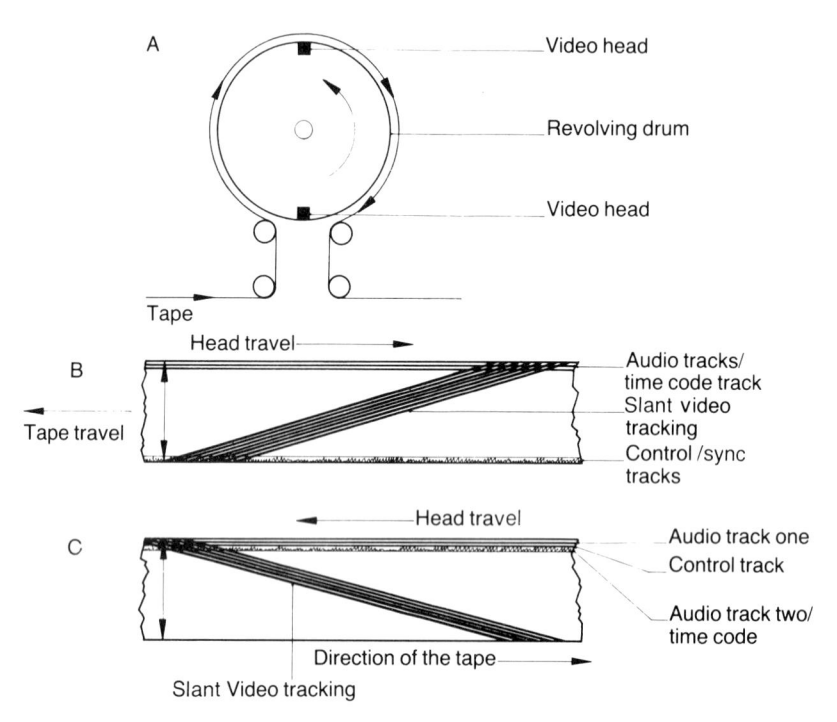

**Figure 7.9** Helical scan wraps/helical scan tape format

A Plan view of tape helically wrapped around drum. There may be more than two heads
B One-inch type 'C' format
C One-inch type 'B' format

around which the tape is wrapped in a skewed path, and at opposite ends of which are situated the recording heads. Each head writes across the tape diagonally. The drum spins round fifty times a second; during each revolution one field is recorded. Thus is takes two revolutions to record a frame or picture.

As large an area as possible on the tape is used for coding the picture. The tape must also carry, in a horizontal stripe across its bottom or top, a control track. This track contains a series of sync pulses that provide a 'lock' for the picture information being written in slanted patterns across the tape. The sync track is the electronic equivalent of the sprocket holes that are perforated along the edge of the film stock. Just as these perforations measure out the number of frames and their regularity of sequence, so the sync track delivers the required reference for the frames and fields on tape. A momentary loss of sync will result in picture instability: the picture tearing, wobbling, jittering, vertically rolling and so on.

The top and/or bottom edge of the tape is reserved for the sound track or tracks (sometimes as many as three of them). In practice, though, one of these audio tracks is used to record 'Time Code

Numbering'. This is a process whereby eight digits, representing hours, minutes, seconds and frames, are coded on to the tape either during shooting or prior to editing. It enables 'takes' to be identified with frame accuracy: Shot 4 Take 1 can be logged as starting at 00:00:08:17 and finishing at 00:00:19:21, the first two zeros are the hours, the second two the minutes, the 08/19 the seconds and the 17/21 the frames. Also logging from time code burnt into the picture facilitates easy and efficient editing of videotape. With film, the entry and exit points for an editing cut can be prescribed by reference to the edge numbers adjacent to the frames. Whereas on videotape, in the absence of time code, you won't know where you are in terms of your start edit point and your finish one (see Section 9.1).

## Tape formats and gauges

The diversity of formats is a veritable jungle of different tape widths, tape speeds, methods of transportation of the tape from the cassette or reel around the drum carrying the video heads, the position of the heads, the mode of head-to-tape contact and the way in which the audio and sync tracks are arranged on the tape. The proliferation of formats continues with, for the most part, a frustrating lack of compatibility between them, and for this lamentable state of affairs the manufacturers of the hardware have, from the point of view of the user, a lot to answer for. That said, there is one common denominator: the basic design system incorporated into most formats is the helical scan one.

As we have seen, one of the determinants of the sharpness and overall quality of the image is the gauge of the tape (the tape speed and the number of video heads being the main others). Just as the very small image area on 8 mm film is too poor for broadcast or professional purposes so the magnetically coded image area on the half-inch tape that we are familiar with on our VHS (video home system) domestic video machines is totally inadequate for the origination of TV commercials or programmes. Two-inch quad and one-inch formats are those standardly in use for TV programme recording and for the shooting and editing of taped commercials.

Matters are, however, not quite as simple as one would wish. For in the world of video—where technical innovations and developments take place with a speed and ingenuity that is awesome—alternatives, exceptions and complications are very much the rule. In the last couple of years a small number of commercials have been made on a format known as Betacam and, evidently, accepted by the ITCA in spite of its specification that all taped ads be made on two-inch or one-inch.[5] The quality of picture recording on Betacam, which has to a large degree been adopted for electronic news gathering (ENG) work, is, given the half-inch tape it uses, astonishingly good.[6] So good that the 'white coat' engineers watchdogging at the ITCA were not able, apparently, to find any appreciable difference between its picture quality and that produced by the specified formats of two-inch and one-inch.

Known as U-Matic in virtue of the 'U' shape described by the path of the tape tugged out of the cassette and around the drum,[7] three-quarter inch U-Matic comes in two 'versions': high-band and low-band. High-band, as its name implies, is capable of coding a much broader range of picture signal frequencies than low-band and so of producing a superior quality of image. Indeed the quality on high-band is sufficiently good for it to be acceptable to Channel 4 (but not to ITV or the BBC).[8] At a pinch the format is probably good enough for the origination of certain kinds of commercials too. Sony, in fact, calls its high-band three-quarter inch format BVU (broadcast video U-Matic), though a cynic or a blunt

| Tape width | Use |
|---|---|
| 2-inch Quad | Broadcast |
| 1-inch | Broadcast |
| 3/4-inch High band U-Matic | Semi-Broadcast and professional |
| 3/4-inch Low band U-Matic | Professional and industrial |
| 1/2-inch Betacam | Broadcast/ Semi-Broadcast |
| 1/2-inch VHS & Beta | Domestic |
| 8mm | Domestic |

Figure 7.10  Tape formats

realist, whether from an electronic engineering background or otherwise, is liable to say that Sony is simply over-selling its product. Whatever, high-band U-Matic is the favoured format for most non-broadcast purposes where high picture quality at a relatively low cost is at a premium; for example: the origination and master editing of video films for use in sales conferences, press receptions, merchandising, etc. Low-band U-Matic play-back machines are used for the presentation of such video films and also by advertising agencies for showing their commercials' reels to prospective clients and other parties.

## 7.2 Comparisons of video and film

### Transfer of film to tape

Commercials are either shot and edited on film (35 mm), shot on film and then edited and/or effects added on tape or realized entirely on tape from start to finish. When a commercial completed on film is sent to the TV station it is transferred to a video signal for subsequent broadcast by a *telecine* machine.

A telecine does not simply effect a transfer from the film medium to the TV one; it also enables a number of other modifications and effects to be performed, principally slow dissolves from one frame to another, freeze frames and broad colour grading of the picture.

In 1986 a telecine colour grader called *da Vinci* was introduced. A highly sophisticated and virtuoso piece of equipment, the da Vinci telecine enables a wide range of individual colours on the original film print to be precisely picked out and altered without affecting the colour of the rest of the image, an inherent and insuperable problem with colour modification with all previous telecine colour grading. Suppose you have a number of shots or scenes for a Campbell's soup ad and that the particular red on the pack label is slightly 'off', much to the consternaton of the ad agency's art director. By using da Vinci, the Campbell's 'red' can be altered to make it as authentic as possible without affecting the colour of the housewife's hair and dress or her kitchen.

Another improvement in telecine design is the pin register gate, a technical device that guides the film by its edge perforations past the scanner that translates the celluloid image into a video one. Before this innovation, telecines were liable to produce a slight movement of the image known as 'weave' or 'bounce'. Though such imperfections are not on the whole apparent when doing a routine transfer to tape from a completed filmed commercial, they do become noticeable when the film material constitutes only a part of the commercial, such as a background, to be subsequently combined with video originated material such as computer graphics or animation.

Suppose you have live action film footage of two people driving along a deserted country road. The script calls for a group of bizarre Martian creatures to appear in a blaze of special effects on the road. The Martians are originated by animation on videotape, ditto the weird and wonderful effects of their landing. When the tape-transferred film of the live action and the video animation and effects are combined they won't fuse with seamless authenticity: the film originated images will appear to move slightly while the video originated material will be dead steady.

Basic transfer of film-to-tape has for a long time been very good, which is what you would expect given that the film image is inherently superior to the video one. While telecine machines can jutifiably lay claim to quantum leaps of progress, the reverse process, transferring videotape to film, is, despite many ingenious technical innovations, and subsequent claims made on their behalf, not very satisfactory. At the end of the day you can't improve on the original, you can't get more from less.

The TV or taped image is ultimately tied to the number of horizontal scan lines making up its picture; and the limitations of such an image will be magnified when converted to film. Other reasons apart, no commercial destined for theatrical showing in the cinema could be or would be shot on videotape and then transferred to film.

### Advantages and disadvantages of film and videotape

(1) In terms of definition and colour fidelity, capturing of tonal range and nuances of tone, the film image cannot be matched by that of video. Moreover the colour on video tends to be unnaturally exaggerated.

(2) With film, the lighting cameraman has a wide range of different types of stock to choose from. Rather like a painter carefully selecting pigments from his palette to achieve a particular effect on canvas, the lighting cameraman chooses a film stock according to its sensitivity to light and colour in order to produce a particular visual impression, mood or other effect. On video the 'look' of a picture can't be determined by the tape stock: there is just videotape and videotape. Saving for differences in particle density and how well the particles are protected from wear from the constant contact with the heads, all videotape is basically the same.

Night scenes to be shot uniquely from point light sources, say, figures moving stealthily around in the dark by the light of torches, necessitate using film that is very sensitive to light – has a high ASA rating. To add light to the scene, necessary for video shooting, would destroy the dramatic or whatever atmospheric quality is desired.

Video cameras can't 'process' a bright, point light source. A torch beam or a car headlamp will comet-tail. You see the trailing flare from lights on TV news, the faster the camera pans across the light the more pronounced is the streaking. Moreover, if you shoot directly at a bright light source for too long you burn a hole on the camera tube. So shots of a character looking up directly at the sun and being blinded are out.[9]

As the scanning spot in the camera tube scans at a constant and pre-fixed rate of twenty-five frames per second, video can't be used to originate slow-motion or speeded-up motion; such effects have to be performed in post-production. Besides, slow-motion sequences to be shot in limited available light require a highly light-sensitive stock which is not available, inherently, on videotape.

(3) Movie cameras are physically robust, video cameras delicate: they won't take much in the way of jostling and banging; their scanning tubes are fragile. They are, after all, scaled-down versions, operating in reverse, of the picture tubes in TV receivers. Knock over a video camera and the chances are, Murphy's and Sod's Law ruling OK, that the tubes will be damaged, writing-off many thousands of pounds, whereas film cameras have been known to survive a flight of stairs!

Film cameras have a portability that most broadcast video ones and their associated recording equipment lack. It's not practicable to shoot action sequences in confined spaces such as the back of a racing car on video. Film, furthermore, 'behaves' in extremes of temperature and humidity. Like the slogan for White Horse Scotch Whisky, you can take a film camera anywhere.

(4) Raw stock costs are cheaper on video. And, of course, the tape can be wiped and re-used, but because of its comparative low cost it seldom is. On tape, too, there aren't the further costs that film involves: of developing, processing and printing.

With video there is the advantage of instant monitoring. The director, producer and client can look at the scene on a monitor as it's being shot, and play it through again at the end of the take.

When using film, the director, though he'll have a very good idea of what's 'in the can', won't know for sure how what he's shot will look until the footage exposed has been printed up in the labs late that evening or the next day. However, it is fairly common nowadays to combine the instant picture monitoring of video with the image superiority of film by having a compact video camera mounted on the side of the movie camera. If, say, there is a cable in shot in a corner of the frame or microphone boom shadow reflected by a polished table the flaw can be picked up straightaway and rectified. Besides, the client and agency people sitting in on the shoot naturally want to see, then and there, the storyboard coming to life.

(5) Video has the big virtue of speed. Firstly during production: with multi-camera set-ups, different shot angles of the scene can, using a vision mixer, be intercut or mixed in real time, i.e., live-edited. Secondly during post-production: a prodigious range of optical effects, such as split screens, freeze frames, wipes and image manipulations, can be realized very quickly as can supers such as slogans or other typographical work (see Section 9.1). Moreover video post-production enables different optical and super effects to be experimented with (if the client can afford the time).

While many commercials can afford to take a couple of months or so to be completed, there are some that, because of the tactical nature of their objectives or the creative incorporation of ideas that are highly topical, have to be turned round in a week. Tactical advertising on TV is dominated by retailers' commercials for limited-period price reductions on goods and by national newspapers plugging what's in store next week in a read-all-about-it idiom.

For sheer speed the TV commercials for *The Sun* are in a class of their own, the fastest turn-around being a day! Producer Hugh Davies at Tape One explains: 'We had a call at 08.00 for a client briefing, and we produced two commercials – with two sets, twenty-four actors and a tiger cub – and the ITCA cleared them at 21.00'.[10] This pace was, Davies concedes, pushing it; the typical schedule for *Sun* commercials runs: the agency gets the brief on a Monday or Tuesday evening; the scripts are ready by the next morning; after a couple of days of pre-production meetings, shooting goes ahead on a Thursday or Friday; editing is done on Friday evening; the finished commercial goes on-air on Sunday.

With tape the completed commercial can be sent to the TV stations via a land line or microwave link; film prints of course have to be physically distributed by air, road or rail.

(6) Summarizing: most commercials are shot on film for its picture quality, versatility and better production values. Tape is largely confined to straightforward productions, like a front-on camera presentation/announcer sort staged in the studio, to those consisting of computer graphics/animation and to those drawing inspiration from pop promos.

At the end of the day the decision on what medium to use is really a question of directorial preference. Some directors simply feel more at home with the discipline of video, others with that of film.

Despite the ever-accelerating technical progress made by video, the tape-or-film decision still manages to incite passionate loyalties and divisions. But when it comes to post-production, at the stage of adding supers and optical effects, there is a virtual consensus of agreement: video rules.

# 8 · Production

## 8.0 Live action

The preparation for and editing of a TV commercial is typically measured in weeks; the actual shooting – the principal photography – in days, usually one to three. How long a shoot takes will depend on whether it's being done in the studio or on location, the number of separate scenes, how complex they are in terms of the lighting set-ups, the camera movements, the action, and so on.

Careful planning is, of course, vital. With the costs of the crew, equipment and studio hire 'on the meter' and running all the time, hold-ups because, say, a special property hasn't arrived or doesn't work are expensive and unforgivable. And someone's head is likely to roll!

What actually goes on during a shoot? To the uninitiated, not apparently very much a lot of the time. All too often it seems there is a surplus of people milling around, waiting, with no *filming* going on. But a single shot will take perhaps an hour or so to set up and rehearse. Film-making is team work: everyone has his or her part to play at different times. At any given moment there may be fifteen people watching and waiting while three people attend to a particular activity (perhaps adjustment of the lighting) that is a piece of the jigsaw which comes together stage by stage and which, when completed, culminates in the director giving the order to start filming.

The director is the key figure; his role is somewhere between the captain of a football team and the conductor of an orchestra. He 'calls the shots' which will have been plotted beforehand as will their sequence. (It is extremely rare for filming to take place in script/chronological order. For cost reasons, all the shots on a given set or location are done together.)

With the camera crew and lighting cameraman the director goes through what's happening in the shot and how he wants it photographed: the type of shot (close-ups, wide-angles, panning, etc.) and the lighting effect required. Meanwhile, the director's assistant will be overseeing the set, getting the actors ready in position and so on.

The lighting cameraman (variously known as the lighting director or the cinematographer) supervises the rigging and positioning of the lights by the gaffers. Another strange species are the grips: they hump, manoeuvre and set up the mounts, tracks or dollies for the camera.

The focus-puller measures the distance from the subject to the lens on the camera. The assistant cameraman loads the film magazine. The sound people work out how best to mike the actors.

While the technical preparations are going on with highly disciplined mayhem the director rehearses the actors: not always easy when all around cables are being laid, equipment manoeuvred into position plus a cross-fire of arcane orders like 'Kill that baby', 'Hit that brute'. The director interprets the scene for the cast, explains how he wants them to say the dialogue, how to react and where to look.

When the sound, lighting and camera technicalities are ready and the actors rehearsed the director calls for a technical run-through. If this goes smoothly and hitch-free, the director or his assistant calls for a take. 'Quiet please, we're going for a take now.' The studio floor hushes; a poised alertness ripples across the set. The director then gives the command: 'Roll sound'. The sound recordist switches on the tape machine, answering: 'Running' or 'Rolling'. Then 'Roll camera': the camera operator pushes the start button on the camera, confirming 'Running'. The director then orders: 'Mark it'. The assistant director or a junior member of the camera team (on some shoots the film loader doubles with a 'clapper' or 'slating' function) holds a slate board in front of the camera: 'Byron After-shave – Vigilante – Shot One – Take One'. Bang! He brings the clapstick down and moves out of the shot. A brief pause. And then: 'Action!' from the director.

The number of things that can foul a take is endless. The actor may not look in the right direction at the right time. Perhaps there's 'dirt' on the sound. Or extraneous noise (more of a hazard on location than in the studio). The camera's panning movement is too slow or too fast. The framing of the shot is not quite close enough or wide enough. A property fails to work: a pack doesn't open or won't disgorge its contents on cue. And if it's a comedy a chair doesn't collapse when it's meant to, or a simulated glass window doesn't shatter at the appropriate moment.

When things go overtly wrong it's pointless to continue with the take: it's a waste of film stock and precious time. The director shouts 'Cut!'. Sound and camera stop rolling. The technical fault is rectified. The technical operators and/or actors are reminded of what they've got to do. And then it's back to another take. 'Byron After-shave – Vigilante – Shot One – Take Two'.

Successive takes will follow until the shot is as near perfect as possible. Usually it's a question of polishing the performance, exacting total belief in the characters, getting the required facial expressions and body language, the required delivery of the dialogue – just the right emphasis, intonation and inflection of the words.

Normally the director will want to get at least two good takes in the can. He will instruct the camera assistant or whoever is logging the shots to have these takes printed up by the labs (these printed takes are the 'rushes').

Suppose things are going badly. Take after take is useless or at best only 'so-so'. The actors are on edge. A psychologically astute director won't berate them as they'll only get more tense. Instead he'll pretend the last take was OK, to bolster their confidence and then say he just wants to go for one more take to be on the safe side. Hopefully, with the actors now at ease, the 'safety' take will prove to be fine.

If after twenty or so takes a good (a 'buyable') one is being held up because the dialogue isn't being delivered in the sought way, the director, ever aware of the exigencies of time and the pressing need to move on to the next shot or scene, may decide to buy the relevant take of the shot for its visuals and have the dialogue recorded (post-synced) during post-production when the overheads are comparatively small, i.e., equipment, crew, studio hire, etc., aren't being paid for.

On the set vigilantly watching everything that is happening are the agency creatives who've devised the script and storyboard, the agency producer (he/she having overall responsibility for ensuring that the advertiser is going to get the TV commercial that he wants) and the client and agency account man. But when or if anybody wants to advise, criticize or comment on what the director is doing, they must do so through the agency TV producer. It is 'not on', practically and professionally, for the agency creative team to usurp the director's role and start telling the cast how to say a line or the lighting cameraman how to adjust the fill of light on the pack.

If a star director has been contracted, he will have virtual *carte blanche* on the shoot. After all, his particular, idiosyncratic even, visual style and flair, his way of dealing with and exacting performances of a certain kind, is what has been sought and paid for.

## 8.1 Animation

### Stop-frame animation

Typically this is used for packs that appear to move and open and unwrap themselves. The pack is set in position on a table or other flat surface. A single frame of film is exposed. Then the pack is moved a tiny fraction. Another frame of film is exposed. The pack is then moved a further fraction. It will take 750 very precise and painstakingly careful movements of the pack, such as the wrapper being peeled off a bar of chocolate, to produce an animated pack ad of thirty seconds (twenty-five minutely progressive movements for each second).

### Cartoons

The principle involved is the same as for stop-frame work. A series of drawings is made, each one being fractionally different from the preceding one. When the series of pictures, photographed one after the other, is subsequently run through a projector or displayed on a TV screen, the twenty-five rapidly successive and incrementally progressive drawings meld together, creating the illusion of motion. It's Donald Duck or Mickey Mouse.

Suppose the commercial consists of a pack, all walking and talking, that bumps into its content benefactor, a chicken, in the aisles of a supermarket. First the background of the supermarket is drawn. Then on a piece of transparent acetate known as a cel the progressive movements of the legs, arms and mouth on the pack are drawn. The non-moving background of the supermarket is placed on a flat bed above which is suspended the camera and lighting. The series of cels showing the pack walking along is placed, one cel after the other, on top of the background and photographed. Then at the point where the chicken makes its entrance the first chicken cel is superimposed on the pack cel and the composite photographed. The frame-by-frame exposure of the minutely progressive action of cartoon chicken and cartoon pack continues several hundred times over.

If a third moving character or object is required in the scene, say a dancing spoon, a separate series of cels will have to be drawn for it and these superimposed on the cells for the chicken which are in turn superimposed on those for the pack.

Crude animation can be achieved without using a camera by painting, drawing, scratching and marking directly on to the frames of the film stock. Usually jerky and splodgy, the results can look interestingly gross and primitive, and when combined with live action material, a mix favoured by some pop promos and one or two commercials, the effect is often startling in its deliberate uncouth flamboyance.

## Computer animation

On the one hand computer-generated pictures still tend to be associated with what is produced on animated video games and from PAC Man programmes for home micros, that is with images consisting of a mosaic of geometrical shapes with large serrated outlines, a limited colour range and a general poor sharpness. Another stereotype is that computer-originated images are limited to wire-frame skeletons like those used for engineering design models and diagrams for cars and the like.

On the other hand there is a widely held belief that computers are capable of producing any image to any degree of finish and sophistication literally from scratch. And thus of reducing manual illustration and the artist's role to a quaint or obsolete craft.

The state of computer animation is such that the first stereotype is a plain insult, the second one still much of a 'brave new world' goal: the human input from the graphic designer or the artist is still necessary.

At one level the computer, in the form of an electronic paintbox, allows the animation artist to produce frame-by-frame illustrations in basically the same way as he does when drawing a sequence of cels to be subsequently photographed.

With an electronic paintbox (the Quantel paintbox has become virtually an industry standard) the artist works with a pressure-sensitive electronic stylus and a touch tablet. The stylus functions just like a brush: it can be used to mix colours and, according to the pressure applied, to lay down varying densities of paint.

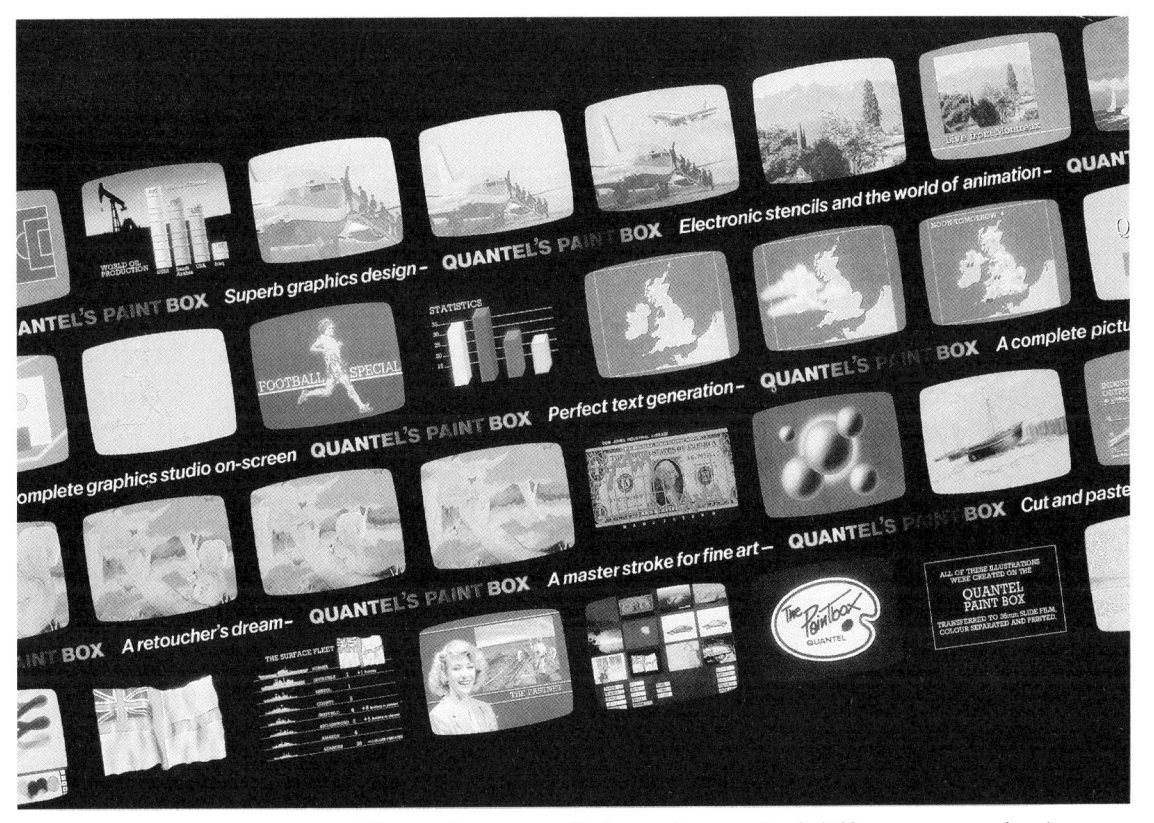

**Plate 2** Quantel's paintbox: the amazingly versatile electronic graphic design system.

The artist can pull down 'menus' of different pots of colour to work with, of different widths of brush, of different modes: the 'paint' mode allows the electronic pigment to be manipulated as if it was oil paint; the 'wash' mode enables images to be executed just like with water-colours; the 'chalk' mode gives the same results as working with crayons; the 'shade' mode allows tints and tones to be worked in; the 'air brush' mode gives the same effect as conventional studio air-brushing.

Paintboxes do a prodigious lot more than replacing the traditional mechanics of cel animation and affording a comprehensive range of execution styles. In addition to artist-originated images ready-made images from 35 mm slides and from video camera and freeze-frame videotape sources can be accessed ('grabbed') and incorporated into an animation sequence either as they stand or modified by cropping, cutting-up and/or enhancing with tints, colours, shades, etc.

Computer animation produces a three-dimensional solidity of image that conventional manual cel animation lacks. More and more commercials are using it for its super-real and 'spacey' effects. Some ads, notably for Smarties and Honeywell, are entirely realized through computer while others integrate computer animated sequences with live action or use computers for bravura logo and slogan work. Like logos that explode, rotate and reassemble. The TV companies, too, have shown enormous interest in the pyrotechnic capabilities of computers; starting with Channel 4's aesthetically exploding and regrouping of the primary coloured '4', logos for station and programme identification manufactured by computer have become commonplace, e.g., LWT's Venetian slat logo, the BBC's spacey and skewed 3-D *9 O'Clock News*.

Sophisticated computer animation is still slow. Well, slow for a client who may be paying out a couple of thousand pounds for each second realized.

A sequence has first to be sketched or 'choreographed' with wire-frame skeleton images either directly from a programme or by way of tracing with an electronic stylus on a tablet. The next stage is to flesh out the frame, to make it solid and real, to 'render' the image by adding the appropriate textures, colours, form and depth.

Some machines come with programmes that will render in real time. But the type or nature of off-the-peg programming for rendering a solid surface look may not be suitable for the particular job at hand. Accordingly, a new programme will have to be tailor-made. Which means time and, of course, money.

Quantel, Bosch, Vax, Sun, Ado, Iris – these are the names most likely to be found in computer graphics and animation facilities houses in London. The state-of-the-art in terms of speed, dexterity and ingenuity is represented by the Cray X-MP computer. But its capital cost is about forty times that of a Bosch or a Quantel. Rolling Stone Mick Jagger drew on its wondrous capability to lend hi-tech pizzazz to his *Hard Woman* video. More sublimely awesome still is the Pixar animation computer researched and developed under the aegis of George 'Star Wars' Lucas.

The rest is future.

# 9 · Post-production

## 9.0 Film editing

At a gross level editing means shrinking down perhaps thirty minutes of film footage into just thirty seconds. Occasionally commercials – such as Levi's 'Stitches' – may have as much raw footage as a full-length feature film to be subsequently distilled and cut into shape.

Editing isn't simply a matter of bolting together shots in script order. A thirty- or sixty-second commercial should be seen as a micro film. As such it needs to be paced; it needs a rhythm. Too fast a pace – too many rapid-fire quick-cuts – tends to be boring. So does a surfeit of slow movements. As with a good music score, an effective commercial needs a variety of tempo.

It is a commonplace complaint that editors, beavering away in some subterranean back room, don't get the credit they deserve. They are the proverbial unsung heroes of the industry. One of the reasons is that good editing isn't noticeable. But a bad cut is. Tough and unjustified it is, to be sure. But the injustice isn't peculiar to editing. The situation is the same for film-music composers. Rarely is a score singled out and lauded. It is only when the music jars with inappropriateness that it is commented on. Like great editing, fitting music doesn't stand out.

A good editor can redeem incomplete or 'so-so' footage. But he or she can't at the end of the day be expected to be a magician. To produce a masterpiece, a prize-winning commercial, the editor has to have material with that sort of potential to start with. An editor, as art director Alan Waldie puts it, 'can make a pig's ear out of a pig's ear and no doubt occasionally arrives at a silk purse (but) if you want a silk purse, kindly supply the silk'.[1]

Why don't directors edit their own material? After all, they know it better than anyone. But this is precisely the point: the director is just too familiar and too involved with what he's shot. He can't see the wood for the trees.

Coming completely fresh to the material, the editor can look at it objectively and impartially. He can view the footage, the way it's cut together, and the effect it's likely to have from the vantage of the audience. Well, up to a point. Because where comedy or suspense is a staple of the commercial the editor, after many hours of working wth the shots and arranging them together, will also become inured to the jokes or the shocks.

To some extent, editing is complementary to script writing. Just as the writer has envisaged the shots/scenes and their sequence, including the manner of transition between them – the cut points, the wipes, the dissolves, etc., – so the editor has to 'write' the script with lots of bits of celluloid, joining them together into a coherent whole that delivers the sought-after effect or impression.

Though the editor's job is to come up with a celluloid translation or version of the script, there is a virtually infinite leeway in the punctuation between the shots. Precisely where and when a cut is to start and finish admits of a wide spectrum of judgement and opinion. The editor's cut points may be thought too early or too late by the director or by the agency people.

Editing a commercial can be as much a committee business as creating a script. From the agency to the client to the production company, everyone wants their say; in differing ways the art director, the scriptwriter, the agency producer and the director have all contributed to the product and, naturally, want to leave their mark on what appears on X million TV screens.

With comments and advice crowding in from all directions the editor needs to have forbearance, patience and a lot of diplomacy.

His loyalties, however, should always be to the director when an argument about a particular cut occurs; their relationship being founded on a very special kind of mutual trust and respect.

### Sequence of steps in editing

(1) The raw material
For each shot there will normally be at least two good takes which

will have been developed and printed by the labs. At the same time the labs will transfer the corresponding sound takes from quarter-inch magnetic tape to perforated film with a magnetic stripe running down the centre or edge. To synchronize the picture with the sound for projection and editing, it is necessary for the sound to be on the same form of stock as the picture.

The master sound recordings and the original picture negative are stored away in a safe place – a vault facility in the labs – after cutting copies or work prints have been made.

## (2) Viewing the rushes

This usually takes place in a small viewing theatre. A double-head projector is used: one set of spools carrying the picture, another set the transferred sound.

Everyone gets in on this. It's both exciting and nerve-racking. It is the first time the editor gets to look at the raw material he's got to work with. And if he's possessed of a sharp political nous, he'll take note of the comments and kibbitzings.

## (3) The assembly

With the takes for each shot to go forward into the commercial decided on, the editor, using a flat-bed editing machine (Fig. 9.1) such as a Steenbeck, will assemble the 'work print' takes in chronological order.

On the editing machine are a set of plates with spindles for the

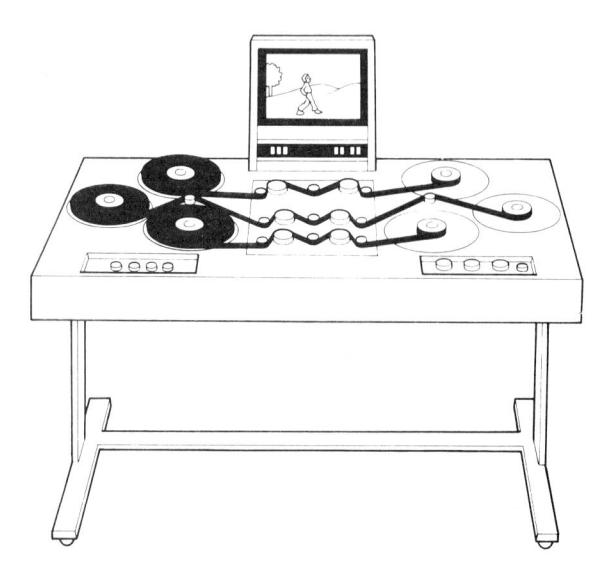

**Figure 9.1** Flat-bed editing machine

picture reel and two lots of sound reels. Between the plates carrying the picture is a device for projecting it on to a small screen; between the plates carrying the sound reels are sets of magnetic heads for playing back the dialogue, the sound effects and other sync sound recorded during the shooting.

To sync up the picture and the sound, the editor first runs the picture reel forward till he gets to what is called the 'strike frame': this is the frame where the arm of the clapboard hits the body of the slate. Holding the picture at this point, the editor then runs the sound reel forward until he reaches its 'strike': the moment when the 'clap' sound is heard. Picture and sound can now be locked together by the deck's sync motor, run forwards and backwards with the sound and picture in synchronization.

### (4) The rough cut

This is where the editor drafts the bolted-together, serially ordered assembly into shape. The rhythm, pattern and pace of the prospective commercial starts to emerge. The clapboard idents are cut out along with the sound (the 'Mark it' . . . 'Shot five, take sixteen', etc.). The various sections of film are further tightened at their beginnings and ends. If wipes, fades and other opticals are required, the editor will indicate these on the edge of the print with a chinagraph pencil.

A working proposal, the rough cut is first shown to the agency people on a double-head projector (until the cut of the commercial is agreed on by all parties involved the picture and the sound have to be kept separate physically. If alterations are to be made, as often they will be, it won't be feasible if the sound and picture are combined. The sound-track on a combined print will precede the picture frame to which it refers by slightly more than one second. To cut it would result in a loss of sync: lip-flap, mouths opening and closing like proverbial goldfish or a muddle of lip movements not coincident with the words being spoken).

Often the film is transferred to U-Matic tape format. And the presentation done on a TV set or monitor. It's 'tidier' and more practical to show a rough cut this way. And, of course, it goes a considerable way to simulating the conditions in which the consumer/target audience will view the ad at the end of the day. The verisimilitude comes at a price: on a small screen the commercial has to work a lot harder to sell itself. Big screen projection and a darkened auditorium lend the commercial an artificial impact.

If the advertising agency is happy with the rough cut it will then be shown to the client for his approval. And if either the product or the treatment is of a 'sensitive' kind it will be prudent to show it to the ITCA for its approval too.

If there is a voice-over to be laid across mute sections of the sound-track, it is sometimes 'scratched': at the production end someone will 'dummy' record the lines of the voice-over to fill in the mute gaps as they occur – usually they are at the end of the commercial.

Assuming the client, the agency and, if appropriate, the ITCA have given their respective seals of approval, the commercial's edit then progresses to the fine cut stage.

## (5) The fine cut

The cutting of the material is polished and tuned until it is cut to the nearest frame. In practice the difference between a rough cut and a fine cut isn't absolute. Rather it's a matter of degree, of progression, of ever-increasing tightening.

## (6) Dubbing

This encompasses all post-production sound operations; it isn't limited to what it means in the vernacular: as in the 'dubbed' version of a foreign language movie – French dialogue being post-synced into English (because the particular audience market won't tolerate the arduousness of reading subtitles).

Dubbing, confusingly, is a term of loose use. It can, for example, include transfer from one medium or format to another. As in: 'dub down from one-inch (tape) to three-quarter inch'.

In the dubbing theatre the various sections of sync sound that have been cut against the fine cut of the picture are transferred to broad-gauge multi-track tape. Because the level of the sound is likely to vary slightly from shot to shot it is 'equalized' during the transfer. In a given scene actor A's voice may be loud in shots one and two but, for reasons of miking and delivery, a bit softer in shots three and four. Obviously this lack of consistency jeopardizes the realism or naturalism of the scene. To maintain it, the voice levels need to be balanced.

At the same time as equalizing, the sound rushes are cleaned. Any noise or dirt will, as far as is possible short of affecting the quality of the desired sound signal, be filtered out.

Any sync sound not recorded during shooting will now be originated and laid down to coincide precisely with the action/movement of the visuals. Typical reasons for having to post-sync dialogue are: on location the sound recording has been plagued by, say, airplanes roaring overhead during takes; the actor/actress, after a frustratingly large number of takes, still hasn't managed to deliver the lines with the desired beat and intonation; the performer is a model: used for his/her looks and aesthetics, he or she just can't do the dialogue convincingly or isn't allowed to do it because of union regulations'; a special, funny or surreal voice effect is called for: a baby speaking in a deep baritone; a cat, frog or monkey (à la PG Tips) has to talk.

Post-syncing of sound effects: as with dialogue, recording of these may have been marred by extraneous noise on location. Or may have been impossible, the source of the sound being simply unreal, unconvincing.

Suppose the commercial is set in the interior of a castle. And that for production/budget reasons the interior has been built in the studio. The sound of footsteps, hard and echo-y, has to be produced. On the boards of the studio stage they sound literally wooden. In this situation a foot artiste will be brought into the dubbing theatre. Watching the footsteps of the character concerned, he or she will walk, stomp, march or whatever on a tray of flagstone to match perfectly the movement of the performer's footsteps.

A shot features a close-up of a ring tab being tugged off a can of beer. The sound effect of the rip, metal out of metal, and the subsequent tantalizing escaping hiss of the lager can't be recorded with the required fidelity or dramatic emphasis. Either it can't anyway, period, or the microphone has to be so close that it will be in shot. So the sound has to be recorded, enhanced and built up in the dubbing theatre.

Paradoxically, many real and live recorded sounds don't sound naturalistic. Well, naturalistic from the point of view of audiences. Their criterion of 'natural' is often determined by a standard derived from repeated exposure to TV and movie sound effects. If you've never heard a gun firing or a bomb exploding other than on TV or in the cinema, then the way it sounds there defines its reality. Sound reality is, a lot of the time, a mythical one.

All the non-sync sound is recorded: the voice-over, typically to reinforce the slogan at the commercial's close; the music, which will have been specially composed or gotten 'off the peg'; and atmos (atmosphere) tracks – the sound of wind, rain, of cicadas or whatever.

Where parts of the commercial are originally mute and then dubbed with sync dialogue and effects, the overall effect will sound different: the ambient acoustics in the dubbing theatre are 'dead', clinically clean compared to the background sound environment on location. During shooting the sound man will record a minute or so of the background: the noise of traffic in the street, the soft but telling murmur emanating from the heart of a forest. Known as 'wild track', it will be laid down at the dubbing stage to render the post-synced work naturalistic and consistent with the sync recordings.

When all the various sound tracks have been recorded at full level, the dubbing supervisor under the direction of the editor will mix them down to one track so that, say, the music will fade up or crash in at the required moment, the levels between the dialogue and sound effects will be appropriately balanced and so on.

The end product of the dubbing will be a mixed, single track magnetic master.

### (7) Master negative cut

Until now the cutting of the picture has been done on a 'work print', also known as the 'cutting copy' or 'slash print'. Along the edge of this are a series of key numbers for each frame. The editor will have logged the numbers for the entry and exit point of each cut. The master negative will now be disinterred from its safe storage and cut to match the cut points on the work print.

In order to safeguard that overlap of the cemented splices between each cut won't appear on the final print and also to facilitate the printing of optical effects and supers the cutting of the master negative is done on two or more separate rolls of film, a procedure known as A and B checkerboard assembly. On one roll of film, the A roll, cuts one, three, five, seven, etc., are assembled; between each are spliced lengths of opaque film that exactly match the number of frames of the missing cuts. On the B roll, cuts two, four, six, eight, etc., are assembled, again with sections of opaque film between them that substitute for the missing odd-numbered cuts. In the same way C and D rolls may be assembled with titles and supers in the required places.

The lab first prints the A roll on to the raw stock. Since the gaps between the cuts are opaque, they will be left as a series of unex-

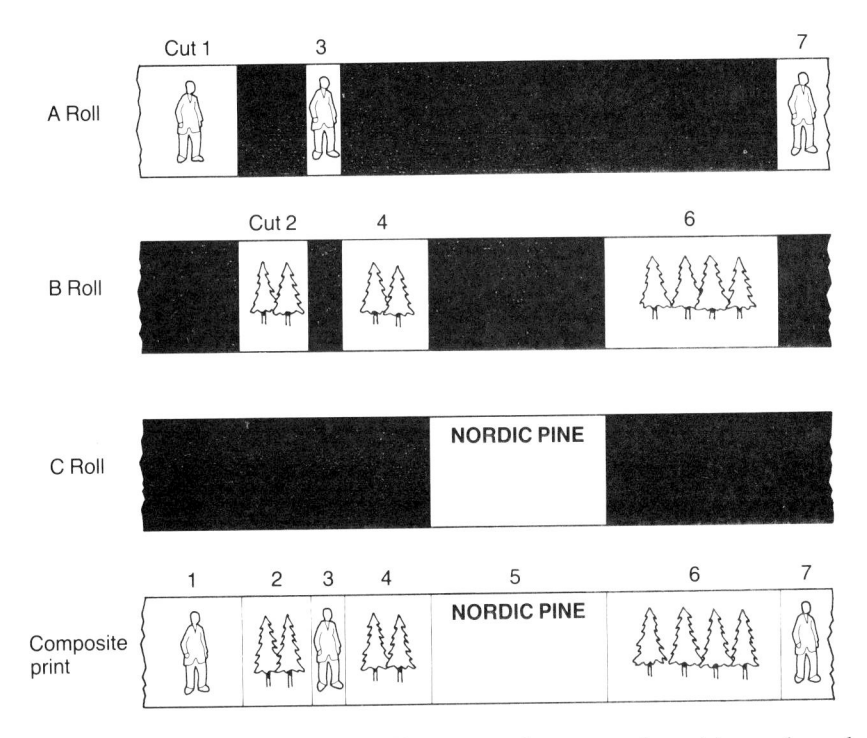

**Figure 9.2** A & B roll assembly

posed blanks. Then the B roll is printed on top: the odd-numbered cuts printing to fit exactly into the unexposed lengths left by the A roll.

The master negative is thus printed join-free; seamless.

## (8) Colour grading and correcting

From shot to shot the colour values are likely to vary. The way a scene is lit may give very slightly different colour qualities for the different camera angles and positions of each shot. Shooting a scene outdoors in available light is the situation that is most likely, despite the best endeavours of the cameraman, to produce discrepancies in exposure levels, especially if the light is changing: at 10.00 a.m. on shot one, the sky is uniformly overcast; at 11.00 a.m. on shot two, patchy sun intermittently breaks through the cloud; on shot three, say half-an-hour later, there's radiant sunlight.

Clearly, the effectiveness of a commercial will be disastrously marred if the actor's ice blue slacks change in hue from one shot to the next. And where pack shots and product demonstrations are concerned the need to get consistency and authenticity of colour is paramount. Tomato ketchup can't look blood red one moment and dark pink the next.

The labs put several sample frames from the master negative through a colour analyser. From the test strips the colour qualities are examined and the amount of adjustment and correction needed is determined. The entire master negative is then subjected to the same correction treatment as the test strips, resulting in balanced and consistent rendering of colour across all the shots.

### (9) Opticals

If mixes, wipes and other optical effects and titles haven't been produced by direct superimposed printing of A, B, C and D rolls, or if they are too complex to achieve in this way, they will be realized on an optical printer. Reduced to its basics, this equipment consists of a projector to show the original fine cut and a highly sophisticated camera which can be moved and positioned in a complex variety of ways in front of the projector from where it films the master material. With this camera opticals such as corner wipes, split-screens, matte effects and so on are created.

The colour-corrected commercial, now with opticals and supers, is vetted by the director, final approval being deferred to the answer print stage.

### (10) Answer print

Also known as an approval print, this combines the treated picture and magnetic sound master on to one piece of film, the sound being represented magnetically or optically. Viewed by all parties ultimately responsible for the commercial, it is the final check.

### (11) Pre-transmission clearance

The completed commercial is sent to the ITCA for final clearance. At the same time as the ITCA's viewing, the commercial is watched by the IBA.

Only about two per cent of commercials fail to get approval. As the ITCA is quick to point out, most of these weren't submitted at the script/storyboard stage. However, the amendments required are usually minor.

### (12) Release prints

Bulk or release prints will be ordered from the labs for onward dispatch to the TV programme companies and, if appropriate, to cinema screen advertising contractors. When a lot of prints are required, a duplicate master will be needed; a master negative becoming worn after about eighty prints are made from it.

### (13) Tape transfer

The above stage is becoming obsolete except for cinema exhibition. Nearly all commercials for broadcast are transferred to videotape prior to distribution to the TV stations.

The reasons are as follows: (a) the stations are tooled up to play out commercials only from computer-controlled VTR's and to computer-assemble the various commercials for each break; (b) the system of auditing the broadcast of commercials, known as EVT (Electronic Verification of Transmission), enables the advertiser/agency to check that the commercial has been put out the contracted number of times and, no less important, at the right time, in the break during the *News at Ten* or whatever. In essence, EVT consists of a coded signal for the advertiser, the agency, the product, the duration, etc., which is recorded on the videotape of the ad before being sent to the TV companies. The code is recorded in what is technically known as 'the field blanking interval'. This means that you and I aren't aware of it when watching the *News at Ten*. But the TV company records it, passing the data on to a contracted bureau. Advertisers and agencies subsequently receive print-out statements showing when and how many times their ad was transmitted.

A further reason is that the majority of commercials are now post-produced on tape.

## 9.1 Videotape editing

Let's assume that the commercial has been shot on tape (probably one-inch, possibly two-inch, very occasionally half-inch, Betacam). The tape rushes will have time code burnt in; equivalent to the frame edge numbers on film, this identifies the start and stop point of each take.

Because one-inch editing facilities are expensive, the time coded rushes are transferred to U-Matic. On this format the cost of the equipment is relatively low. Indeed, paying for the editor's time is usually greater than the hire of the two-machine edit desk.

Known as 'off-line' editing, this way of working allows the editor and director to take their time in experimenting and playing around with various assemblies and different cut points for each shot. Though, strictly speaking, the term 'cut' is a misnomer in the video medium, as shots are joined together by being copied one after the other, on a virgin reel or cassette of tape.

The rushes are played through on the 'source' VCR and the best takes for each shot recorded in script order on to a blank cassette on the 'edit' VCR (Fig. 9.3). The editor, having got the feel and pace of the commercial from this assembly, will then put the

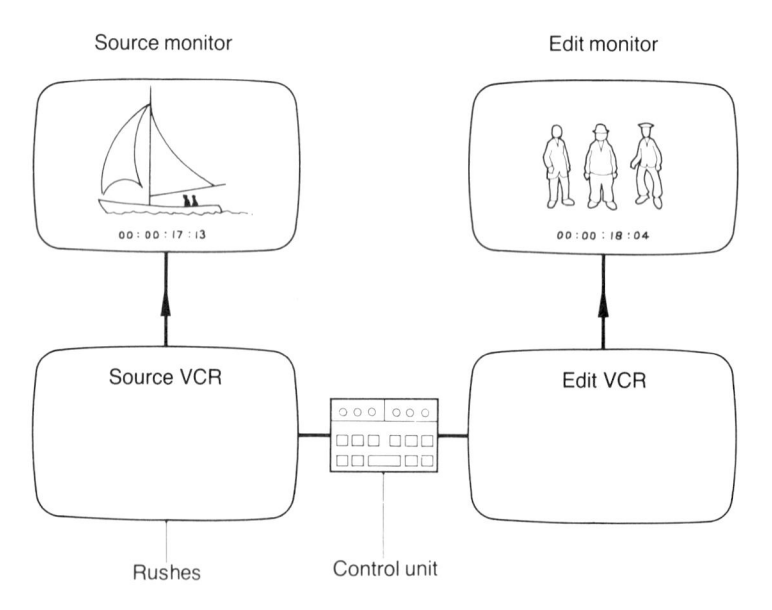

**Figure 9.3** U-Matic off-line editing

assembly cassette into the source machine and record the sequence of shots, tightening the beginning and end of each, on the edit machine. This is the rough cut for showing to the client/agency.

The entry and exit points of each of the sections is logged from the time code. It will look, at its simplest, as follows:

|  |  | Hours | Minutes | Seconds | Frames |
| --- | --- | --- | --- | --- | --- |
| Edit One | Start | 00 | 01 | 07 | 23 |
|  | Stop | 00 | 01 | 11 | 07 |
| Edit Two | Start | 00 | 03 | 51 | 01 |
|  | Stop | 00 | 03 | 57 | 09 |
| Edit Three | Start | 00 | 19 | 16 | 18 |
|  | Stop | 00 | 19 | 19 | 01 |

The time code for all the edit points is entered on to a punched tape or magnetic disk. The coded data can then be used as a programme to conform the one-inch master material to the edit points on the U-Matic. Thus costly VTR time in a one-inch edit suite is saved.

A drawback of video editing is this: once you've recorded an edited sequence, other than inserting a new shot into the assembly, you can't change it – shorten or lengthen a cut here or there – without copying the whole assembly all over again from scratch. Unless you're prepared to accept a generation loss.

Let's say you have forty-two shots electronically cut together on your edit reel. But you (or someone else) isn't happy with the edit point of shot thirty-six; you (or they) decide it comes in too quickly. With film you can simply retrieve the rush for the shot, cut it to add the desired extra twenty frames or whatever, and then physically splice it into the otherwise finished edit. But with tape you have to load the rough/fine cut material on to the source machine, record edit points one to thirty-five, then stop, then load the rush material for shot thirty-six on to the source machine, record the lengthened version on it, and then record the remaining sequence of shots thirty-seven to forty-two. Thus the whole of the commercial has suffered from a generation loss saving shot thirty-six.

However, video editing is currently undergoing a major revolution with the introduction of disk-based digital systems like Quantel's Harry. These liberate editing from the constraints of linear assembly of cuts and the degradation that comes from repeated copying. In short it means that tape rushes can be cut and re-cut and played around with in the same fashion as film footage. There is no loss of quality. And results can be viewed instantly.

The limitation, at least at the moment, is frame memory storage. Quantel's Harry is at full capacity with a few minutes. Thus editing and effects adding an entire commercial is not yet a practical option. But, doubtless, it soon will be.

### Supers and special effects

Once approved, the edited one-inch 'master' is ready for titles, supers and optical effects to be added.

Film edited material is usually transferred to one-inch tape after the rough or fine cut stage. During the telecine process the footage

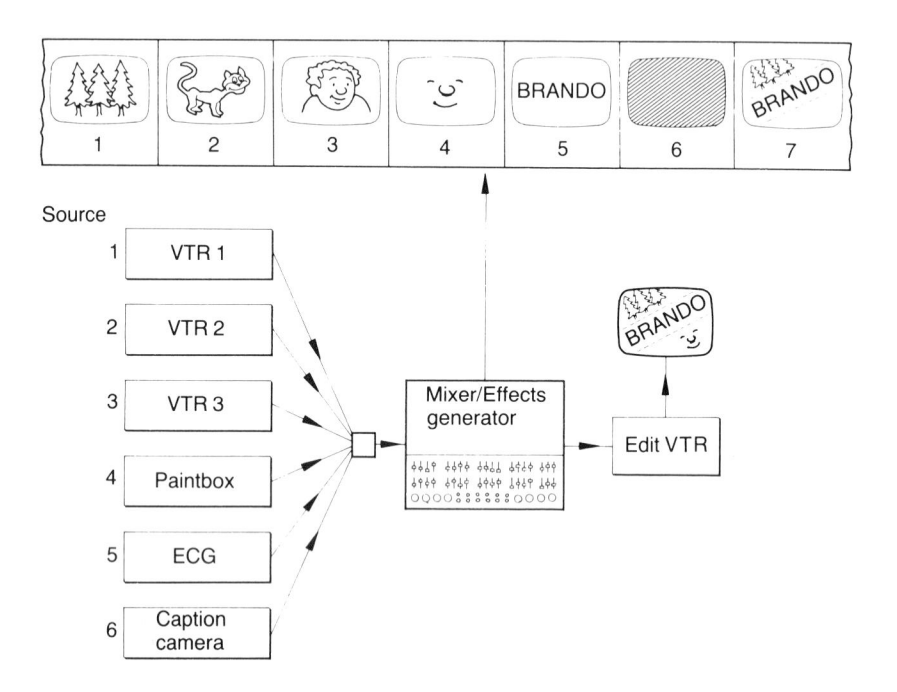

**Figure 9.4** Configuration for one-inch editing

will be colour-adjusted, though sometimes this will have already been done by the labs.

Text, slogans and captions are keyed on to the required frames by an electronic character generator (ECG) or from the text-generating facilities of an electronic paint-box.

A wide variety of typefaces and sizes can be accessed and entered. The layout can be tried out; characters can be squeezed, stretched, colourized; a slogan can be spelt out, the characters appearing one after another in rapid succession. When the desired display has been achieved, it is previewed and then recorded.

By contrast, producing titles and slogans on film is a laborious process. The supers have to be originated by rub-down transfer lettering or other means, then filmed, and then printed on top of the relevant series of frames. There is no scope for playing around with positioning and composition. And it takes days rather than an hour or so.

With devices such as Cypher, text can be produced with a 3-D effect. Characters can be made to stand out with stonemason solidity or suspended in curved space.

For special effects, Quantel's Mirage must rank as one of the most wizardlike and versatile tools available. Its repertoire of 'standard' effects includes: the frame flip-over; the page turn – as if it were a page in a magazine the frame is lifted up by the corner and folded over to reveal a new image; the pixel explosion: the picture erupts into an anarchy of fleeing dots of colours; the 'tile whoosh': the frame is broken up into a mosaic of tiles which then whizz off the screen, whizzing back, the tiles meld to form a new frame.

Pre-programmed, these sort of effects can be realized by the proverbial push of a button. They look amazing; they grab attention. Until the viewer, after repeated exposure to them, gets blasé. The impact and surprise of the effect wears off. The effect then tends to get in the way of the content/message rather than enhancing it. The bottom line is reached when the whoosh, flip, tumble or whatever deteriorates into the pornography of effects.

The value of systems such as Mirage lies in eschewing the menu of 'off-the-peg' pre-programmed effects and, instead, exploring and harnessing its virtually limitless potential for manipulating images and space to suit the purposes of the particular commercial or other job. The problem, however, is this: you need to imagine what you want in advance. Which isn't that easy, even if you're endowed with a singularly gymnastic and surreal imagination. It's a chastening fact that experienced Mirage operators have conceded that they don't know what moves and effects can be produced. Quite often one or more of these has been realized by serendipity: playing around, trial, error and then – wham! – success.

Basically, Mirage is a device that takes in images and then performs spectacular operations on them. It is a virtuoso shape-shifter, elasticating, squeezing, moulding, rearranging and grafting picture frames to fit any shape or form. In computerese, Mirage is a tool for 'texture mapping', marrying together shapes and contents.

A pack shot, for example, can be wrapped around any number of computer-generated forms: a cube, a cylinder, a rhomboid, a pyramid, etc. To obviate the bizarre distortion caused by mapping the frame of a pack on to a coin shape (part of the image would be fitted on to one side, another part on to the flip side, and another part folded around the bevelled rim), the pack shot image is 'sectorized', a process which enables the required part of the image, or all of it, to be mapped on either side of the coin and/or around its edge free from weird distortion.

Imagine a detergent commercial: the housewife retrieves a football vest from the washing machine. The pack mixed with the image of her footballing son can be mapped on to the tousled and shape-changing form of the vest. More dramatically, a man's face can be fitted on to and into the head of a vampire bat or other creature.

**Part three · Into print**

# 10 · Creativity in print advertising

## 10.0 The creative teamwork

The starting point is the creative strategy. This provides the framework or the grate for the creative fire-lighting. The strategy, as we've seen (Section 5.1), sets out what the objectives of the advertising are; who it is being aimed at; what proposition is to be communicated and what impression is to be left; the way the communication is to be put over, i.e., the tone and the appeal(s) to be used; and the range of media to be used, including the space sizes and positions.

A creative team thrives both on mutual respect and fertile chemistry. The writer and the art director should be able to spar with each other with total trust, bounce ideas back and forth, catch and run with the ricochets. Ideas may surface in the form of a copy line, an image, a mix of both, a made-up character, a vision of an entire layout or in any number of other ways. There are no set procedures to the process[1] just as no one creative team puts its heads together in exactly the same way as another.

Though the art director's job is to envisage and supervise the way an ad will look (deciding on the subject and executive style of the photography, the typefaces and sizes, the design and layout of all the graphic elements), he may, at the ideas stage, come up with a slogan. Conversely, it may be the writer who hits on a particular visual approach. Neither should be proprietorial about their 'official' roles or labels.

Once in a while a great idea may come 'out of the blue'. But on the whole the work in getting ideas is not unlike using a metal detector. After a lot of frustrating and fruitless sweeping over an area that has been mapped out in advance by the strategy, you at last get a tell-tale 'click'. And then excitedly start to excavate and, finally, to sift. You may have hit on a rusty nail, and if so it will very quickly be nailed. Or you may not recognize straightaway what you've got. And occasionally you may have struck gold.

To optimize the prospecting, the creatives will vicariously enter the world of the target consumer. What is she (or he) like? As a real person rather than a category, a C2 or whatever. What are her hopes, wishes, desires? What's her domestic and social life like? What does she think of the product generally and the various branded versions of it? At the same time the writer and art director will get hold of as much information as possible about the product and the company behind it, and to this end will work closely with the account planner whose job is to interpret all the market data and if necessary to augment it.

Between the customer and the product there is the potential for a rapport, a dialogue or a bond to be set up and maintained. The basis of the relationship may rest with an image or a straightforward proposition – a USP, while the appeal to be used (love, pride, nostalgia, economy, etc.) provides the catalyst.

## 10.1 Copywriting

Philip Dusenberry, the creative director at the BBDO agency in New York, once wisecracked[2] that copywriting is the second most lucrative form of writing, the first being writing ransom notes. Pecuniary considerations apart, the comparison isn't – well, up to a point – that wild. Both can be short, tersely so. And both are to the point. Never mind the style, it's the content that counts. Its purpose is to get the reader to *act*. Ultimately by paying up for goods, beans or live bodies. Or, as a prelude or softening up to this end, instilling or reinforcing attitudes or impressions.

Viewed more closely the simile crumples. The kidnapper has got a captive audience that reads, re-reads and dwells on every word, that in anguish plumbs and probes for sub-text. Whereas the copywriter doesn't start with built-in attention and interest; these have to be variously induced or manufactured, to halt the reader in his/her page-turning tracks. And reading between the lines is pretty well the preserve of clients, agency creatives and accounts people and a smattering of academics.

Over to another analogy: poetry! It says more with less than ordinary prose. It won't translate; the meanings of the words being inherently bound up with their sense, the very language of their expression. It is sensitive to typographical get-up: the 'look' of the words on the page, the line length and so on.[3] It cues the reader to supply the visual imagery. And it uses words alliteratively and musically, sets them in collision, makes them work overtime.

Now look at some of the main features of copywriting:

- A slogan or headline, particularly if it involves a pun, won't translate; the style, the expression and the content are fused.
- Alliteration and sound resonance are frequently used: so, famously, 'Beanz Meanz Heinz'; 'Esso's Put a Tiger in Your Tank'.
- Typographics are an integral part of the effectiveness of copy.
- Words are measured and weighed with a care, sensitivity and precision that 'regular prose' doesn't or can't afford.
- Copy excites or directs visual imagery (especially in radio commercial scripting where the pictures are uniquely provided by the listener's mind theatre).

## Headlines

Though some art directors might disagree, if the headline doesn't work, the ad isn't likely to either. Because however striking, intriguing and aesthetically resplendent the picture is, it needs a copy line, if only as an anchor, caption or directive. As Alastair Crompton says: 'A great picture deserves a great line to back it up, even ... the *Mona Lisa* ... needs a small brass plate underneath'.[4]

What makes for an effective headline? Or a good slogan? (Repeatedly used headlines acquire the status of slogans; conversely, a slogan may function as a headline even if it isn't a *head line* but instead appears at the close of an ad.) Simply, it's one that you don't have to think about to *know* that it's great; it's one that triggers the response: 'That's it!'; it leaps out fully armed, grabbing and convincing immediately.

One of the dreams of a copywriter bent on immortality is to

come up with a line that enters the vernacular and becomes famous. Slogans that have become culturally canonized include, notably: the riff of Smirnoff's much-loved classic campaign, 'I used to be a (librarian, accountant, etc.) ... until I discovered Smirnoff' ... 'The effect is shattering'; Heineken's 'Refreshes the parts other beers can't reach'; 'Tell Sid' (British Gas flotation); Audi's up-market strapline '*Vorsprung durch Technik*' (as we say in German); Schweppes' 'Schh ... You know who'.

Such is the litany status of lines like these that some of the agencies concerned have wittily and ironically played around with their idiomatic properties. So, Smirnoff's subsequent campaign: 'Well, they said anything could happen'. One ad showed a girl water ski-ing on Loch Ness, the monster substituting for the speed boat; another, an overt role reversal: the executive husband wearing a pinafore and all the trappings of housewifedom saying goodbye at 8.30 a.m. to his spouse, sharp-suited, carrying a leather brief case and bound for a hard day arbitraging pork bellies or whatever.

A fairly widely used 'technique' for headlines is that of inverting or otherwise altering a proverb or saying (Fig. 10.1). So: Unigate's 'When Unigate went bananas, strawberry and chocolate, sales went crazy'.[5] If imitation is the sincerest form of flattery one of the highest tributes that can be paid an agency is when one of its slogans is borrowed. Schweppes' 'You know who' was appropriated by Amstrad: 'Comparable with you know who. Priced at only we know how'.

There are no formulae for writing headlines, though there are quite a few dogmas, e.g., that headlines shouldn't be long or have full-stops at the end. Firstly, creativity can't be rule-bound; if it is, it ceases to be innovative. Secondly, recipes for headlines are artificial as they remove the copy from the context of the artwork. That said, it is useful to look at some of the favoured approaches to headlines that have worked well in the past. The common denominators are mixes of attention, interest and involvement that are product relevant.

### (a) Questions

How? Why? What? Where? enjoin involvement in a way a statement doesn't.

'If Phurnacite were a person, who would it be?' (Frank Bruno. Both he and the product have concentrated energy.)

# Creativity in print advertising 147

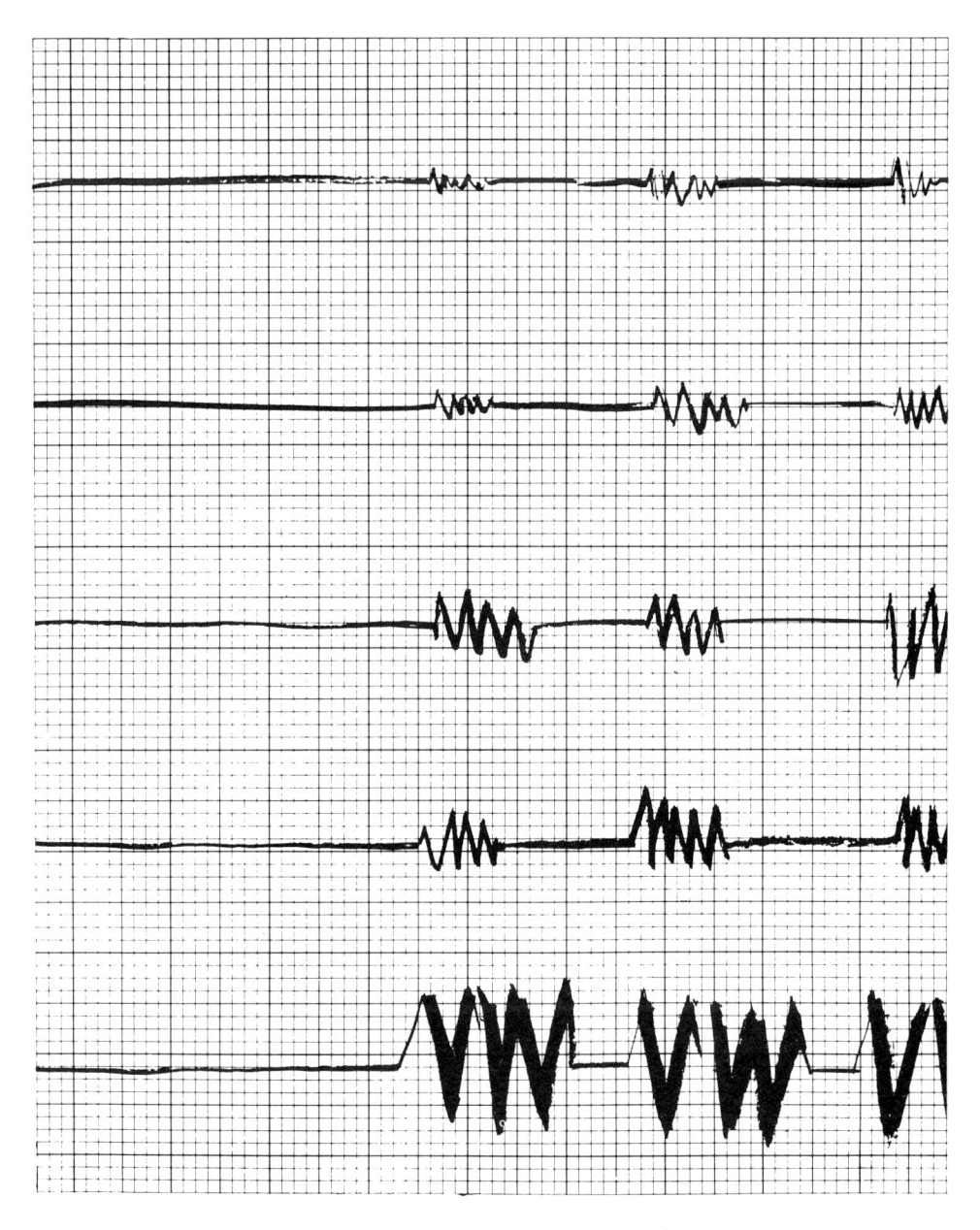

## It can save your life.

In London, the doctors of the city's 'Dial-a-Doctor' service rely 24 hours a day on a fleet of Volkswagen Polos to save lives. In an emergency, thanks to its rigid steel safety cell, a Polo may well save yours.

**Figure 10.1** A brilliant visual pun on the logo/ECG trace

'What do *you* do after you've mown the lawn?' It's an odd thing to ask. Till we realize it's keying the benefit of Qualcast mowers. The Qualcast owner gets out a deckchair. Not so the hapless chap with a hover; he has the bother of raking up all the mess of the scattered cuttings.

### (b) Paradox
Saying black is white. The intrigue here is: how is the ad going to crack the paradox?

'If you feel like a dog, count yourself Lucky'. The body copy in this much-acclaimed Healthcrafts ad has the job of explaining the apparent contradiction (dogs don't eat junk food, smoke or drink, or stay up late; if your pattern of living doesn't quite measure up to the dog's life, then you need the dietary supplement provided by Healthcrafts' range of vitamin pills).

### (c) Story appeal
Typically a unique and startling fact about the product (Plate 3). 'At Waterford, we take 1,120 times longer than necessary to create a glass'. Even if you habitually drink out of free glasses from petrol stations, the line intrigues.

### (d) Narrative
Often tied to the product as a source of personal transformation (shades of the classic Smirnoff riff).

'On Thursday I was that new kid in dispatch. On Friday I was that bright young man on the ground floor' (thanks to Red Star express parcels service).

### (e) Quotes
Usually in the form of an endorsement. 'It had to be shot at dusk, or I'd have been shot at dawn'. David Bailey on the Olympus OM40 camera.

'It's with my brush that I make love.' What! No, it's Renoir speaking about the erotic passion in his painting. And was used as a strapline for an art book-club subscription ad.

### (f) USPs
'A great man admits his mistakes. A great pen erases them' (for the Eraser Mate ball-point pen that erases as easily as a pencil).

### (g) Puns

Though a veritable minefield, there's no stopping them. 'The Sovereign. Worth any number of Deutsche marques' (Jaguar 'Sovereign').

## Subheads and body copy

Subheads act like signposts; they direct the reader through the ad; they catch the skim-reader's attention as a series of hooks, incentivizing him/her to start again and enter the text. If there are a lot of points to be put across, as in selling off-the-page ads, they are essential both as mini chapter headings/summaries and as routine points.

Body copy: there's a view that nobody reads it, especially if it's long. Certainly it's true that it's not given the attention of a headline and to this end individual words or punctuation marks don't have to be weighed with quite the same laboratory precision and 'feel' for every shade of nuance and implication. If you've got ten words to say something rather than five hundred you are of course going to consider those ten with a care where no nit is too small to pick. Nevertheless, if the body copy is inherently interesting and compelling, it will be read no matter how long it is. One might as well declare that no one reads long novels. Truistically, they don't if the material is boring and hard work. Good body copy possesses the equivalent of the book's 'page turner' effect: you no less effortlessly than captivatingly sail through line after line, paragraph after paragraph, the typography and layout playing a crucial role in assisting the passage.

Copy language: it's often maintained that there are near 'magic' words such as 'free', 'improved', 'new'; use them, particularly in headlines, and you're made. The trouble with words like these is that – not to put too blunt a point on it – they are worn out. Not only are they cliché-ridden, they reek of advertisingese – they are 'addy'. With great mastery their jaded currency can be redeemed but in most cases they alienate readers. Copy should use the language of the people that it's talking to; it should be realistic and natural, like good dialogue.

**Plate 3** (overleaf) Great story appeal. And a deft borrowing from de Beers. It matches Ogilvy's famous Rolls ad. (Mick de Vito – Art Director; Giles Keeble – Copywriter)

**150 Into print**

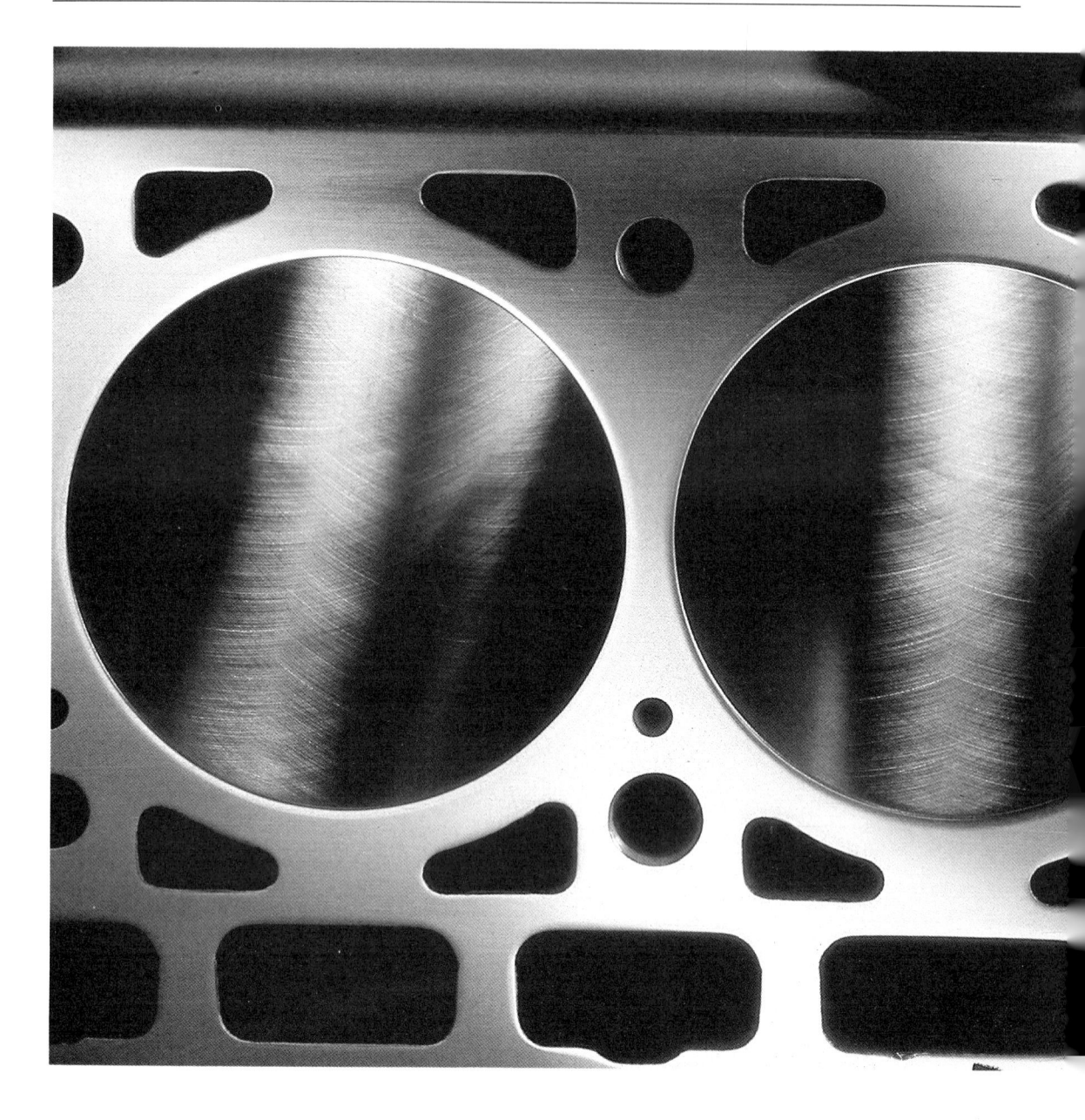

To cross-hatch the surface of their cylinders, most manufacturers use ceramics.

For BMW, that isn't good enough. We use diamonds.

Cross-hatching retains engine oil so that the pistons and the cylinders don't overheat. Unlike diamonds, ceramics aren't really cut out for the job: they soon wear down, leaving shallow grooves of uneven depth.

By having deeper grooves, a BMW's cylinders retain more oil, which means they last longer than other cylinders.

In fact, the etch lines are clearly visible after 125,000 miles.

Insisting on diamonds may seem a small detail, but BMW have always worked to the philosophy that a long-lasting reputation isn't built by taking short cuts.

Here are some other examples.

One in every five men at the factory is a quality controller.

THE BMW RANGE, FROM £7,995 TO £35,450. PRICES, CORRECT AT TIME OF GOING TO PRESS, INCLUDE CAR TAX AND VAT BUT NOT DELIVERY
FOR A BMW 3, 5, 6 OR 7 SERIES INFORMATION FILE AND THE NAME OF YOUR LOCAL DEALER PLEASE WRITE TO: BMW INFORMATION SERVICE, PO BOX 46, HOUNSLOW,

**Creativity in print advertising** 151

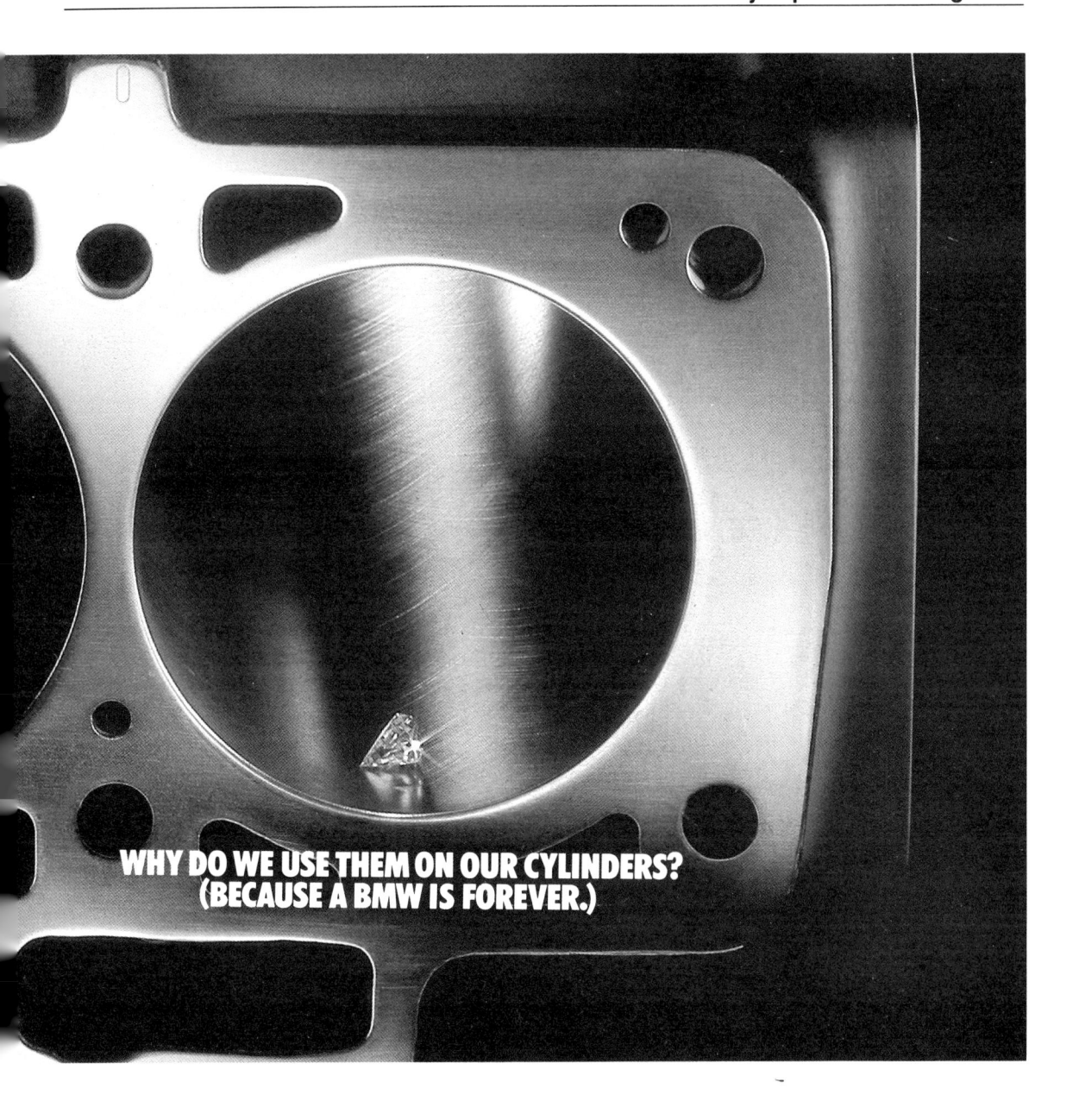

## WHY DO WE USE THEM ON OUR CYLINDERS?
## (BECAUSE A BMW IS FOREVER.)

Samples of all paints are tested in salt water for up to 480 hours to see if they withstand rust.

Every conrod is measured 24 ways, and conrods that go into the same engine are matched by weight and diameter. (No wonder BMW engines are so finely balanced.)

The value of such an attitude will be appreciated when you realise how little your BMW has depreciated.

In a recent survey, for example, the BMW 316 lost less of its value over three years, than 75 other cars tested.

Of course, hardly anybody keeps their car for ever. In BMW's case, however, three out of four owners go on to buy another BMW.

For them, at least, the pleasure of owning The Ultimate Driving Machine never dies.

**THE ULTIMATE DRIVING MACHINE**

OR NUMBER PLATES. INCLUSIVE DELIVERY CHARGE. INCORPORATING BMW EMERGENCY SERVICE & INITIAL SERVICES. £225 & VAT.
MIDDLESEX, OR TELEPHONE: 01-897 6665 (LITERATURE REQUESTS ONLY). FOR TAX FREE SALES: 56 PARK LANE, LONDON W1. TELEPHONE 01-629 9277.

## 10.2 Art direction

The art director, as we've seen, has a special and symbiotic relationship with the copywriter. In addition he works in close co-operation with the typographer, the production manager, the art buyer and the art studio. In their respective different ways these parties will advise on the feasibility and practicalities of realizing the visual and graphic ideas for an ad into a finished, production-ready form.

Roughs or 'scamps' showing the ideas, headlines and design elements in a variety of layouts are rigorously appraised by the senior creatives (the group head and/or the creative director) and then put through a marketing mill by the account people – to check that the proposals are 'on strategy'. If the agency is satisfied that these represent the best way of meeting the client's objectives, the roughs are worked up to a presentation standard and then put before the client, explained, rationalized, in a word 'sold'.

With the exception of production costs, which are often a source of contention because they turn out to be greater than anticipated, TV commercials' presentations tend to have an easier passage than those for press work. Often overawed by the mysteries of TV production, clients are likely to be relatively temperate in their comments and criticisms. But when it comes to print advertising, they, like a lot of people, are prone to think they can write and design a full page ad. Hence the need for a wide variety of layouts.

### Pictures

Some images more or less sell themselves on the basis of the core idea(s) underlying them. Original analogies, visual puns and concrete idioms have something of the instant 'hit' of a great, lethally telling slogan. For example: 'A fly in the ointment' got up as a picture of a bluebottle wallowing nastily in a jar of Germolene is intrinsically arresting. As is Kit-Kat's elongated chocolate strips doubling as the wooden planks of a park bench. The surrealist painters, Magritte especially, have been a rich 'borrowing' source for art directors in search of visual wit and surprise (so, much of the classic Benson and Hedges artwork).

Photography: principally it's through the stylistic handling and execution of the visual idea/subject that a great piece of artwork comes into being. The most obvious example is pack shot photography. A picture of a bottle of beer can be a visual bromide, at the other extreme, it can have all the aesthetics of an old master still-life. A close-up of a plate of bangers and mash can look like sullen, greasy-spoon fare. But with the right lighting, presentation and theatre it can be metamorphosed into virtual *nouvelle cuisine*, so luscious and appetising that you'd want to eat it off the page.

Photographers specialize – in cars, food, fashion, people, landscapes, etc. One of the art director's skills is choosing and commissioning the right photographer for the particular job, communicating his ideas about how he wants the product and the setting to look and then overseeing the subsequent shooting of it.

Commissioned photography is expensive. And it may be that the material the art director is looking for can be obtained from library stock. Obviously it's a waste of time and money to pay for original photography of such subjects as wild animals, famous buildings, woods and coastlines. However, a possible drawback of library sources is that some of the stock pictures may be on 35 mm format only and so won't be good enough for large size, high quality reproduction. OK perhaps for a low-cost brochure but not for a double-page spread in a colour supplement.

## 10.3 Appraisal of press ads

### Salignac (Plate 4)

*'After five hours' talking, Messieurs Picasso and Braque separated on the most cordial of terms'. Montparnasse, 1907.*
This is very much an art director's ad. On a practical plane it is a superb example of the closest co-operation between a skilled art director, highly talented photographer and production executive.

Recalling USPs (Section 2.1), nothing is said about features or properties inherent in the brand. Its individuation is achieved solely, and very successfully, through projecting an outstandingly memorable image.

The ad locates the brand in a cultural and historical context. You aren't subjected to an art history lesson about Picasso and Braque. The ad's far too subtle and clever for that. Rather you are flattered to be participating in a slice of cultural history. The ad effectively holds up a mirror which reflects your culture and edu-

**Plate 4** A young-master still-life.

cation and also invites you to enter the Montparnasse café world of 1907 with your imagination left free to roam.

The great artists have left the table. You're given 'the opportunity' to get into those empty seats. If Salignac was OK for Picasso, then it's more than OK for you. The fantasy implication, which can be taken or left, is that people who consummate a meal with Salignac are likely to have had heated, though amicable, discussions about art during the course of their dinner.

The ad is refreshingly free from 'plug' pack shots. Unlike the majority of drink ads, tiresomely featuring bottle-and-glass packs on an invisible plinth, this ad gets the Salignac bottle on to the end-of-meal tableau in a way that's fully integrated with the picture while simultaneously enabling the brand to stand apart as a 'hero'.

Everything in an ad is, or ought to be, saying something about the product. Here, all the props and accessories, such as the half-drunk wines and coffee, the barely eaten peach, and so on, combine to produce a mellow, deliciously haunting ambience, radiant with the well-being aftermath of a great occasion. But there is no ostentation. The debris of the meal testifies to quality rather than gluttony. An especially nice touch is the still-full glass of cognac. Of course the advertiser wants to show the product in glass. But as with the cognac bottle, it's not overtly plonked down bottle-and-glass pack shot style; its presence is fully justified by the terms of the scene – casual abandon.

It's a version of the star/celebrity treatment, only here the personalities are disembodied. The big names departed, the brand remains. You know the company it keeps, its diplomacy, pedigree and heritage.

## Parker Lady (Plate 5)

*'A ridiculous alternative to the 10p ball pen'*
Predominantly a copywriter's ad, this instantiates the candour approach (Section 3.1) and the use of a paradox headline (Section 10.1). The ad doesn't fight shy of the price of the product: it boldly proclaims it's downright silly. Having said so, the reader is intrigued: how is the ad going 'to get out of it'?

The writer turns the tables in a series of adroitly paced, brilliantly manipulated manoeuvres. First come the exclusive product points: the rolled gold finish and so on. More tension: the copy spells out just how crazy the price is – you could buy 100 biros for

## A ridiculous alternative to the 10p ball pen.

The ridiculous alternative we're talking about is the new Parker pen on your right, The Lady.

It's finished in white or yellow rolled gold (of sufficient thickness to ensure that it won't roll off again).

It comes in four point styles, extra fine, fine, medium or broad.

And every time you press the button, the point turns to a new angle so that it wears evenly.

In our opinion, it's the one ball-pen that wouldn't look cheap in a Dior handbag.

So far, so sane. Now for the ridiculous bit.

The Lady costs £9.95.

Roughly what it costs to buy one hundred 10p ball-pens.

And there's no doubt that it would be sensible and thrifty to buy the throw-away pens.

Just as it's sensible and thrifty to buy paper handkerchiefs instead of Irish Linen.

Plastic knives and forks instead of Sheffield cutlery.

And cardboard cups instead of bone china.

Hmmmmm…

Might we suggest a solution to the problem?

You be sensible and thrifty. Persuade your man to be ridiculous and extravagant. ♦ PARKER

*Recommended retail price including VAT. £9.95 in white rolled gold, £9.95 in yellow rolled gold.

The Parker Lady. £9.95.

**Plate 5** Compelling candour in the tradition of Bill Bernbach (Copywriter: Tony Brignull; Art Director: Neil Godfrey).

what a Lady Parker costs. And then comes the punch that starts the veer into the U-turn. Do you really want chuck-away biros? Wouldn't you prefer Irish linen handkerchiefs to paper ones. Or Sheffield cutlery to plastic knives and forks?. . . . As the copy concludes: 'You be sensible and thrifty. Persuade your man to be ridiculous and extravagant'.

# 11 · The type world

## 11.0 Typography

There are thousands of typefaces available; and their proliferation would appear to be unstoppable.

Are all these typefaces necessary? It has been estimated that a mere five faces – Garamond, Goudy, Bembo, Futura and Franklin Gothic – account for around one third of press advertising work.[1] If a sprinkling of other traditional faces, notably Caslon, Plantin, Times, Helvetica and Univers is added, then given the ardent support and preference from many leading typographers for using designs of long-proven worth like these, it is a fair bet that getting on for half of all advertising is set in perhaps a dozen or so faces.

The platitudinous answer to the alleged surfeit of typefaces is: it all depends on what you want to achieve. Faces for setting text and body copy need, obviously, to be easy to read; they shouldn't draw attention to themselves, or get in the way of copy points. The choice of faces for most copy setting work is thus likely to be limited to a small pool of tried and tested designs.

The irony in all this is that the typesetting houses have been largely responsible for – and castigated for – the proliferation of faces, foisting on to the market, if only by way of mammoth catalogues thumping on to the desk of typographers, a vast and prodigious range of typefaces. Several major houses boast two thousand-plus faces. It doubtless makes for great PR in terms of credibility and overall image-psychology. But who really wants them all? Not, apparently, that many typographers. At least not for a lot of the work they do.

The typesetting houses are, moreover, wont to agree. As Maurice Turner of The Setting Room explains: 'Even though eighty per cent of the paint Dulux sells is white, it still has a huge range of colours. Similarly, though eighty per cent of the work we do is in traditional faces, there is still a demand for other faces and if I didn't have them I might lose the business'.[2]

Which is fair enough. And who could argue?

Some typographers would. Their grouse is that big design houses aggressively push new faces to typesetting equipment manufacturers. And that a lot of the designs aren't new; worse still, some are revamped versions of classic faces devoid of respect for the integrity of the originals.

Back into the court of the typesetters, counsel for their defence: too many typographers are just too conservative; they won't risk experimenting with new faces; they are hidebound *vis-à-vis* what designs are legible and 'good' and what ones are 'bad' and illegible. As a result a lot of text, graphic and other work ends up by being 'samey' and monotonous.

There is, doubtless, much to be said on both sides.

But once one departs from the bread and butter of text setting and design choices for it, the situation changes. For display work, the get-up of brand names in verbal-visuals, the design of pack labels and so on, a wide range of typefaces is a vitally needed resource. With company and brand names there is a premium on design versatility. The chosen face is an integral part of an overall design element.

## 11.1 The grammar of typography

A principal feature of the design of a face is the presence or absence of serifs, the short cross strokes at the base or stem of the characters. Such strokes can be hairline, fine, thick, slabbed, wedge-shaped.

The majority of typefaces could be categorized, and indeed often are, into those with serifs and those without them — sans serifs.

### Classification of typefaces

The taxonomy instituted by Maximilien Vox is one of the most widely used; it has, for example, been adopted as a British

The type world 159

1/2 Goudy Old Style
**Goudy** Extra Bold
Goudy Handtooled
Garamond
*Garamond* Italic
Bembo
Caslon Antique

3 **Century Schoolbook**
Baskerville Old Face

4 **Bodoni** Bold
**Bodoni** Extra Bold

5 **Rockwell** Bold Condensed 359
**Rockwell** Extra Bold

6 Univers 45
**Univers 59**
Futura Light
Futura Medium
**Futura** Bold
Helvetica Light
**Helvetica** Medium
**Helvetica** Extra Bold

7 Albertus
**Perpetua** Bold

8 *Palace Script*
*Vivaldi*
*Young Baroque*

9 YANKEE Shadow
NEON
STACK
Shatter
SLIPSTREAM
CHROMIUM ONE
Tiptopetto
YAGI LINK DOUBLE
Transmission

10 Alte Schwabacher
Weiß Rundgotisch
Walbaum Fraktur
**Blackmoor**

**Figure 11.1** Typeface groupings: examples

Standard (BS 2961) and by A Typ I, the Association Typographique Internationale. However, it's not entirely perfect: the categories aren't always mutually exclusive (Fig. 11.1).

(a) Groups one and two
Respectively known as *Humanist* and *Garald*. Seriffed, the characters are rounded and open, with the thickness or weight of the strokes forming them being largely uniform. Faces in this category are also known as 'old face' or 'old style roman'. Prominent examples are: Centaur, Goudy, Garamond, Bembo and Caslon, all evergreens for text setting.

(b) Group three: *Transitional*
The serifs are more pronounced and sharper; the characters have a vertical emphasis. Into this group fall Baskerville and Fournier and, arguably, the 'innovations' faces of Century and Times, the latter being widely used for a lot of magazine, book and newspaper text printing.

(c) Group four: *Didone*
(Also known as '*modern*' – a rather misleading term as the faces were cut in the eighteenth century).

The characters are distinguished by their very fine serifs and their thick vertical stress.

Not a popular choice for text setting. With the fineness of the serifs and the lateral strokes forming the characters these designs, of which Bodoni and Walbaum are the best known, are not recommended for reversing out (printing white text on a black background).

(d) Group five: *Mechanistic*
(Also known as *slab-serif* and *Egyptian*). The serifs are as thick as the strokes forming the characters. As a consequence the characters have an aesthetically pleasing uniformity of design.

Rockwell and Memphis are probably the best known examples. In their pure form these faces work best for display. Though light versions can, exceptionally, be used to good effect for text purposes.

(e) Group six: *Lineal*
(Variously referred to as '*sans serif*', '*grot*' and '*gothic*'.) Devoid of serifs, the characters have a uniform skeletal look and are rather short on 'personality'. On the whole they don't make for easy reading and are largely reserved for subheads and headlines in advertising and for headlines and captions in editorial.

Being 'pure', they allow for a wide number of permutations to be made on their basic design. The characters can be squeezed, stretched, made heavy or light without unduly affecting the integrity of their core design.

The best known and most frequently used faces are: Univers, Helvetica, Futura and Franklin.

(f) Group seven: *Incised*
Typefaces in this category were originally designed as cuts in stone or metal and, accordingly, work best as capitals; examples are: Perpetua, Albertus, Columna.

(g) Group eight: *Script*
These faces have a running, flowing form, resembling handwriting. Their elaborate, cursive design makes them very difficult

to read. Consequently they are limited to headlines, letterheads and other display work where a highly stylized, elegant look is required. Examples are: Palace Script, Young Baroque, Commercial Script, Vivaldi.

(h) Group nine: *Manual*

('Variously known as '*Graphic*' and '*Decorative*'.) This category comprises a no less prodigious than exotic range of faces that are, basically, designer ones. Usually they come in upper-case (capitals) and read, or are decipherable, only in large type. Accordingly, they are rarely, if ever, used for text and are the preserve of rub-down transfer lettering. Examples are legion: Yankee, Neon, Sprint and Stack are just some.

(i) Group ten: *Black Letter*

Northern European these faces are traditional in German newspaper text. Indeed, they tend to be thought of as 'Germanic' or, misleadingly, as 'Gothic'.

A book title like *Inside the Third Reich*, or whatever, is highly likely to be set in a face such as Fraktur or Weiss Rundgotisch.

Possibly as a hangover from the newspaper tradition, the masthead of the *Daily Mail* is in black letter design.

The Olde Englishe Tea Shoppe design is another example.

## Anatomy of type

The unit of type size is the *point*, seventy-two points approximately equalling one inch.

The point size refers to the distance from the top of an ascender (of an 'h' or 'l', say) to the bottom of a descender (a 'y' or 'p'). However, it is the height of the body of the characters, the 'x' height, that creates an overall impression of the type size (Fig. 11.2). The exact size of the type can often be deceptive: a design with a squat 'x' height, such as Centaur, will *appear* to be of a smaller point size than one with a big 'x' height, such as Times New Roman.

Body copy and text typically uses nine, ten, eleven and twelve point type (Fig. 11.3); subheads: twelve, fourteen, eighteen and occasionally twenty-four point; headlines (Fig. 11.4): thirty, thirty-six, forty-eight, sixty and seventy-two point. Tabloid newspapers are wont to run headlines in a minimum of 192 point and to scream them in deafeningly much larger sizes. Footnotes and 'small print'

## TYPOGRAPHICAL MEASUREMENT

The POINT is the basic unit of measurement,
a POINT is 0·013833 of an inch (0·35mm) approximately $\frac{1}{72}$ of an inch.
The width and depth of a page is measured in 12 POINT EMS,
a 12 POINT EM is 0·166 of an inch (4·22mm) approximately $\frac{1}{6}$ of an inch.
There are six 12 point ems to the inch (25·4mm)

## TYPOGRAPHICAL DIMENSIONS

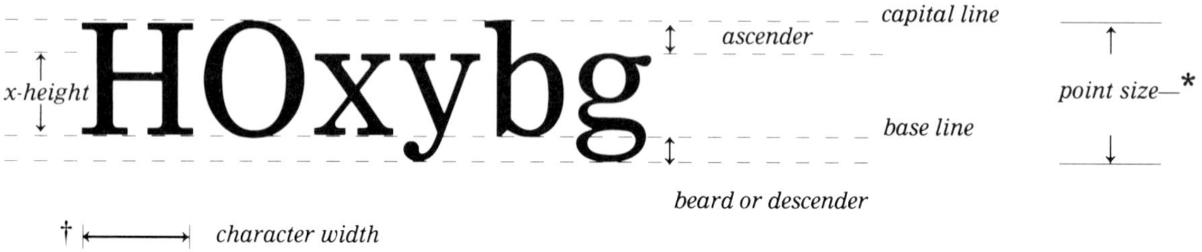

**HOxybg**

x-height · ascender · capital line · base line · point size—* · beard or descender · character width

**Figure 11.2** Anatomy of point size

are typically set in four and six point. Legibility is arduous, though this is, in some situations, intentional: hence the cliché about the small print on the back or bottom of insurance policies!

Typesetters measure the width and depth of type by 'ems'. The 'em' refers to the letter 'M', the width of which is the same as its height, the character being cast on a square body. A column of newsprint will be described as, say, sixteen ems wide. A measure of so many ems, unless otherwise specified, means twelve point or *pica* ems, there being six picas to the inch. Halving the em measure refers to an 'en' one: the width and depth of the character 'n' being half that of an 'm'. Compositors' old-fashioned slang for 'ems' and 'ens' is 'muttons' and 'nuts'.

A *font* (or fount) of type refers to the standard range of characters – upper case A to Z, lower case a to z, numerals 1 to 9, punctuation marks, brackets, £ and $ signs, etc., in a given point size and face design. A typewriter contains a font of ten (élite) or twelve (pica) type on a golf-ball or daisy wheel.

A *series* of type is a group of different-sized fonts in a given typeface. Series come, standardly, in a range of point sizes from six to seventy-two.

**6** abcdefghijklmnopqrstuvwxyz
ABCDEFGHIJKLMNOPQRSTUVWXYZ&
£1234567890$   .,:;'"!?-()[]—

This essay is the fruit of many years' assiduous labour—a real labour of love—in the service of the art of printing. Printing is the final outcome of man's most beautiful, ingenious and useful invention: that I mean, of writing: and its most valuable form where it is required to turn out many copies of the the same text. This applies still more where it is important to ensure uniformity, and most of all where the work in question is one which deserves transmission in clearer and more readable form for the enjoyment of

**8** abcdefghijklmnopqrstuvwxyz
ABCDEFGHIJKLMNOPQRSTUVWXYZ&
£1234567890$   .,:;'"!?-()[]—

This essay is the fruit of many years' assiduous labour—a real labour of love—in the service of the art of printing. Printing is the final outcome of man's most beautiful, ingenious and useful invention: that I mean, of writing: and its most valuable form where it is required to turn out many copies of the same text. This applies still more where it is important to ensure uniformity

**9** abcdefghijklmnopqrstuvwxyz
ABCDEFGHIJKLMNOPQRSTUVWXYZ&
£1234567890$   .,:;'"!?-()[]—

This essay is the fruit of many years' assiduous labour—a real labour of love—in the service of the art of printing. Printing is the final outcome of man's most beautiful, *ingenious and useful invention: that I mean, of writing: and its most valuable form where it is required to turn out many copies of the same text. This applies still more where it is*

**10** abcdefghijklmnopqrstuvwxyz
ABCDEFGHIJKLMNOPQRSTUVWXYZ&
£1234567890$   .,:;'"!?-()[]—

This essay is the fruit of many years' assiduous labour—a real labour of love—in the service of the art of printing. Printing is the final outcome *of man's most beautiful, ingenious and useful invention: that I mean, of writing: and its most valuable form where it is important to ensure*

**11** abcdefghijklmnopqrstuvwxyz
ABCDEFGHIJKLMNOPQRSTUVWXYZ
£1234567890$     .,:;'"!?-()[]—

This essay is the fruit of many years' assiduous labour—a real labour of love—in the service of the art of printing. Printing is the final *outcome of man's most beautiful, ingenious and useful invention: that I mean, of writing: and its most valuable form where it is required to turn*

**12** abcdefghijklmnopqrstuvwxyz
ABCDEFGHIJKLMNOPQRSTUVW
£1234567890$   .,:;'"!?-()[]—

This essay is the fruit of many years' assiduous labour—a real labour of love— in the service of the art of printing. *Printing is the final outcome of man's most beautiful, ingenious and useful invention: that I mean, of writing: and its most*

**Figure 11.3**   Text sizes: 6 to 12 point

A *family* of type is a collection of series that have a number of variations on the basic design theme. The most obvious variant is the italic: the slanting or sloping of the upright or roman master design.

Otherwise, the principal modulations are: making the characters lighter (finer) or heavier (bold), or squeezing the pattern and shape of the characters (condensing) or expanding them (Fig. 11.5). The more the basic design, usually the medium width and weight, is exaggerated, the more the legibility of the face suffers. On the whole it is only the skeletal sans-serif designs, such as Univers, Helvetica and Futura, that will withstand breeding into large families. Seriffed faces lose their identity after a small number of permutations with their width and weight. While decorative faces disintegrate rapidly. Just as they won't withstand reduction in size beyond a certain level.

**164 Into print**

24 required to Turn out many Copies of the Same Text. This applies still more where it is Important

30 to Ensure Uniformity, and Most of all where the Work in Question is one

36 which deserves its Transmission in Clearer and more Readable

48 form for the Enjoyment of Posterity. When we

**Figure 11.4** Display sizes: 24 to 48 point

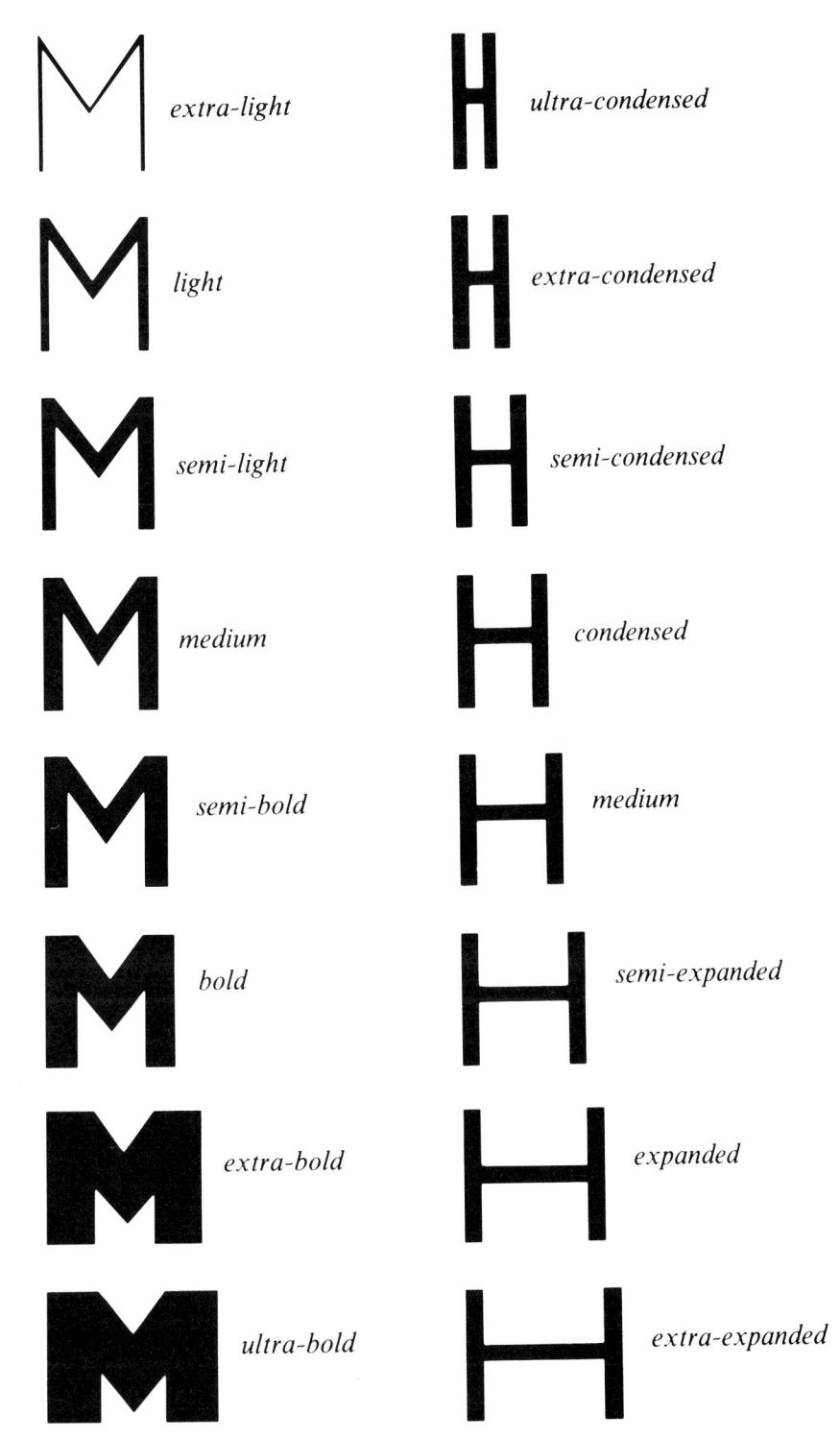

**Figure 11.5** Weight and width variations

### Legibility

This is an area that has been the subject of copious perception-psychological and physiological research, the upshot of a lot of the findings simply corroborating the instincts and intuitions of typographers.

Faces with serifs are easier to read than those without. As are roman or uprights compared to italics. Other factors affecting legibility are line length, justification, interline and inter character spacing.

### Line length

Most studies suggest that a line of around forty-two to sixty characters (Fig. 11.6) optimizes reading efficiency. Too long a line causes the eye to 'drift' and frustrates its finding the entry point of the next line. Too short a line slows down perception, the eye spending too much time scanning back and forth across the text.

### Justification

Lines of type are conventionally squared-up on the left- and right-hand side to form vertical columns (i.e., justified). Forcing the squaring up of a stack of very short lines, as in newspaper columns, invariably results in extreme differences in the spacing between characters and between words. Also words frequently have to be broken at the end of lines. The combination of irregular spacing and hyphenation not only hampers reading but also looks aesthetically unattractive.

Text set with left-hand justification and an uneven, ragged right margin is the easiest to read. Furthermore it looks different. On both grounds quite a lot of advertising copy is set with flush left margins and ragged right ones.

That said, unsquared text/copy is liable to be stigmatized as 'slovenly'; it doesn't look tidy; it's not what the reader is used to. So, regrettably, there are no fail-safe rules or laws. And in all likelihood there never will be.

Whatever, advertising copy, free from the procrustean constraints of short-line column editorials and the time pressures of setting the same, can achieve the best of both worlds: eye-pleasing justification along with uniformly spaced characters and words.

### Interline spacing

Spacing between lines is referred to as 'leading', a hangover from

The sound of tools to a clever workman who loves his work is like the tentative sounds of the orchestra to the violinist who has to bear his part in the overture; the strong fibres begin their accustomed thrill, and what was a moment before joy, vexation, or ambition, begins its change into energy. All passion becomes strength when it has an outlet from the narrow limits of our personal lot in the labour of our right arm, the cunning of our right hand, or the still, creative activity of our thought. Look at Adam through the rest of the day, as he stands on the scaffolding with the two-foot ruler in his hand, whistling low while he considers how a difficulty about a floor-joist or a window-frame is to

**6 point solid**
**12 ems measure**
**average 60 letters to a line**

The sound of tools to a clever workman who loves his work is like the tentative sounds of the orchestra to the violinist who has to bear his part in the overture; the strong fibres begin their accustomed thrill, and what was a moment before joy, vexation, or ambition, begins its change into energy. All passion becomes strength when it has an outlet from the narrow limits of our personal lot in the labour of our right arm, the cunning of our right hand, or the still, creative activity of our thought. Look at Adam through the rest of the

**8 point solid**
**16½ ems measure**
**average 60 letters to a line**

The sound of tools to a clever workman who loves his work is like the tentative sounds of the orchestra to the violinist who has to bear his part in the overture; the strong fibres begin their accustomed thrill, and what was a moment before joy, vexation, or ambition, begins its change into energy. All passion becomes strength when it has an outlet from the narrow limits of our personal lot in the labour of our right arm, the cunning of our right hand, or the still,

**9 point solid**
**18 ems measure**
**average 60 letters to a line**

The sound of tools to a clever workman who loves his work is like the tentative sounds of the orchestra to the violinist who has to bear his part in the overture; the strong fibres begin their accustomed thrill, and what was a moment before joy, vexation, or ambition, begins its change into energy. All passion becomes strength when it has an outlet from the narrow limits of our personal lot in the labour of

**10 point solid**
**20 ems measure**
**average 60 letters to a line**

**Figure 11.6** Justified text with an 'easy to follow' length of line.

the days of hot-metal typesetting. To effect a space between lines the typesetter would place a thin strip of metal, conventionally lead, between them.

Type set without any space between the lines is said to be 'set solid'. The bottom of the descenders in line one grazes against the top of the ascenders in line two.

When not set solid, interlinear spacing is specified or referred to in terms of so many points of 'leading': one point, two point, three point.

Other things being equal, the decision on line spacing is largely determined by the type design. Typefaces with a small x-height read reasonably well when set solid. Those with a large x-height signally improve in reading ease when set with leading of one point or more (Fig. 11.7). Depending on the typeface design, too much leading hampers readability as does too little.

### Inter-character spacing

Text set in a sans-serif face can be compressed to a large degree and still remain legible. On the other hand serif faces, if bunched together too much, will cause the characters to foul, impairing legibility.

Allocating the same unit of space to each character, as the

The sound of tools to a clever workman who loves his work is like the tentative sounds of the orchestra to the violinist who has to bear his part in the overture; the strong fibres begin their accustomed thrill, and what was a moment before joy, vexation, or ambition, begins its change into energy. All passion becomes strength when it has an outlet from the narrow limits of our personal lot in the labour of our right arm, the cunning of our right hand, or the still, creative activity of our thought. Look at Adam through the rest of the day, as he stands on the scaffolding with the two-foot ruler in his hand, whistling low while he considers

**6 point. 1 point between the lines**
**13½ ems measure**

The sound of tools to a clever workman who loves his work is like the tentative sounds of the orchestra to the violinist who has to bear his part in the overture; the strong fibres begin their accustomed thrill, and what was a moment before joy, vexation, or ambition, begins its change into energy. All passion becomes strength when it has an outlet from the narrow limits of our personal lot in the labour of our right arm, the cunning of our right

**8 point. 2 points between the lines**
**18 ems measure**

---

The sound of tools to a clever workman who loves his work is like the tentative sounds of the orchestra to the violinist who has to bear his part in the overture; the strong fibres begin their accustomed thrill, and what was a moment before joy, vexation, or ambition, begins its change into energy. All passion becomes strength when it has an outlet from the narrow limits of our personal lot in the labour of our right arm, the cunning of our right hand, or the still, creative activity of our thought. Look at

**9 point. 2 points between the lines**
**20 ems measure**

Figure 11.7 Interline spacing – because it increases legibility a longer line can be used.

traditional typewriter does, neither looks attractive nor is conducive to ease of reading. Proportional spacing, whereby four or five units of space are allocated to intrinsically wide characters such as the 'm' and 'w', three units to the 'body' characters of the 'a', 'e', 'h', etc., and two units to the inherently slender characters, the 'i', 'j' and 'l', is preferable.

## Against legibility

For general text purposes and conveying information, body copy for an ad for a tech product such as an SLR camera or photocopying machine in a specialist or trade publication, legibility is a prime requirement. But for a lot of advertising and publicity work it isn't. Whereas noticeability, recognizability and distinctiveness are.

Brand names, magazine titles and newspaper mastheads need to grab attention. And to do it repeatedly. No less importantly, they need to be instantly recognizable.

Salience and even idiosyncrasy is at a premium in the typographical get-up of brand names and logos. The design of the face serves to shape, fix and lock up the nature and business of the product or company. The type design uniquely upholsters and positions the brand's personality (and if it doesn't it ought to); it is

People will argue forever about whisky. But, anytime you want to cut the arguments short, simply mention that Black Label is the best-selling de luxe whisky in the world. An even more powerful argument for you to be stocking it this year is the half a million pounds behind it, including for the first time a national 48-sheet poster campaign. With that heavy a punch the message should really hit home.

**All arguments about whisky end with Black.**

Black is the ultimate in whisky.

**Figure 11.8** The creative use of typography. Though low in legibility the ad is both striking and involving. ('Best use of typography' Campaign Press Awards 1981)

part and parcel of its identity. Campbell's soup or Coca-Cola wouldn't be Campbell's or Coke if set in Helvetica or Bodoni.

'Shatter' isn't the easiest of faces to read but it projects a forceful emotional set of shock and suspense. It would be ideal for the headline titling of a psycho-chiller movie.

The highly articulated graphic form of Palace Script would work well for proclaiming the elegance and refined style of a de luxe hotel or shipping line. Just as Neon or Transmission would be leading candidates for effectively communicating the pioneering, high-tech spirit of a computer company.

Ogilvy[3] recommends that 'reversing out' should be avoided because it's difficult to read; black type on a white background should always be preferred (Fig. 11.8). But which is the more noticeable? A ten per cent (or whatever) decrease in legibility is a small price to pay for looking different and grabbing attention.

Respectfully, what Ogilvy ought to have advised is that reversing out should be avoided in newspaper ads: the consistency of saturation of the black background is all too often wanting, appearing unevenly dark grey. Indeed, some newspapers won't accept ads with dark reversed-out areas.

Headlines: Ogilvy declares that these shouldn't be set in upper case as capitals are more difficult to read. True; they are. But are headlines actually *read*? Unless they are very long they are likely to be seen as a *Gestalt*, taken in as a verbal-visual all-at-once pattern. Different or even quirky typographics can serve as a 'hook' as much as the picture or graphics.

## 11.2 Typesetting

Movable type is the first appearance of the form of the mass-assembly production line. Letters that were previously handwritten, each one being different, are standardized. Writing becomes mechanized, transformed into a linear, uniform and repeatable process.

Type is still — occasionally — set by hand, the process being basically the same as it was in the mid-fifteenth century in Gutenberg's day. The typesetter uses a 'composing stick' into which he assembles the type characters, one by one, into lines. Each of the entered characters is cast in metal as a raised, reverse-reading shape like the individual characters that strike on to the paper immediately following the key taps on a conventional typewriter.

The method is a luxury and limited to a small and ever-dwindling number of very specialized text-setting jobs, almost entirely non-commercial, where the traditional values and qualities of craftsmanship are both revered and sought after.

## (a) Hot metal

Using relief metal characters and developed in the late nineteenth century, this method of typesetting is an automated version of traditional setting. The operator types in the copy on a keyboard: as each key is struck, the machinery retrieves a matrix (a mould) for the letter concerned from a magazine containing a given font of type. As required, the operator can retrieve a different font: a different point size of type and/or typeface design.

When a line of words has been completed, molten metal is poured into the succession of matrices. Released from the line-matrix, the cast line of type is known as a slug.

Later machines cast the type character by character (Monotype) rather than as a line (Linotype). As the operator keys in the text the information is punched on to a tape as a perforated code which subsequently slaves a casting machine to cast the characters individually. Monotype casting enables corrections to be made without resetting the whole line.

Hot metal typesetting was the preserve of letterpress printing, which, until the early 1960s, was the main way of printing of all magazines, newspapers and advertising material. While print quality is affected to a large degree by the paper stock and inks used, relief metal setting of text yields an incisive crispness that is, arguably, hard to match.

## (b) Cold setting

Also known as 'strike on', this was a popular, low-cost alternative to hot-metal setting made possible by the advent of litho printing and IBM golf-ball composing typewriters in the 1960s. The latter enable text to be originated in point sizes from six to twelve in a range of about twenty faces, with the lines justified and the characters proportionally spaced.

The designer has a large degree of control over the way the text looks and is laid out. Once set, the pages of text are then camera-ready for making a litho plate. If composition with pictures and other artwork is required, the text is cut out and pasted up in the required layout with the graphics, and then photographed to produce a plate. As the plate is realized photographically, the original text doesn't have to be the same size as the intended printed version: usually reduction to half size or even smaller will be required but occasionally the requirement will be for enlargement.

### (c) Photo-composition

The fonts are stored on film strip. A beam of light is passed through the matrix negative for each character, rapidly one after the other, and the positive images are fixed on to light-sensitive paper that is subsequently processed to yield a proof.

The compositor keys in the copy along with a series of codes for the required setting: the point size, the typeface, the spacing between the lines and characters, the line justification and so on. All this text information and the formatting of the same is transferred to disk which then slaves the photocomposing machine.

Film or photosetting is versatile. The processed text can be realized as a positive or negative, as right-reading or reverse-reading, or combinations thereof. Also, by using special lenses and altering the exposure time, a variety of effects on the point size, the definition of the images of the characters and the spacing can be achieved.

For a lot of routine text-setting work (brochures, leaflets, reports), it makes sense to obviate the duplication of effort of the compositor key-stroking the text, for example where the text is originated on a word processor and stored on a floppy disk. If the 'text file' is not, as often happens, acceptable to the input system of the filmsetting machinery, it can be converted into the appropriate 'readable' format. Alternatively, by using a modem, the formatted text data can be transmitted down the telephone line to the typesetting house and there be intercepted and subsequently set, proofs being relayed back via fax.

### (d) Electronic composition

This method of typesetting is broadly the same as electronic character generation (ECG) of title and super work for TV commercials. The type fonts are held on computer software in digital form, i.e., they are stored as figures rather than spatial images. The characters in the required face and point size are accessed from the software and the text set, and laid out on a VDU which provides a 'window' on the page inside the circuitry.

Full-blown systems, variously known as 'direct entry' and page make-up terminals (PMTs), enable graphics and photographs to be electronically pasted up into position with the text. Original art work in the form of colour transparencies, illustrations, hand-drawn or rub-down transfer lettering, etc., is scanned, converted into digital form, and fed into the system. When making up the page, the operator can blow up, reduce or crop the inputted digitized artwork, rearrange and order it to produce the required composition and layout. State-of-the-art terminals produce complete, finished plates for onward printing.

## Headline setting

The largest type size carried by most film-stored and digitally-held fonts is thirty-six point. Low-cost ways to produce big headline characters are to use a photo-mechanical transfer machine (confusingly also known as a PMT) to enlarge the filmset type or, if using a page make-up terminal, to magnify the required set of words electronically. Neither expedient is that satisfactory, and it becomes less and less so as the magnification required increases, the characters tending to break up and lose definition. Furthermore, inter-character spacing that looks fine at a relatively small point size becomes critical and noticeable when blown up massively; this is particularly true of the spacing between capitals and a string of lower case characters.

In filmsetting, headlines are produced on a special machine such as a Photo Typositor. Each character can be moved laterally, meticulously positioned and spaced, and the result 'fixed' on to a strip of photographic bromide paper for subsequent paste-up.

Where decorative or script typefaces are required, photo or software stored fonts won't usually be available. The typographer will originate the headline with transfer lettering. Laborious as it is, it permits a level of exactitude and control that isn't available with machine-generated faces.

## Proofing

The typesetting house returns the set text as a galley proof. This must be checked for misspellings, either in the original typescript or introduced by the typesetter (literals or typos). As must the layout of the text. Have all the instructions for setting been carried out exactly? Are, following hyphenation and justification, the inevitable word breaks at the end of lines acceptable? Or do some of them look unsightly and/or impair ease of reading? Are some of the lines suffering from excessive bunching up or spreading out? Are there unsightly 'widows'? (A single word being carried on, all alone, on to a new line on a new page.) If the text is set left-hand justified only, is the right-hand side unduly ragged looking? Is the density of type even throughout?

# 12 · Printing processes

These involve different methods of holding or recording an image (words, pictures, graphics) on a plate and different ways of inking the image and then transferring it on to the surface of the material to be printed.

## 12.0 Letterpress

The image to be printed is in relief. Developed around 1450 by Gutenberg, this is the oldest method of printing.

When an ink roller is passed over the raised image it covers it with ink, leaving the non-image area below untouched. A succession of sheets of paper pressed against the inked design will bear an impression of it. The rubber stamp and the notoriously fiddly – and messy – children's John Bull printing kits are homely illustrations of the relief principle (Fig. 12.1).

Traditionally, all text matter is set in hot metal. Pictures, too, are represented in metal, the product known as a block. First a negative is made from the line artwork to be reproduced. If photographs are to be printed, they are first converted into *halftone* negatives – broken down into a pattern of dots (Section 13.0). Light is beamed through the negative on to a plate, usually copper or zinc, treated with a light sensitive emulsion. The pattern of light and dark is imposed by photoengraving on to the plate. The light passing freely through the image area, the white parts of the negative, causes the emulsion to harden; conversely, the light is blocked by the opaque parts of the negative leaving the emulsion

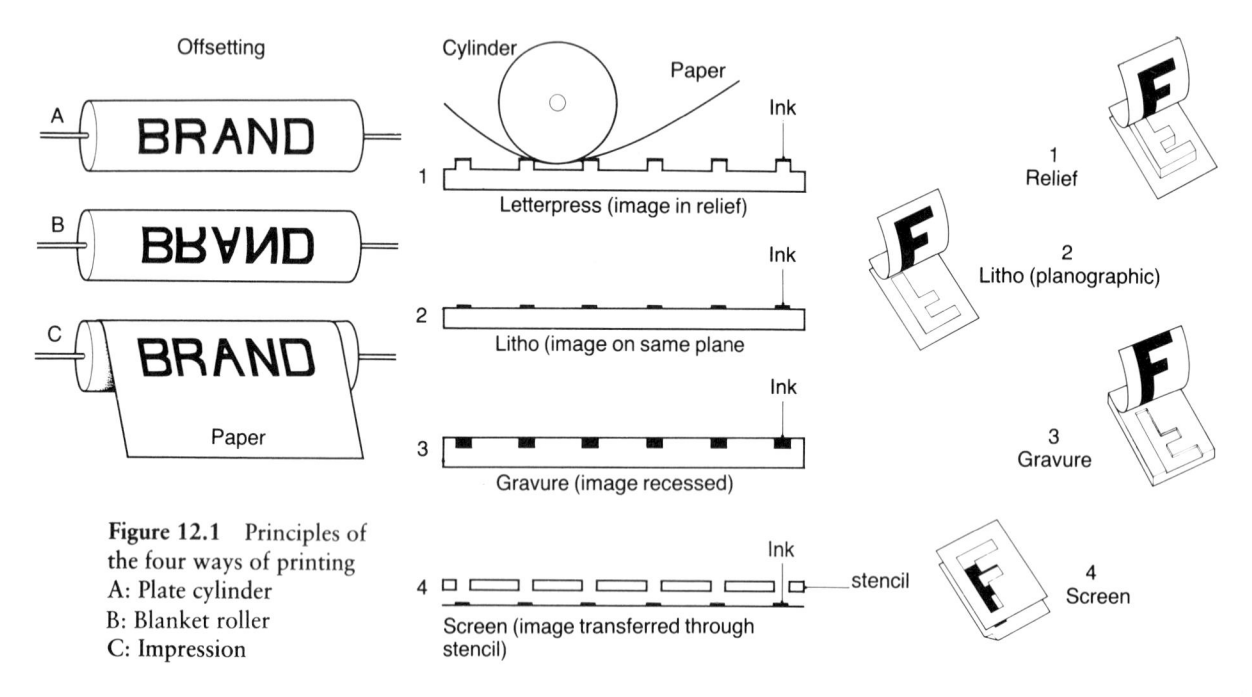

**Figure 12.1** Principles of the four ways of printing
A: Plate cylinder
B: Blanket roller
C: Impression

untouched, soft. When the plate is subsequently treated with acid, it etches the soft areas (the non-image) but not the hardened ones (carrying the image) as these are etch-resistant. The plate is thus engraved with a relief pattern that corresponds to the original picture, the raised parts carrying the line and dot information of the image.

The various sections of type and the picture blocks are arranged together in the required layout, known as a 'forme', and then locked up into a frame (a 'chase'). The result provides the composite relief plate for subsequent printing.

Production from such a flat plate limits printing to platen and flat-bed cylinder presses. In the former, the paper is inserted between the printing surface and a pressure plate on a sandwich principle. In the latter, the printing plate is locked into the flat bed, ink rollers run over its relief image, then the cylinder transports the sheets of paper across them. As the base on which the type is mounted is thicker than the metal used for blocks, these have to be built up in the forme so that their image surface is exactly level with that of the type.

For high-speed printing, rotary presses are used. The paper, fed on a web – a continuous roll rather than a stack of sheets sequentially picked up and routed into the press – is passed between, at its most basic, two cylinders: one carries the plate with satellite rollers coating it with ink, the other provides the transport for the web of paper to take off the impression. For rotary printing, a single flexible metal plate that can be wrapped around the plate cylinder has to be made from the type and blocks held in the forme.

Modern letterpress has to a significant extent abandoned continuous, single plate-making in floppy metal for plastic. Polymer materials are more versatile and better suited to long-run high-speed work. Plate-making is quicker and cheaper (zinc, copper and other metals are more expensive than plastics); print runs can be longer as the wear on the plate surface is reduced as is also the number of duplicate plates (stereos) required; further, plastics have better curving and moulding characteristics for plate wrap-around.

As plastic has replaced metal as the plate medium, so filmsetting of type has taken over from metal casting. Photo-set, the text is produced as a series of film negatives of the words/lines. Instead of a forme of various bits of raised metal, plate make-up consists of a sheet of acetate or film base containing the composition of the negatives for the text, for the pictures and graphic work. From this negative film master of the page(s), a plastic relief plate is struck by photoengraving, the process being essentially the same as that described for making metal blocks from line work and halftone picture negatives. Since all the elements are of the same height, the labour of adjusting block heights to match type heights is eliminated.

Using filmsetting and plastic plates, letterpress has effectively shaken off its origins and evolved into a process known as *flex-ography*. To reduce plate wear further and also to enable printing on a wide range of different stocks and materials, the plates are often made from rubber compounds.

Conventional letterpress, from the point of view of an advertising agency's design, typographic and production departments, is restrictive. There isn't enough control over the way the eventual reproduced material will look. Too many decisions on the final appearance are, inevitably, left with and vested in the printer. Moreover, the quality of half-tone reproduction, particularly in colour, isn't as good as that realized by litho processes.

Apart from the laboriousness of plate-making, letterpress suffers from further disadvantages: it doesn't print happily on cheap paper; the image tends to squash, to spread slightly, the more so the poorer the quality of paper. Rubber plates used in flexography are prone to stretching and shrinking. But the liability is compensated for, flexography printing well on cheap, rough surfaces.

Relief metal printing, though inexorably on the decline, still finds diehard support. Purists insist that, on high-grade paper and with care in plate making, letterpress production from halftone engraving and metal type gives a brilliance and clarity that is hard to beat.

## Uses

Invitation and visiting cards, letterheads, newspapers (though in the wake of the production innovations spearheaded by *Today's* former owner Eddie Shah and the success of Murdoch's 'Fortress Wapping' most national newspaper titles are either printing on litho or scheduled to switch to it); basically, print jobs that don't call for sophisticated layouts of artwork.

Flexography: newspapers, paperbacks, wrappers, leaflets, labels; plus a variety of work requiring bold, brightly coloured, simple visual designs to be printed on to miscellaneous surfaces – cellophanes, polythenes, coarse papers, cardboards; for example: carrier bags, window stickers, display material, 'box' packaging (as for cereals, detergents), plastic packaging (for margarine tubs, frozen food bags, etc.).

## 12.1 Lithography

Think of an oil slick. Or French dressing for that matter. Oil and water mutually repel. This simple phenomenon lies at the heart of the chemical complexity of litho printing.

The plate is treated so that the parts of it that are to carry the image to be printed attract the grease of the ink while the parts that constitute the non-image absorb water and repel the ink. A sheet of paper pressed against the plate receives an impression of the greasy inked design. Thus the separation of the image from the background is chemical rather than physical, as with letterpress. As both areas are on the same level, litho is described as a *planographic* process.

The basis of litho seems so obvious that it is a wonder that the process wasn't invented or harnessed until the end of the eighteenth century. From Archimedes in his bath tub to Madam

Curie stumbling upon the existence of radium, momentous chance discoveries are wont to become sources of the anecdotal and apocryphal. One story goes that Alois Senefelder, in Munich in 1798, was outside making out a laundry list with a wax crayon on a piece of slate when it started to rain. And *voila*!, litho printing was discovered. Well, it makes a nice story!

Traditionally, litho uses stone for the printing surface (hence 'lithography', from *lithos*, Greek, a stone and *graphein*, to write). The commercial application of litho took off with the development of inks resistant to dilution when in contact with water, the introduction of highly porous metal plates, usually zinc or aluminium, for wrapping around rotary press cylinders, and innovations in the mechanics of offsetting.

With offsetting, the image on the plate cylinder is transferred on to an intermediate rubber-coated roller known as a blanket. The image is then transferred on to the paper as it is transported round the impression cylinder. Because of the resilience and cushioning of the blanket roller, the inked design can be transferred without undue pressure. Squashing or spreading of the image, a liability with letterpress because of the pressure of the raised surface bearing directly on to the paper, is largely eliminated. The image on the plate is protected from wear from the paper, thus print runs can be longer and the number of duplicate plates needed reduced. And printing can be done on a wide variety of surfaces: metals, foils, plastics, coarse papers, etc.

Further virtues of offsetting are: the amount of water getting into contact with the paper is reduced; paper which becomes too damp invariably causes problems, particularly in colour printing. And the type and artwork in plate make-up can be right-reading, as on the blanket the image appears in reverse, and so when transferred to the impression surface it reads the right way round.

Almost all litho printing is offset. In fact the terms have become more or less synonymous. Nevertheless, it is arguable that the 'bad press' received by letterpress is not wholly justified, for the majority of the advantages of litho stem from its use of offsetting rather than from its inherent planographic characteristics. Moreover, letterpress occasionally incorporates offsetting, the relief metal image being transferred to a blanket and thence to the impression surface. The process is known as 'indirect letterpress' or, as no dampening is involved, 'dry offset'. But it has to be conceded that the overall advantages are slight. Plates still have to be photoengraved which, as ever, is expensive and time-consuming. Dry offset is confined to specialized work such as the printing of playing cards and paper currency.

Litho plate-making is relatively quick, easy and cheap. Also it allows the advertising agency or design studio a large measure of control over how the material will look in the end. The printer is supplied with a mechanical, a board representing what is to be produced as a printed image. The mechanical consists of the previously photo-set text stripped into position along with any line artwork. The positioning, scale and size of the photographs is clearly indicated (often by photocopies), the photographs themselves being supplied separately. If a headline is to run across a picture, say, as a reverse-out, it is fixed on to a sheet of clear acetate which is superimposed on the camera-ready material.

The printer makes a photographic negative or positive from the mechanical, reducing or enlarging it to the size of the printed page. The photographs – prints or transparencies – are converted into half-tones and fixed into the designated positions on the main piece of film. The composite film is then laid over a light-sensitive metal plate and exposed to light in a contact vacuum frame. In the process the image areas are translated on to the plate as water-resistant and ink-attracting ones, the non-image areas as water-attracting.

This is the 'classical' procedure. For plate origination from the physical assembly of photographic-based material has largely been superseded by electronic methods, almost universally so where colour is to be reproduced. All the text and line artwork on the mechanical together with the various pictures that are to be printed are separately scanned by a sweeping spot of light. Reflected back, the light information is converted into a pattern of electrical impulses which is stored in digital form on disk. Accessed, all the elements are electronically pasted up and arranged into the prescribed layout. The pattern of electrical impulses representing the finished layout is then fed into a plate-making machine.

## Uses

(1) Small, sheet-fed presses taking A3 or A4 stock, are the staple of 'in-house' and 'instant'/franchise high-street printing. Principal jobs: short run – a few thousand copies – of simple, basic work,

perhaps in one colour. Price lists, letterheads, leaflets, business forms.

(2) Larger sheet-fed presses capable of printing on to paper stocks up to A0 in size in two or more colours, with runs ranging from 5,000 to 20,000. Typical work: commercial brochures, catalogues, leaflets, posters.

(3) Big, high-speed web-fed machines printing in four or more colours on to stocks twice A0 size and upwards, with runs going up to 500,000 or more. Main uses: local newspapers which, despite the coarse, thin stock can reproduce full colour reasonably well; colour magazines; mail-order catalogues; door-drops and leaflets; labels.

Litho is also used for printing on to materials for packaging: foils, plastics, metals, cardboards.

## 12.2 Gravure

Gravure printing evolved from the artist's technique of engraving and etching on metal; ink wiped across the surface fills the recessed lines that make up the design. When paper is pressed against the metal the ink-filled image is transferred. Known as an *intaglio* process, gravure is the reverse of relief printing.

Modern gravure printing uses rotary presses. The image to be printed is etched on to the plate cylinder in the form of a series of tiny pits or cells which vary in depth, or both depth and area. The plate cylinder is partially immersed in a trough of ink or has ink sprayed on to it. To scrape off excess ink and to ensure that all cells are perfectly filled, a steel blade is set against the plate as its surface rolls clear of the ink; known as a 'doctor blade', pressure is applied to it pneumatically. Under pressure from the rubber-coated impression cylinder, paper, mostly web-fed, runs directly across the ink-filled dot pattern on the plate.

Plate-making is a lengthy process as conventionally the plate can't be etched directly from a filmed original; image transfer takes place via a sensitized gelatine medium called carbon tissue which has first to be impressed with a 'honeycomb' pattern that will form the walls for the ink-holding cells. Accordingly, a glass screen bearing a fine mesh of transparent lines that describe a lattice of tiny opaque squares (similar to that used for making halftones, see p. 186) is placed over the carbon tissue and the two elements locked in a vacuum contact frame and exposed to light.

A film positive of the original (text, line work and continuous tone photographs) is superimposed on the screened layer of carbon tissue and, again, the two are exposed to light. Transmitting freely through the highlights, the light hardens the gelatine; where it is blocked by the deep shadows, it leaves the gelatine soft. Intermediate tones register as varying degrees of hardness and softness in proportion to their tonal value. Thus treated, the gelatine is laid around the copper plate surface and treated with etching fluid. Left totally unetched, the transparent criss-cross lines on the screen leave a mosaic of tiny walls. Into these partitions the very light areas etch shallow recessions, the dark areas deep ones, with middle tones being etched in proportion to their lightness or darkness. The plate cylinder thus carries a pattern of cells of varying depths corresponding to the tonal range of the original artwork/photographs. Halftone black-and-white and colour reproduction is extremely good – on the whole far superior to that produced by litho and letterpress – because the tones are produced by greater or lesser amounts of ink transferred on to the paper. The fidelity of gravure printing becomes even better when the continuous tone originals are first screened as halftones (the method used for reproduction of photographs by litho and letterpress): the ink cells on the plate now vary not only in depth but also size. This procedure is now virtually universal.

Costly and long-winded, chemical plate origination has given way to electronic engraving which is quicker and cheaper. Wrapped around a cylinder, the image to be printed is 'read' by a flying light spot, the modulation of the beam by the images on the copy being coded as electrical impulses. These drive an engraving stylus to 'write' the variable depth and size cell pattern on to the plate. Increasingly, this method of electro-mechanical writing is being replaced by electronic-slaved laser engraving. And to facilitate this, plastic based plate surfaces are commonly used.

The drawbacks of gravure are: (1) original artwork/text – the mechanical – must be the same size as that to be printed; (2) with electronic engraving the mechanicals, if mounted on stiff board – a form preferred by art departments and studios – must be capable of being stripped off it for subsequent wrapping around the cylinder to be scanned; (3) proofing from the printing plates is expensive as the proofing press is elaborate. If the colour is unsatisfactory, corrections normally have to be made directly on to the plates by hand. Accordingly, it is important to get everything right before proofing; (4) since *all* the elements in the layout are screened, the line work and type is reproduced as a shape composed of minute dots rather than a solid. The edges around hairline serifs, for example, can appear as slightly indistinct.

The advantages are: (1) consistency of colour and tone quality over long print runs from a single set of plates; (2) high fidelity of picture reproduction; (3) good quality colour printing on cheap papers; (4) *very fast*: in terms of sheer speed and efficiency of printing it is superior to litho, its main rival: because the evaporative inks used dry rapidly and, more importantly, because of the absence of having to keep just the right proportions of inking and wetness throughout the run. Gravure is, literally, a 'dry run'; and so in contrast to litho is free from problems associated with dampness causing paper stretch.

## Uses

Long-run mail order, brochure and magazine work; 400,000 being about the economic threshold.

Nearly all the Sunday colour supplements are gravure-printed, runs ranging from around 700,000 for the *Observer Supplement* to 5,000,000 for the *News of the World*'s 'Sunday'. Other major publications include the TV programme papers and the higher circulation women's monthly and weekly titles. To take advantage of the process's superior production values, some comparatively smaller circulating magazines (e.g., *Company* with around 200,000) print the covers by gravure, the 'body' being litho produced.

Packaging materials; postage stamps and other security work: cheques, banknotes, etc.

A variety of work where the premium on high quality and finish takes precedence over the normal considerations of economic viability of the run: 'designer' wallpapers, lavishly illustrated books particularly with fine art subject-matter, such as *Great Treasures of the Louvre*. Since gravure prints impressively on cheap stock – as any colour supplement bears testimony – on high quality paper it produces an image of stunning magnificence.

## 12.3 Screen printing

Unlike the other production processes described, the image isn't transferred *from* a plate but rather *through* one.

The method is the same as stencilling. The non-image areas are masked, the image areas left open. Take 'crate box' lettering. The words or letters to be printed on to the side of a tea chest, carton or truck side are cut into a cardboard or plastic plate which is placed over the impression surface. When ink or paint is squeezed or airbrushed across the stencil it passes through the open pattern of the letters and deposits their shape on to the crate or other surface.

With hand-cut stencilling, special double-layered film material is laid over the artwork to be printed. The image is carefully cut out of the top layer, the bottom one being left intact. The result is then heat-sealed to the underside of a screen of silk, synthetic fibre or fine wire mesh which is stretched across a frame. The protective backing is then peeled off. Now holding a film stencil, the screen is superimposed on the paper or other surface to be printed on. As ink is squeezed across it, it goes through the mesh and through the image areas and so transfers the design to the paper.

For printing photographs, text and line work, the manual excision method is, obviously, not suitable. Photo-stencilling is required.

A film positive of the artwork is made and placed in contact with the screen, previously treated with a light-sensitive solution. The two are then locked up in a vacuum frame and exposed to light. After chemical washing, the image is rendered as a free, open pattern, the non-image as a masked one. On the press a squeegee runs ink across the photographically cut stencil. Passing through the open areas the ink transfers on to the impression surface; blocked, it doesn't.

### Advantages

The ink can be deposited very thickly (at least thirty times heavier than with litho). Powerfully dense blacks and deep, saturated colours can be printed. Thus reversing out can be produced with immaculate contrast.

Any type of ink can be used – fluorescent, metallic, day-glo (unlike litho where the inks necessarily have to maintain a high water-resistant chemistry).

The process is versatile. It can be used to print on any surface: every type of paper stock, plastic, metal, fur, leather, ceramic, cork, wood, rubber, glass, textile.

It can be used to print on to pre-formed shapes: bottles ashtrays, tumblers.

It is economical for short runs, say, a few hundred.

It is a virtual axiom that when a printing job gives rise to problems, however apparently insuperable, the screen process will be able to solve them (though in some cases not economically and not, too, with the desired fidelity to detail).

## Disadvantages

Production machines are slow. Partly because they are sheet-fed, partly because the ink can't physically be squeezed across the stencil rapidly, especially where thick deposits on the impression surface are required. 6,000 impressions per hour (i.p.h.) is about the commercial ceiling.

For halftone production, coarse screens are necessary. Thus fine or subtle tone gradations can't be realized. As can't small point type, and type with inherently fine or intricate face designs. Overall, the process is limited to big, bold text and artwork.

## Uses

Posters, where the impact from strikingly deep and impactful colours (to be 'read' from one hundred yards distance or whatever) is at a premium, where there is no requirement for small text and where the print runs are short (perhaps a few hundred or at most a few thousand).

Point-of-sale and promotional material: T-shirts, badges, key rings, ties, window stickers, umbrellas, awnings, ashtrays.

Fine art printing: Andy Warhol's silk screens of Campbell's soup cans and Marilyn Monroe being celebrated examples.

Electronic printed circuit boards.

# 13 · Reproducing pictures

**13.0 Halftones**

Pictures made up of lines and solid areas are reproduced in the same way as type matter: as far as plate-making and subsequent printing is concerned, the lines forming a string of characters are no different from those delineating a tree or a house. We've seen (pp. 175–176) how a line drawing is photoengraved and how the resulting relief image is assembled with the raised type matter to form a printing plate.

A photograph consists of continuous tones. Between the darkest shadows and the brightest highlights is a sliding scale of grey tones: dark grey – medium grey – light grey – very light grey. Saving gravure, which because of the varying depths of the cells on the plate corresponding to the varying lightnesses and darknesses of the tones in the original photograph, the other print processes are restricted to a 'yes–no' principle. Either ink is transferred or it isn't; there is no way to lessen or increase the ink transfer to produce the gradations of grey tones in the original. Everything is deep black and white or dark grey and white.

To print continuous tones, the gradations of grey in the original have to be 'processed' in a way that will simulate, through subsequent printing of solid areas, the tone variations. Known as a halftone, the process involves breaking up the original continuous tone image into a pattern of tiny dots of different sizes.

The photographic original (or other artwork) is fixed in position in front of a process camera. Superimposed on the film plate in the back of the camera is a glass or acetate screen scored with a fine pattern of criss-cross lines. The grid of lines on the screen serves to decompose the continuous tones into a series of dots; widely-spaced small dots representing the light tones, the smaller and more widely distributed they are the greater the lightness of tone eventually produced; large dots bunched together representing the dark tones, very big dots very close together merging into areas of solid black.

The stock-in-trade for reproducing editorial pictures is the screen structure, producing dots. But for a lot of advertising work diagonal screens and combinations of line and dot screens (the main form is the 'grey-cut line' – lines running in the mid-tones, dots in the highlights and dark areas) are used as they give superior results in both tone ranges and sharpness.

The definition, subtlety and detail of continuous tones 'faked' by screening is determined by the gauge and structure of the screen and also by the quality and nature of the paper stock to be printed on. Screen sizes are measured by the number of lines to the inch or centimetre. The more lines per unit inch or centimetre, the better the quality of the simulated tone (Fig. 13.1).

Fine screens won't reproduce satisfactorily on low grade, absorbent paper, the result blurs and smudges. For newspaper work the screen is necessarily coarse: twenty-four to twenty-six (metric), sixty-five (imperial). For magazines, brochures and books printed on cartridge or coated paper the screen sizes range, as a rule, from eighty-five lines per inch to one hundred and fifty (thirty-five to sixty lines per centimetre). On top quality paper used for specialized book and other production the screen may go as fine as three hundred (imperial). For halftone printing by the screen process the practical limit is one hundred (imperial), forty (metric).

Aside from the screen size and paper stock, the quality of the printed picture image is of course determined by the quality of the original. Photographs with excessive contrast and a lack of mid-range tones reproduce poorly. The missing tones, along with the softening of hard shadows and exaggerated highlight, should be put in or modified by manual or electronic retouching. An alternative to retouching is to rescue detail and adjust contrast through darkroom procedures: having a new print made from the original negative.

One of the outstanding techniques for reproducing continuous tone photographs is the *Schafline High Definition System*. Developed primarily for reproduction work in newspapers, it enables

**188　Into print**

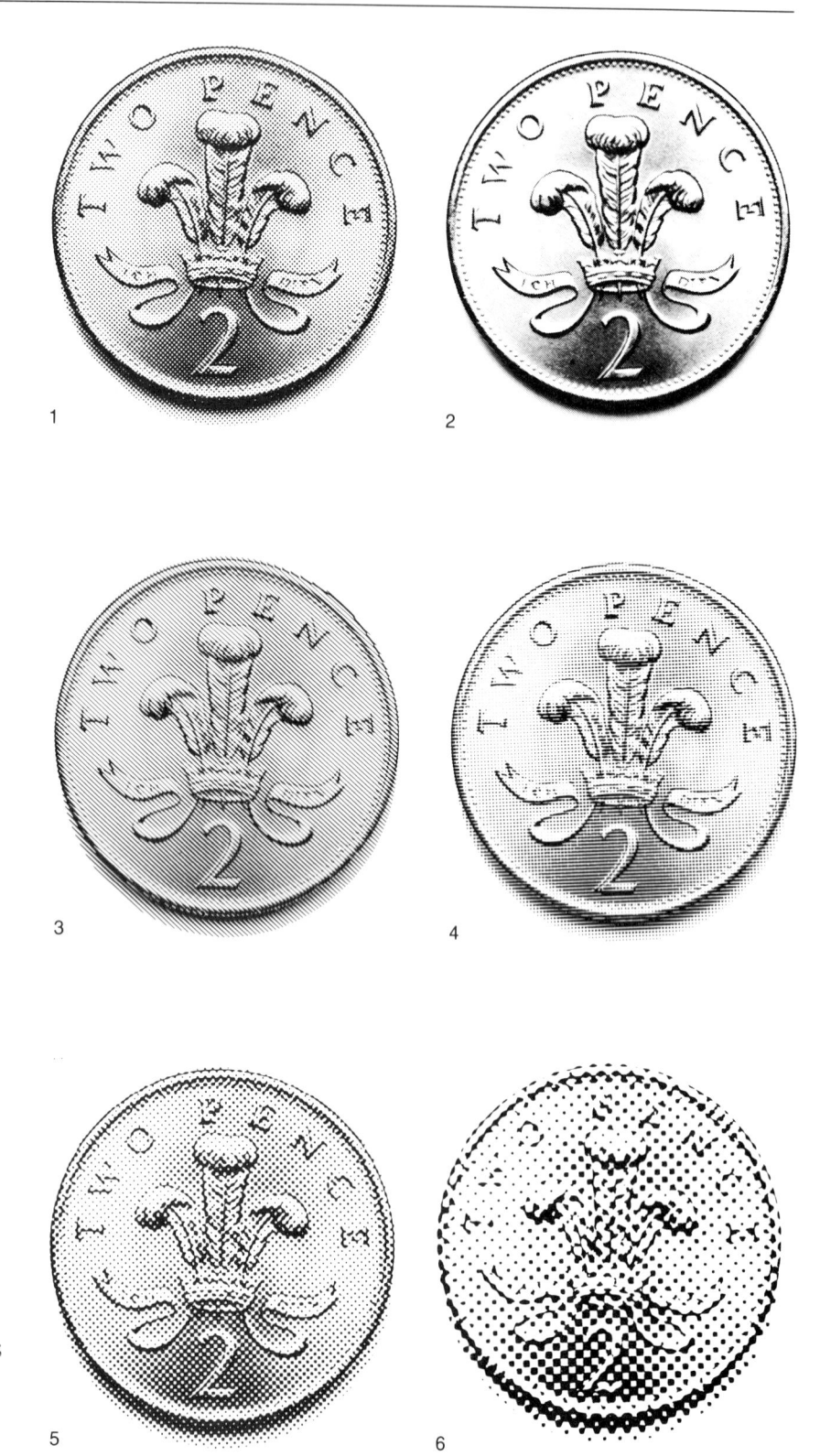

**Figure 13.1** Forms and sizes of screen: (1) 55-dot; (2) 150-dot; (3) 55 linear line; (4) 55 grey cut line; (5) 30-dot; (6) 15-dot

**Reproducing pictures** 189

**Figure 13.2** Schafline: (1) 55-line; (2) 65-dot; (3) 120-line; (4) 50-dot; (5) coarse mezzo; (6) bottom extreme left, fine mezzo; (7) left, 55-line; (8) 120-dot

**Figure 13.3** Schafline: 55 diagonal screen

photographs to be printed with exceptional clarity, detail, impact and realism (Figs 13.1 and 13.2). It is much favoured – and with good reason – by agency production departments for pack shot photography reproduction in national newspapers.

Instead of simulating tones by the use of screens, the original artwork can deploy tone effects directly, in a way that will be camera-ready. On the artwork, tones are laid down as tints: patterned dots, line gratings of varying densities and so on. Laborious to produce by hand, tints are normally effected from mechanical or ready-made sources such as rub-down transfers like Letratone.

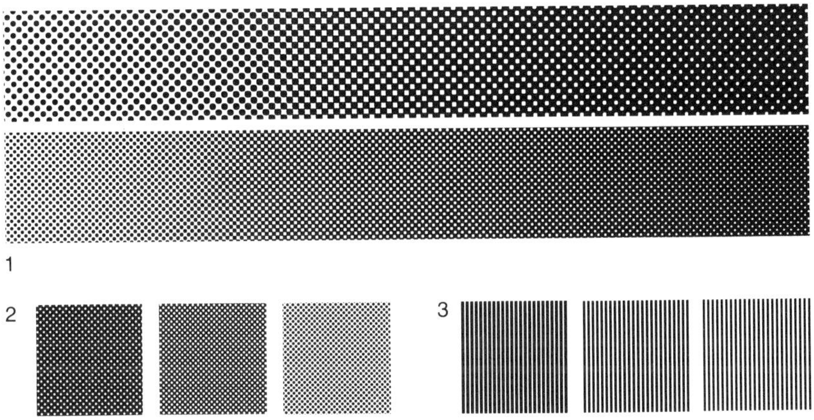

**Figure 13.4** Tints: (1) graduated dot; (2) dot; (3) line

Another method of producing tones through patterns of fine, close lines is *scraperboard*. This consists of a chalk-based background overlaid with a coating of black. The artist cuts or scratches into the top black layer to reveal white lines. Scraperboard origination reproduces well in newspapers.

## 13.1 Colour reproduction

Just as printing has to simulate black-and-white photographic tones by breaking them into lines and dots on the plate, so to print a full colour photograph or illustration requires breaking down the range of colours into their constituents and varying proportions and then, using separate plates, reconstituting the original colour image on the printed surface.

We've looked briefly (p. 108) at how colour TV produces the colours in the spectrum by adding various amounts of red, green and blue light. The principle involved is illustrated by superimposing on to a screen a beam of red light with a beam of green light: it produces yellow. A blue light made to overlap with a green one produces a sky-blue (a colour known in the printing world as cyan). And a red beam converged with a blue one produces magenta. Known as additive primary colours, the red, green and blue when mixed form white light.

Using mixtures of pigment rather than those of light, the pro-

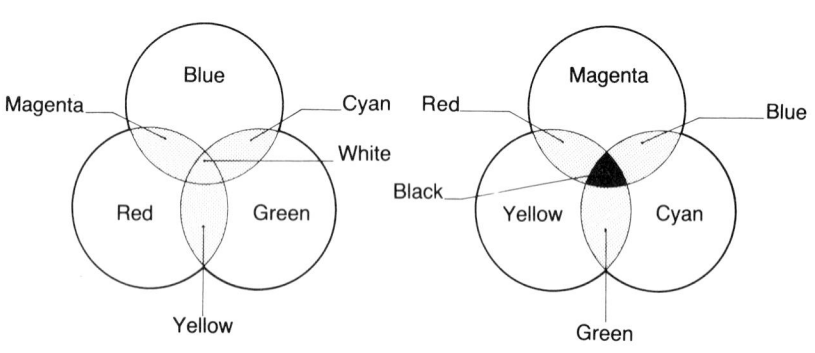

**Figure 13.5** Colour mixing principles

(1) Mixing additive primary colours

(2) Mixing subtractive primary colours

duced colour works by the absorption of some colours and the reflection of others. Thus black pigment appears black because it absorbs red, blue and green. A white surface is seen as white because it reflects red, blue and green. Yellow pigment appears yellow because it absorbs blue and reflects red and green (red and green being 'read' by the eye as yellow). Magenta pigment absorbs green and reflects red and blue. Cyan absorbs red and reflects green and blue. Thus yellow, cyan and magenta are known as subtractive primary or secondary colours: yellow is minus blue, cyan is minus red, magenta is minus green.

## Film separation

The original colour photograph or artwork is placed on the copyboard in a process camera. Shot through a blue filter, all the yellow values in the original are isolated and recorded as a yellow film negative. Through a green filter, the magenta values are recorded. Through a red one, the cyan values are recorded. Lastly, by using a composite filter the monochrome values are separated.

The original full colour photograph is thus discomposed into primary subtractive colours. However, the product is still in continuous tone and so not in a state suitable for onward plate-making and printing. The colour negative separates are converted into positives and then, one by one, filmed through screens to produce halftone separations. Sometimes the colour separation and halftone screening is performed at one and the same time, the 'direct' method.

The angle of the screen is critical. If the position of the screen is the same for each of the colour separations it results in 'clashing', the dots for each of the colours printing with excessive overlap or, worse, on top of one another. Not only is the right blending of the colours vitiated but also interference patterns are set up. Accordingly, when making halftones, the screen is placed at a different angle for each of the colours. Screen rotation for three-colour printing is thirty degrees. With four-colour printing consideration

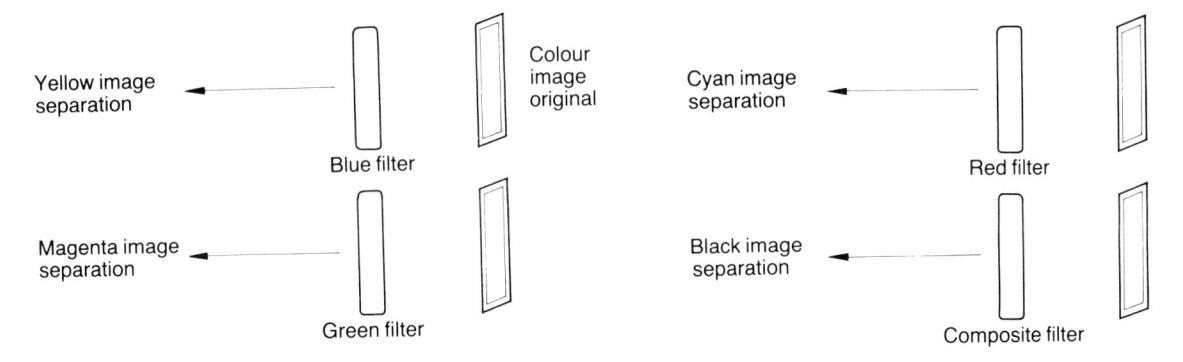

**Figure 13.6** Colour separation

needs to be given to the yellow and the magenta, the least (palest) and most noticeable colours respectively. Normally the screen angle for yellow is ninety degrees to the film negative to make its halftone dots more prominent in the mosaic of the process colours. Screening of the magenta is usually done at forty-five degrees to lessen its subsequent visibility.

### Electronic separation

Colour breakdown by film filtering has largely been taken over by electronics-based separation methods. These are faster, more controllable and much more accurate. The industry 'leaders' are the scanning processes developed by Dai Nippon, Hell, Crosfield and Scitex.

The original artwork is wrapped around a drum. A scanning spot or laser traverses across it. Via an optical colour-splitting system the flying beam analyses the image into its different quantities of cyan, magenta and yellow. The process is basically the same as a three-colour tube video camera scanning a subject and translating the different colour (chroma) and luminance values into electric impulses. During the scanning the operator, checking against the original with a densitometer – a device that quantifies the density of the colour – can adjust the level and intensity of the colour as well as the tonal values, increasing or reducing. In addition the desired screen size can be entered into the system as can requirements for enlargement or reduction.

Digitized in computer storage, the output of the scan signals then drives cyan, yellow and magenta light sources to record the respective colours on to film as fully screened halftone negatives or positives from which printing plates can be struck. Even better, many scan systems will directly output plates that are production press ready.

Origination by electronic scanning can be used to pre-empt some of the problems that are wont to occur on printing presses, particularly litho ones. Firstly, *dot gain*: because of ink compression and other factors the size of the dots on the plate increases on the printed surface, causing a loss of image sharpness and alterations in the tonal values. To avoid this the dots are made slightly smaller on the origination film and so are correspondingly smaller on the plate. Secondly, *under colour removal*: when printing very dark areas the four colours, appearing as large dots bunched together, demand heavy inking levels which tend to cause problems with drying and so of mixing with other colours ('trapping'). To forestall this hazard, the dark areas on the artwork are scanned in a way that cuts out all the colours except black and, occasionally, cyan.

## 13.2 Proofing

The printer supplies the agency (or client) with a set of *progressives*. These show the sequential build-up of the colour separations. The usual progression is (a) yellow, (b) yellow superimposed by magenta, (c) yellow-and-magenta superimposed by cyan and (d) yellow-and-magenta-and-cyan superimposed by black.

Press proofs aren't a totally reliable and faithful indication of how the printed colour will look. The proofing press can't replicate the conditions of the actual press on which the job will be done. Proofing presses are small, slow running and sheet-fed with the four coloured inks being applied wet-on-dry; production machines are, as often as not, web-fed, high-speed and print the colours wet-on-wet.

The term 'proof' is something of a misnomer; it doesn't *prove*, it approximates. Nevertheless, a high degree of simulation can be achieved by proof printing with the same inks and paper stock to be used on the production press. A proof may look wonderful on top grade, heavy paper but on the final job, on coarse, thin stock, the reproduction may turn out to be a distant relative in terms of accuracy and faithfulness.

Comparing the original work with the proof by eye is unreliable; such is the subjectivity of colour vision and the differences in viewing conditions. What the art director, say, sees as one shade of red may be seen as a slightly different one by the printer. Thus proofs come with standard colour bar strips so that the colour densities, gauged by a densitometer, can be determined and compared objectively.

Press proofing is necessarily expensive: the machine has to be set up, inked and run. A widely used alternative is 'soft' or 'dry' proofing which uses an electrostatic/photographic process and eliminates the need for plate-making. The prevalent systems are Dupont's Eurostandard *Cromalin* and 3 M's *Match Print*. Primary coloured dusts are deposited on to the image areas on each of the colour separation films which are then superimposed one on top of the other, i.e., placed in register. Processed, a four-colour proof is realized. This is checked against a 'control strip' consisting of a series of squares showing the standard process colours and their various combinations.

Dry proofing is more accurate than press proofing. And if only a small number of proofs is called for, significantly cheaper. When a lot are required, say for a multi-page brochure, they are usually produced on the press as 'scatter' proofs: the various pictures and artwork are shown randomly rather than in the page and position order in which they will appear in the finished work.

## 13.3 Colour correction

Printing inks have characteristics inherently different from the chemicals used in photography. Thus it is more than likely that the result of a progressive proof won't have the desired fidelity to the original material. Naturally, if verisimilitude between the original and the printed version of it was likely to be very high, the whole business of proofing would be unnecessary or a luxury.

Colour correction can be achieved: (a) by re-scanning the originals with appropriate adjustments to the colour densities; (b) by very fine, local etching on the plates, increasing or diminishing the halftone dots. This is a highly skilled and, needless to say, time and cost intensive process; (c) by manually retouching the original photography using dyes. Not only is this expensive but it also incurs a generation loss as the retoucher starts with a duplicate transparency. And if he makes a mistake he has to begin again with a new duplicate; (d) by retouching electronically. Speed apart, the advantages are: alterations can be played around with and experimented – if something goes wrong there is no problem as the errors can be wiped; adjustments can be made with lethal accuracy as the image of the original is broken down into a multitude of picture cells (pixels) which can be 'addressed' individually. (Electronic retouching is as much, if not more, used for creative origination: adding borders and tints, putting in tones, montaging images, extending backgrounds, shifting subjects up and down, to the left or right.)

The outcome of proofing and the subsequent consideration given to correction will of course vary with the nature of the work to be printed. An ad that is to appear in a glossy magazine will be given a great deal more care and attention at the correction stage than, say, a door-drop leaflet.

## 13.4 Machine press production: common faults

Basic presses print colour serially: first the paper passes over the plate inked with yellow, then that inked with magenta, then the cyan ink is applied and lastly the black. As the paper is transported across one plate cylinder to the next, the sequentially transferred inks are likely to dry. Wet-on-dry superimposition of colour can cause problems if the dry (or drying) pigment doesn't have enough 'tack' or take-up with the wet colour overlaying it.

On sophisticated high-speed presses the process inks are applied virtually simultaneously. The separately inked plate cylinders are positioned around a common impression cylinder. Passing across it, the paper receives all four colours in rapid succession, their superimposition being wet-on-wet. But as we've seen, unless anticipated and compensated for, excess wet inking can produce dot gain and imperfect colour mixing.

Other causes of defective impressions are paper stretch, using the wrong paper or failing to condition it adequately before running, over and under inking, ink stray, too much or too little pressure between the plate, impression and blanket rollers.

Faults that can occur contingently during the running of the press – and so are not going to be evident at the proofing stage – are outlined below.

### Misregister

The alignment of the four colour process inks becomes slightly displaced. One or more of the colours gets out of its correct relative position. Though the flaw is obvious – a misregistered colour showing up as a peripheral fuzz, halo or blurr – on a high-speed web-fed machine it may be difficult to trouble-shoot quickly enough to prevent a large number of spoiled impressions. In litho printing one of the most common causes of misregistration is the paper getting damp and stretching. Another culprit is paper slip ('slurring').

### Tracking

When broad expanses of solid colour are being printed alongside predominantly white areas such as blocks of fine, widely-spaced type, the inking level required for the former can be too much for the latter, and result in its being smudged.

### Show-through and strike-through

This is where the image on one side of the paper is distractingly visible on the other side. The paper may be too thin or too absorbent. And if this is the case there is no excuse: the stock has been unsuitably specified at the job's start. On the other hand the paper may be adequate but there is an excess of ink in the system.

# References and notes

*Chapter 1*

(1) Wittgenstein, L., *Philosophical Investigations*, Blackwell (1953).

(2) Bernstein, D. *Creative Advertising*, Longman (1974).

(3) On definitions in general: Georg Lichtenberg, writing in the mid-eighteenth century, possibly got it about right: 'What a chattering there would be if people were determined to change the names of things to definitions'. Lichtenberg, G., *Aphorisms and Letters*, Cape (1969). For some way-out 'chattering': Sigue Sigue Sputnik – famed for selling the blank intervals between the tracks on their album to advertisers – with their definition of advertising as 'the rock-and-roll' of the eighties' is in a class of its own!

(4) Nor how effective the budgets allocated to it are. Thus Lord Leverhulme's classic remark: 'Half the money I spend on advertising is wasted; the trouble is I don't know which half'.

(5) Industrial designers may also be viewed in a similar way. The invested hope is that the designer will magic a saleable product into being. It's as though product research and consumer testing can't be wrong. And that industrial design will midwife the product into a sales success.

(6) For an excellent critical discussion of the use of magic in advertising, see: Williamson J., *Decoding Advertisements*, Chapter 6, Marion Boyars, London (1985).

(7) Ogilvy, D., *Ogilvy on Advertising*, Pan (1983).

(8) Reeves, R., *Reality in Advertising*, Alfred Knopf (1961).

(9) Benton & Bowles is now part of D'Arcy McManus (DMBB).

(10) Cited in Ogilvy, D., *Ogilvy on Advertising*, Pan (1983).

(11) Creative ideas for scientific theories/models tap into the same imagination wells as do advertising ideas. Ogilvy records how he dreamt of the idea for the ad campaign for Pepperidge Farm bread. How he saw

the old baker driving a horse and carriage along a country lane. The scientist Kekulé day-dreamt, on the top of a tram, seeing a snake eating its head. The image led to his model of the carbon chemistry ring.

(12) Sweeney, P., *Direction*, September 1986.

(13) *The Art of the Ad*, London Weekend Televison, *The South Bank Show* (1981).

*Chapter 2*

(1) Colley, R.H., *Defining Advertising Goals*, New York (1961).

(2) For how the formal or inherent characteristics of media shape or dictate our reception of the messages, see McLuhan, H.M. *Understanding Media*, Routledge & Kegan Paul (1964) and McGraw-Hill (1971).

(3) Reeves, R., *Reality in Advertising*, Alfred Knopf (1961).

(4) Ogilvy, D., *Ogilvy on Advertising*, Pan (1983) p. 15.

(5) The references of some long established brand names are lost. Why PG Tips, Bovril? Bovril has an interestingly quirky provenance. The Latin *bos, bovis* – an ox – of course designates the product's meat extract composition. But 'vril' refers to a subterranean super race, the *Vril-ya*, in a Victorian novel *The Coming Race* by Bulwer Lytton, 'vril' being an all-purpose beneficent force used by the race to control its world.

(6) Bernstein, D., *Creative Advertising*, Longman (1974).

(7) A literal logo can communicate the brand identity forcefully. e.g., Swan lager and a silhouette of a swan. A black swan, moreover, stamps the Australian pedigree.

*Chapter 3*

(1) If someone find the 'facts' as presented in a particular paper's news story disagreeable, he or she may say the paper is biased. Well, it may be. But another paper with a different editorial stance and carrying a different headline, a different picture and different report is equally subject to the charge of bias. Just what is the truth? From a strict logical point of view there are no facts, only interpretations.

(2) McLuhan, H.M., *Understanding Media*, Routledge & Kegan Paul (1964) and *The Mechanical Bride*, Vanguard Press, New York (1951).

(3) McLuhan's position, which has been given deserved attention by Barry Day of McCann-Erickson, has to be put into perspective. Print media are inexorably influenced by the moving-image media of TV and video where images reign supreme in 'telling the story' of a product. People, especially those under the age of thirty and brought up on television as the third parent, *demand and expect* print advertising to have a close similarity in grammar and language terms to TV commercials.

McLuhan, writing in the late 1950s and early 1960s, was advancing a thesis that the potential of new media are not, in the early stages, really appreciated or grasped. We see the new media in terms of the old: a radio is a wireless; a car a horseless carriage; TV a scaled down version of the cinema and so on.

Notwithstanding his bold embrace of the (then emergent) grammar of television, McLuhan is himself apparently locked into the supremacy of print. His bravura use of puns and pregnant chapter headings, where all manner of meanings collide with energy and brilliance, illustrates: 'Is Bogart America's Shropshire Lad?'; 'Say it with tanks'; 'The Bold Look: The Face that launched a thousand hips'. How do you argue with headlines like these?

(4) When Ogilvy came out with his celebrated rule on 'no humour', print media were predominant. Ogilvy borrowed from Claude Hopkins writing at a time when advertising was virtually confined to print (hence Hopkins' definition of advertising as 'salesmanship in print'). Still, Ogilvy says his recantation of the role of humour was brought about by research showing that 'humour can now sell'.

(5) This is enshrined in McLuhan's famous, if misleading, slogan 'The medium is the message'. See McLuhan, H.M. *Understanding Media*, Routledge & Kegan Paul (1964).

(6) See Packard, V. *The Hidden Persuaders*, Penguin (1967).

(7) For a rivetting fictionalized treatment of subliminal techniques, see Koontz, D.R., *Night Chills*, Star (1984).

(8) A light-hearted effective use of subliminals was recounted to me by a producer at a commercials production company. The company had been commissioned to make an army training film. Each time the rough cut of the film was shown to the client, a group of brigadiers and colonels, for approval it was met with all sorts of criticisms and reservations, even though the film had been thoroughly approved at the script stage. As it happened the production company had just been editing a sex picture. Before the next client presentation of the training film one of the production company editors, in a fit of naughty desperation, cut in a few frames of the soft porn movie. And, yes, the military client was delighted with the new version of the training film! (The story is bound to be tall.)

*Chapter 4*

(1) See Goldman, W., *Adventures in the Screen Trade*. Goldman makes the point that, from a scripting point of view, the first episode of a new TV series is the most difficult. The 'grabber' of, say, a car chase and shoot-out, doesn't involve the audience as it doesn't know the characters and so can't care about whether they narrowly escape death or whatever.

(2) For the record: Cooke's 'Wonderful World' (and Marvin Gaye's 'I heard it through the grapevine' were painstakingly re-created for use in the Levis 501 commercial by Karl Jenkins and Mike Ratledge (ex-Soft Machine) of Mooz Music. The cult success of the commercial prompted

*Chapter 5*

(1) Depth of field is not only determined by the focal length of the lens: the distance between the lens and the subject affects it as does the aperture (the f-stop number) – the amount of light reaching the lens. The more the lens is 'stopped down', the greater is the depth of field.

(2) A brilliantly effective hand-held subjective camera shot is the opening of John Carpenter's *Halloween*. We stalk with the camera towards a clapboard house. . . . We push through the door, slowly climb the stairs, cross the landing. . . . We're subjectively involved. It's a piece of very scary branding!

(3) Film buff corner: Raymond Chandler's *The Lady in the Lake* (1946), directed and starring Robert Montgomery as private-eye Philip Marlowe, is shot entirely from Marlowe's point of view using a subjective camera. We only see Marlowe in reflections – in mirrors (and the eponymous lake). The narrative is conveyed through Marlowe's voice-over.

(4) ITCA *Technical Standards and Transmission Requirements*; p. 4, 1(e).

(5) As above: p. 6, 3(c).

(6) As above: p. 4, 1(d).

*Chapter 6*

(1) *The Art of the Ad*, London Weekend Television, *South Bank Show* (1981).

(2) *Creative Review*, Vol. 5, No. 5, May 1984.

(3) *IBA Code of Advertising Standards and Practice*, Independent Broadcasting Authority, 70 Brompton Road, London SW3 1EY.

Independent Television Companies Association, 56 Mortimer Street, London W1N 8AN.

*Notes of Guidance*
No. 2: Copy Submission Requirements
No. 3: Visual Treatments
No. 4: Special Problem Areas
No. 5: Advertising for Investments, Insurance and Finance
No. 6: Medicines, Treatments and Health Claims
No. 7: Advertising of Foods and Drinks
No. 8: Copy Clearance: Why and How
No. 9: Cash with Order Advertisements
No. 10: Agency Registration and Credit Listing Procedures

(4) Instead of a double-head version of the commercial the agency can submit 'for preliminary viewing and advice' a Sony U-Matic Cassette.

(5) ITCA *Notes of Guidance*, Visual Treatments, p. 3.

(6) It is estimated there are around 90 active commercials production companies chasing approximately 2,000 scripts a year.

(7) *Campaign*, 14 November 1986 p. 17.

(8) The traffic is predominantly one-way: commercials directors to films and TV drama rather than the reverse. Acclaimed, prize-laden directors of commercials have over the last eight years or so graduated to the big time of movies. Ridley Scott with *Alien, Blade Runner* and *Legend*; brother Tony Scott with *Top Gun*; Alan Parker with *Midnight Express, Shoot the Moon, Birdy*; Hugh Hudson with *Chariots of Fire, Greystoke, Revolution*; Adrian Lynn with $9\frac{1}{2}$. And very successfully too. Whereas directors who have made their mark, artistically and commercially, in features have seldom 'reversed' into a successful commercials career. Though either way, the reservations tend to be of comparable sorts: movie producers (and their money men shadows) aren't on the whole confident that a director of shampoo and lager commercials will be able to adapt to the scale, narrative demands, stamina and cumulative pace of 120 minutes or whatever. Conversely, agency producers and those that influence them—agency art directors and copywriters—are wont to have deep misgivings about the ability of a director habituated to the luxuries of long schedules, elastic artistic licences, to be able to meet the tyrannical time constraints of a thirty-second ad and its equally strict message disciplines—selling a product.

(9) *Campaign*, 8 August 1986, p. 17.

(10) *Campaign*, 8 August 1986, p. 17. In the USA the production company with lowest bid usually lands the job.

(11) *Direction*, December 1985.

(12) Ziessen, M., *The Production Budget*, privately circulated (1984).

(13) Low-budget films have been known to make the sun look like the moon.

(14) A thorough-going treatment of the pros and cons of the methods of budgeting is given in *Procedures for the Production of TV Commercials*, February 1987 (the Pliatzky Report). Published jointly by the associations representing the production companies (AFVPA), the agencies (IPA) and the advertisers (ISBA), the report lays down a comprehensive code of practice for making TV commercials.

(15) In the opening months of C4's operation, commercials were restricted to animation/cartoons, those made overseas with non-Equity labour and those featuring performers playing themselves—like cat owner Mrs Williams testimonializing. But it was far from enough to fill the IBA-allowed six minutes of advertising per hour. The protracted dispute prompted quite a few advertisers and advertising agencies to

review the worth of using live action Equity member advertisements. A significant result was an upsurge in animation.

(16) See *Agreement for the employment of Performers in Television Commercials* (approved by the AFVPA, the British Actors Equity Association and the IPA), Schedule 7.

*Chapter 7*

(1) There is anger and controversy over the TV companies' habit of cutting feature films shown on television. The cutting may take place because excessive violence and/or sex or four-letter dialogue in a film is thought likely to offend 'the general viewer' or to a lesser extent because of tight scheduling demands. Directors are, with good reason, savage at seeing their work 'mutilated'. However, 'lay' custodians of the integrity of feature films persist in charging TV companies with unjustifiable cutting of the films they broadcast. The argument rests on a knowledge of the running time of the film and then timing the film as shown on TV: the TV version is always shorter. Therefore the TV companies are guilty of cutting films.

But of course a made-for-cinema film with 24 fps is going to be shorter when shown on TV at 25 frames a second. A two-hour film will lose 7,200 frames, i.e., it will be shorter by 300 seconds (5 minutes). The overall shrinkage is four per cent.

'Hiccups' have been known to occur in cinema screening. The director Michael Winner (of *Death Wish* fame) took issue with the management of the Curzon Cinema in Mayfair for 'short-timing' audiences to the film *Room With a View*. It transpired that the theatre had been used in the morning for pre-viewing TV commercials; to this end the projector's speed had been increased to run at 25 fps. But the projectionist had failed to adjust the projection rate back to 24 fps when showing the feature film in the afternoon and evening. Thus the audience had been deprived of several minutes of cinematic experience.

Composers of the original scores complain too. And with justification: broadcast on TV their music is fractionally altered in pitch.

(2) In still photography, compensation for poor light levels can be made by decreasing the shutter speed instead of, or as well as, increasing the f-stop.

(3) Occasionally a director will stipulate or try to insist that the sale of his film to TV will be subject to the condition that it won't be adjusted to the TV screen proportions when broadcast, though only a handful of directors are in a sufficiently powerful position *vis-à-vis* the producers and finance people to exact this condition. Whatever, the director – naturally – doesn't want to see his work cut: to have the extreme left and right sides of the shots chopped off, the integrity of the framing and composition of the scenes spoiled.

(4) Independent Television Companies Association's *Technical Standards and Transmission Requirements*, p. 5, (f) 'Sound Tracks'.

(5) Independent Television Companies Association's *Technical Standards and Transmission Requirements*, Section 3, VTR Commercials: 'The original recording of a commercial should be made using a broadcast quality video tape recorder conforming to the ITCA Equipment Specification for VTRS (namely EBU one-inch helical scan C-format or two-inch quadruplex transverse scan format).... Commercials for transmission must be supplied on EBU one-inch C-format or two-inch quad format'.

(6) Given the narrow width, the exceptional picture quality achieved by Betacam can be put down to two factors: the tape runs at six times the speed for normal half-inch machines and the colour (the chrominance) and the black-and-white (the luminance) are coded 'componently'.

(7) Like 'videotape' or 'formica', U-Matic has become generic. U-Matic, though Sony's development, has become synonymous with three-quarter inch recording. A National Panasonic or JVC three-quarter inch recorder will be described as a U-Matic.

(8) The policy of Channel 4 is to buy in a percentage of programming from Independent TV programme makers. The concession to high-band origination is to help the independents: the costs of producing programme material on this format being a great deal less than on one-inch or two-inch.

(9) It's risky to make statements about the limitations of video cameras and video equipment in general such is the awesome rate at which technical developments take place. The problems of comet tailing, and many others too, have largely been overcome by a new generation of camera that is completely solid state, i.e., the conventional picture tube is replaced by chip circuitry. Market-led by Sony and generically known as CCD (Charge Coupled Device) this new breed of camera, if the claims made on its behalf stand the test of rigorous trial and time, can do virtually anything that a movie camera can: shoot directly into the sun without risk of 'burn', fast pan from the sun to a darkened wood without comet-tailing and go virtually anywhere, as happy in a helicopter as in the back of a racing car, equally at home in the most sultry tropics as in the frozen wastes of the Antarctic.

(10) *In Vision*, April 1986 p. 35.

*Chapter 9*

(1) *Creative Review*, May 1984.

*Chapter 10*

(1) Except, paradoxically, that the more you concentrate the less likely you are to be successful. This is because, so neuropsychologists tell

us, concentration activates the left brain hemisphere (the site of logical and rational thinking) to such a level that the 'current' in the right brain hemisphere (the site of imagination, fantasy and irrational modes of thought) is shut off.

(2) *The Art of Persuasion*, Channel 4 (1985).

(3) The renowned typographer Sir Francis Meynell recommended that poetry be set in italics to ensure that it was read slowly.

(4) Crompton, A., *The Art of Copywriting*, Business Books (1979).

(5) Runner-up 'Best Food Advertisement', Campaign Press Awards (1981).

*Chapter 11*

(1) Cited in Douglas, T., *The Complete Guide to Advertising*, Macmillan (1984) p. 186.

(2) *Direction*, December 1986, p. 41.

(3) Ogilvy, D., *Ogilvy on Advertising*, Pan (1983).

# Glossary

**'A' Paper Sizes**  The international standard. A0 is a square metre (841 mm×1189 mm). All the 'A' sizes have the same proportions (1:1.414); folded lengthwise the higher 'A' size produces the next size in the series. Thus A0 folded produces A1; A1 folded, A2; A2 folded, A3 and so on. A4 (210×297) is standard for letterheads and stationery; A5 (148×210) is typically used for leaflets and small brochures; A6 (105×148) is the standard postcard size and A7 (74×105) common for labels, business cards and slips.

**A & B Rolls**  Assembly of alternate cuts/shots on separate rolls of film to enable join-free printing of the edited commercial and low-cost realization titles and simple *opticals*.

**Airbrush**  Using an aerosol principle, an instrument for producing a very fine spray-jet or ink or paint. Chiefly used for retouching work and illustration origination.

**Animatic**  A development of the TV storyboard into a number of sequences of moving-picture illustrations. Used to give the client a better idea of what the commercial will be like.

**Answer print**  A check print returned from the labs after *colour grading* of the final edited negative master. Once approved by the director and agency *release prints* are ordered.

**Aperture**  The amount of light transmitted by the lens to the film or to the target area of the camera tube; controlled by a variable diaphragm and measured in *f stops*.

**Art paper**  Stock coated with china clay to give it a smooth surface, usually shiny.

**Artwork**  Any non-text material: original line drawings, illustrations, photography, graphics.

**Ascender**  In lower case characters like the 'h', 'b' and 'd', the distance from the top of the *x-height* to the end of the upward stroke.

**Aspect ratio** The horizontal and vertical proportions of the screen. The TV ratio is 4:3.

**Assembly** A preliminary stage in editing: joining the shots together in script sequence either by physical splicing (film) or re-recording (video).

**Atmos** Atmosphere sound effects; background noise such as wind, traffic, 'jungle' *dubbed* from a loop tape from library sources.

**Back projection** A device for faking backgrounds in the studio. The action is performed in front of a translucent screen on to the rear of which is projected the background, either still or moving.

**Bandwidth** The range of frequencies that can be 'handled' by a TV camera or video recording system. The wider the range the better the picture quality.

**BCU** Big Close-Up.

**Beta** A high quality half-inch broadcast or near-broadcast video format mainly used for electronic news gathering (ENG).

**Blanket** A rubber-coated roller used in *offset* printing. It accepts the inked image from the plate and then transfers it to the paper or other impression surface.

**Bleed** Refers to the printed picture being run to the edges of the page.

**Block** A metal plate photoengraved from filmed *artwork*. Normally what is supplied by an agency to a publication printed by *letterpress*.

**Blow-up** An enlargement of a photograph.

**Blues** A low-cost method of proofing by contact printing, usually as a white image on blue. Also known as an Ozalid.

**Bold** A thicker and heavier version of the basic form of a typeface design.

**Bromide** A photographic print on silver bromide paper. Different papers give variations in hardness and softness contrasts. A general term for photographic material.

**BSF** Basic studio fee: the agreed daily fee paid to a performer on which *repeats* are based.

**Calendering** Conditioning paper to give it a smooth finish by passing it through metal and fabric rollers.

**Camera-ready** Artwork that is in a state suitable for filming and subsequent plate-making.

**Carbon tissue** The conventional gelatine-based medium for transferring an image on to a cylindrical plate for *gravure* printing.

**Cast off** Working out the amount of space that will be taken up by the typescript copy when set in type of a given size.

**Cel** In animation: one of the series of clear acetate sheets on which is drawn each of the fractionally progressive images.

**Cell** One of the tiny recessions or pits which holds the ink on the *gravure* printing plate.

**Chase** A rectangular metal frame locking up the various sections of typeset matter and *blocks* ready for printing by *letterpress*.

**Chroma** The part of the video signal carrying the colour (chrominance) values as distinct from the luminance values – the brightness level on a sliding scale between total black and total white.

**Chroma key** A means of electronically inserting a foreground subject into a background picture. The subject to be keyed in is shot against a blue background and the camera output electronically combined with the output from another picture source in such a way that in the composite all the blue in the subject is subtracted. Blue is used because the image to be inserted is usually a human subject, flesh tones being devoid of blue. Also known as CSO – colour separation overlay.

**Cold setting** Any method of typesetting other than *hot metal*, e.g., strike-on setting from an IBM composing typewriter or *filmsetting*.

**Colour bars** A series of vertical stripes or rectangles of the primary colours, yellow, cyan, magenta, red, green and blue used as a reference to check the densities of colour in proofing colour printing and also as a test signal for TV cameras.

**Colour grading** A process carried out by the labs: adjusting and rendering consistent the colour values throughout the *fine cut* of the master footage.

**Colour separation** Using photographic filters, the process of separating out the different quantities of the primary colours in a colour picture to enable printing plates for each of the colours to be made.

**Commag** A film print on which the magnetically recorded sound is combined (married) with the picture.

**Comopt** A film print on which the sound in the form of an *optical track* is combined (married) with the picture.

**Crab** Moving the camera sideways on a *dolly* or rolling spyder.

**Cromalin** Made by DuPont, a system of proofing colour work that eliminates the need for plating up a press; known in general as dry proofing.

**CU** Close-up.

**Cutting copy** An ungraded print made from the master *rushes*; the material on which editing decisions are taken. Also known as a work print or slash print.

**Definition** The sharpness or *resolution* of an image.

**Densitometer** A device for measuring colour and tone density; used in proofing and the control of inking levels on presses.

**Depth of field** The distance between the nearest and farthest points in a shot that are in focus. It varies with the *lens length* and the *aperture*.

**Descender** In lower case characters such as the 'p' and 'j', the distance from the base of the *x-height* to the end of the downward stroke.

**Die stamping** A method of producing a moulded relief image from an incised die. Used to emboss characters, logos and words on letterheads, packs, etc. When no ink is used, known as blind embossing.

**Dissolve**  A shot/scene transition mode: as the old shot is faded out the new shot is faded in. A cross-fade.

**Doctor blade**  In *gravure* printing, a metal blade set against the plate cylinder which scrapes away surplus ink before the image is transferred to the impression surface.

**Dolly**  A mobile trolley on which the camera is mounted. Thus: to dolly in/out, to dolly left/right.

**Dope sheet**  A record kept by the cameraman during shooting of the footage used, the exposure and other data, shot by shot.

**Dot gain**  The increase in the size of the dots on a *halftone* during printing which results in a marred impression.

**Double-head**  A projector enabling the uncombined sound and picture to be laced up separately and screened in sync. Used for showing the *rough cut* to the client/agency.

**Dry offset**  *Letterpress* printing incorporating the *offset* principle. Also known as indirect letterpress.

**Dubbing**  Post-production sound operations: *post-syncing* dialogue, laying down *voice-overs*, music and effects tracks and mixing them together. Also the transfer of sound and videotape from one format to another, e.g., dub from quarter-inch to magnetic striped film; dub down from *one-inch* to *U-Matic*.

**Dupe**  A duplicate negative made from a positive print.

**ECG**  Electronic character generator. Used for inserting captions and *supers* on to commercials and for typesetting directly into a page make-up terminal.

**ECU**  Extreme close-up.

**Electro**  A duplicate *letterpress* plate. A mould is made from the original plate and then by electrolysis coated with a film of copper or other metal.

**Em**  A unit of type measurement based on the space occupied by the upper case 'M'. Line lengths or column widths are described in terms of ems. Unless otherwise specified an em means a *pica* (a 12 *point*) em.

**En**  Half the width of an em (traditionally ems and ens are known as muttons and nuts).

**Equalizing**  Balancing and rendering consistent the level of the sync sound during dubbing. The sound equivalent of *colour grading*.

**EVT**  Electronic verification of transmission. A code inserted on to a taped commercial that enables the agency/client to check the actual transmission schedule for the ad.

**Family**  A typeface with common and peculiar design features. The variations on the core design are derived from differences in weight (light, medium, bold, extra bold) and width (expanded, condensed).

**Field** The pattern of odd or even scan lines forming the TV image; two fields combined (interlaced) make one *frame*.

**Filmsetting** Typesetting from *fonts* held as negatives on photographic film. A beam of light is shone through the matrix for each letter, the image being fixed on sensitive paper.

**Fine cut** The stage where the commercial is cut to the nearest *frame*.

**Flexography** Form of relief printing using rubber or plastic plates.

**Font/Fount** A complete set of characters in a given typeface and *point* size.

**fps** Frames per second; there are 25 for TV (in the UK), 24 for film projection.

**Frames** One of the series of individual and fractionally progressive pictures that when projected on a cinema screen or displayed by scanning on a TV tube creates the illusion of motion.

**Freeze-frame** The effect of a still image; produced by the repeat printing or scanning of a given frame.

**F-stop** A calibrated control of the *aperture*; the smaller the f number the less the light passing through the lens and the greater the *depth of field*.

**Galley** Short for galley proof: a general term for checking typesetting output before doing the layout.

**Glitch** Any transient fault (such as picture tear or jitter) in a video/TV picture.

**gsm** Grammes per square metre (g/m$^2$). A measure of the weight of a paper stock. Newsprint is usually 50 g/m$^2$; bond paper, 80 g/m$^2$; coated papers, 100 g/m$^2$ plus.

**Gravure** Method of printing where the image to be printed is recessed into the surface of the plate and then filled with ink; the principle is the opposite of relief printing.

**G spool** A small diameter spool for videotape; the form for supplying commercials to the TV stations.

**Halftone** A means of reproducing in print the gradations of tones in a photograph by representing them as a pattern of black dots of different sizes.

**Halftone screen** A glass plate carrying a grid of opaque criss-cross lines used to break down continuous tone into halftone. The finer the grid the better the simulation of tone range and detail.

**Hot metal** The traditional method of typesetting: by pouring molten metal into a matrix for each letter the characters are cast in relief.

**Imposition** The arrangement of the pages on the plate so that when folded and cut after printing they will be in the right order.

**Intaglio** Any method of printing from a recessed image.

**Interline spacing** See *leading*.

**Justification** Squaring up type into columns: both margins, left and right, form a vertical line. In left-hand justification the right margin is ragged, the left is flush.

**Jump cut**  A jarring cut usually caused by an abrupt change in the position of the subject(s); one moment A is on the left of the screen, the next on the right.

**Leading**  Traditionally a thin strip of lead placed between lines of type to create a space. Used generally to describe interline spacing; measured in *points*, typically one or two. Where there is no between-line spacing the type is 'set solid'.

**Lens length**  A long focal length (telephoto) lens gives a narrow angle of view; it enables close-ups of the subject to be shot without moving the camera nearer to it but at the cost of reducing the *depth of field* and flattening perspective. A short focal length lens gives a wide angle of view but exaggerates perspective, the wider the angle the greater the distortion.

**Letterpress**  Method of printing where the image is cast in relief metal.

**Lip flap**  A momentary loss of sync in dialogue; the performer's lips move before the sound of the words is heard.

**Literal**  A mistake made in typesetting as distinct from one in the copy.

**Lithography**  Method of printing where the image is on the same plane as the non-image, separation between the two being maintained chemically: the grease defining the image area rejects the water adhering to the background area and vice versa.

**Mark up**  Detailed instructions to the typesetter on how the copy is to be set. Also instructions for reproduction on the *artwork*.

**Matte**  A mask used to stop light exposing certain defined areas on the film frames. Often used for faking-in backgrounds.

**Mechanical**  The finished layout of all the artwork and text; usually what is supplied by the agency to a publication printed by litho.

**Mixing/mix**  Adjusting the levels of the various sound tracks when combining them on to a single track ready to be striped on to the edited picture. Also a video term for a *dissolve*.

**Normal lens**  A lens giving a medium angle of view and a natural perspective.

**NTSC**  National Television System Committee. The broadcast TV system used in the USA.

**Offset**  The transfer of the image on the plate to an intermediary roller, the *blanket*, and thence to the impression surface. Virtually universal in litho printing.

**One-inch**  Principal tape gauge for originating and editing commercials.

**Opticals**  In post-production, the addition of titles and *supers* and shot transition effects—*dissolves*, wipes, 'page turns', etc. Once the preserve of the labs, opticals are now almost entirely realized with video facilities.

**Optical track** A photographic representation of the magnetically recorded and mixed sound; performed by the labs when producing a *comopt*.

**PAL** Phase alternating line. The broadcast TV system used in the UK.

**Pan** Swinging the camera left or right on its support mounting to follow action or survey a scene from the subject's *POV*.

**Paste-up** Arranging all the elements of *artwork*, headlines, text and so on on a board. Increasingly done electronically for editorial (see *PMT*).

**Pica** 12 *point* type; one pica is approximately one-sixth of an inch.

**Pixel** Picture cell; the smallest unit on an electronically displayed image that can be altered—'addressed'.

**PMT** (1) Page make-up terminal. Electronic means for laying out input text and *artwork* in the 'window' of the *VDU*. Also used to originate text and graphics and to retouch *artwork* with *pixel* precision. (2) Photo-mechanical transfer. Process for making photoprints from *artwork*. Chiefly used for enlarging, reducing and screening for subsequent *paste-up* and for presentation of proposals to the client.

**Point** The unit of type size; there are approximately 72 points to the inch. The distance from the top of the ascender to the bottom of the descender.

**Post-syncing** In post-production, recording dialogue and sound effects to synchronize with the action. Necessary where sync sound hasn't been recorded during shooting or where it needs enhancing; or where 'dubbing' into a different language is required.

**POV** Point of view; as seen through the eyes of the subject.

**Press proofing** Impressions (often called 'pulls') taken from a printing press that is a scaled down version of the production press to be used for the actual print run.

**Process colours** The yellow, magenta, cyan and black inks that blended in different quantities produce the full spectrum of colours in colour printing.

**Progressives** Proofs showing each process colour separately and then in a series of progressive superimpositions—yellow+magenta, yellow+magenta+cyan, yellow+magenta+cyan+black.

**Quad** Quadruplex: a two-inch tape format for broadcast purposes.

**RA** Reverse angle: a shot that shows the opposite or reverse viewpoint.

**Raster** The pattern or image traced by the scanning spot on a TV tube or *VDU*.

**Register** In colour printing: the correct positioning of the overlay of one *process colour* image over another. In video cameras: aligning the red, green and blue electron beams so that they converge and blend in the correct way.

**Release print**  A print of a filmed commercial for cinema exhibition or for dispatch to TV stations.

**Repeats**  A use fee, based on the number of times the commercial is shown and the *BSF*, paid to a performer.

**Resolution**  The amount of detail that a video/TV system can discriminate and reproduce.

**Reversal stock**  Film that produces a positive image on the originally exposed material.

**Reversed out**  Type matter appearing as white-out-of-black or other solid colour.

**Rostrum**  A special mount for holding a camera above flat *artwork*; used for titles and for filming animation work.

**Rough cut**  An intermediary stage in editing between making the *assembly* and making the *fine cut*. What is shown to the client/agency/ITCA on a *double-head* or *U-Matic* transfer for approval.

**Rushes**  The takes ordered by the director to be printed up by the labs; the raw material of editing. In the US known as 'dailies'.

**Scatter proofs**  A set of proofs in random order i.e., not in the sequence and position in which they will appear in the final printed work.

**Screen**  See *halftone screen*.

**Screen angle**  The rotation of the screen when making *halftones* from continuous tone *colour separations* in order to avoid clashing or interference patterns.

**Screen printing**  Method of printing in which the image is transferred by squeezing ink through a stencil held on the underside of a fabric mesh and thence on to the paper.

**Serif**  Cross strokes of varying weights, such as hairline or slab, at the end of the strokes forming the characters.

**SFX**  Sound effects.

**Shooting ratio**  The amount of film exposed or tape used as compared to what is actually used as the raw edit material. An index of the number of takes for each shot averaged over the shoot.

**Show-through**  Where the reverse side of the page is visible; caused by over-inking and/or the paper being too thin or insufficiently opaque.

**Speed rating**  The sensitivity of a film stock to light; measured by ASA – American Standards Association – ratings. The higher the rating the 'faster' the stock, i.e., the less the light needed for exposure.

**Strike frame**  The *frame* where the arm of the clapboard hits the body of the slate. Used in editing as a reference point to sync the picture with the sound-track: the two are moved forward until the action of the strike and the sound of the 'clap' are coincident.

**Super**  Superimposing words on to the picture.

**Thermography**  A low-cost method of simulating embossing produced by *die stamping*. The image to be embossed is coated with a resinous powder which when subjected to heat causes it to stand out in relief.

**Telecine**  A device for transferring film to videotape.

**Tight shot**  Loose specification for a close shot or close-up.

**Tilt**  Moving the camera up or down in a vertical arc.

**Tints**  Patterns of dots or lines used to put tone and shading effects directly on to line artwork; often used to create solid backgrounds or to fill in areas described by lines.

**Tracking**  Physically moving the camera on a *dolly* or along purpose mini 'railway lines' to get closer to or further away from the subject, or to maintain a constant lens-to-subject distance. Since the lens used is the same there is no alteration of the perspective.

**U-Matic**  A three-quarter-inch cassette tape format, the high-band version being semi-broadcast quality. Often used for presentation of *rough cuts* and, after transfer of the taped rushes from *one-inch*, as the equivalent of a *cutting copy*.

**VDU**  Visual display unit.

**Voice-over (VO)**  A non-sync voice recorded in post-production; usually a commentary. Occasionally used to externalize the thoughts of a character on-screen. FVO – female voice-over; MVO – male voice-over.

**Web**  A paper feed from a continuous roll as opposed to feeding from sheets.

**Wet-on-wet**  Printing one process colour on top of another before the first colour has dried.

**Wild track**  Background sound recorded non-synchronously during production which is later dubbed on to any shots which have had to be left mute while filming.

**Wipe**  A means of exiting one shot and entering a new one without cutting or *dissolving*. Classically the new shot shunts the old one off the screen in a horizontal left-to-right movement. Common wipe modes are for the incoming picture to emerge from the outgoing one in the form of a square or circle.

**x-height**  The height of lower case characters without *ascenders* or *descenders*.

**Zooming**  Getting closer to or remoter from the subject by optical means: changing the length of the lens.

# Bibliography

Advertising Agency Production Association, *The Pocket Pal.*
Bann, D., *Print Production Handbook*, MacDonald (1986).
Bernstein, D., *Creative Advertising*, Longman (1974).
*Black and White Book*, Mirror Group Newspapers.
Book, A.C. and Schick D., *Fundamentals of Copy and Layout*, Crain (1985).
Brewer, R., *Print Buying*, David & Charles (1986).
*British Code of Advertising Practice*, The CAP Committee, Brook House, Torrington Place, London WC1.
Busch, H.T. and Landeck T., *The Making of a TV Commercial*, Collier Macmillan (1980).
Chambers, H.T., *The Management of Small Offset Print Departments*, Business Books (1979).
Crittenden R., *Film Editing*, Thames & Hudson (1984).
Crompton, A., *The Craft of Copywriting*, Business Books (1979).
Croy, O.R., *Camera Copying and Reproduction*, Focal Press (1975).
Douglas, T., *Complete Guide to Advertising*, Macmillan (1984).
Hulke, M., *Writing for Television*, A & C Black (1980).
*IBA Code of Advertising Standards and Practice*, IBA, 70 Brompton Road, London SW3 1EY.
Independent Television Companies Association, *Notes of Guidance on Television Advertising*, ITCA, 56 Mortimer Street, London W1N 8AN.
*Letraset Graphic Design Handbook*, Esselte, Letraset Ltd (1986).
Marner, T. St J., *Directing Motion Pictures*, Tantivy (1972).
Martineau, P., *Motivation in Advertising*, McGraw-Hill (1971).
McLean, R., *Typography*, Thames & Hudson (1980).
McLuhan, H.M., *Understanding Media*, Routledge & Kegan Paul (1964).

McLuhan, H.M., *The Mechanical Bride*, Vanguard (1951).
Millerson, G., *The Technique of Television Production*, Focal Press (1983).
Millum, T., *Images of Woman*, Chatto & Windus (1975).
Newman, W. and Sproull, R.F., *Principles of Interactive Computer Graphics*, McGraw-Hill (1979).
Ogilvy, D., *Ogilvy on Advertising*, Pan (1983).
*Procedures for the Production of TV Commercials*, AFVPA, IPA and ISBA, February 1987.
Reeves, R., *Reality in Advertising*, Knopf (1961).
Roman, K. and Maas, J., *How to Advertise*, Kogan Page (1976).
Spencer, H., *The Visible Word*, Royal College of Art (1968).
Walter, E., *The Technique of the Film Cutting Room*, Focal Press (1976).
Williamson, J., *Decoding Advertisements*, Marion Boyars (1985).

# Index

A & B rolls 134–135
Abbott, David 78
Advertising
  above-the-line 2–3, 40
  and creativity 8–11, 75–76
  below-the-line 2
  definition 3
  expenditure 3–4
  informative versus persuasive 24–26
  models 12–14
  objectives 5, 60
  relationship with sales 4–8
  strategy 61, 143
  theories 12–23
  versus advertisement 27–28
Advertising agency
  account handling 60–61, 75
  as magician 8
  media department 45
  USP 17
AFVPA 87–89
Agency TV producer 78–80, 85, 87, 90, 123, 129
AIDA 12
Ajax 15, 20
Alka-Seltzer 42
Alliance Building Society 49
American Express 21
Ampex 111
Amstrad 49, 146
Anachronism 54–55
Andrex 56
Animals 55–56, 84–85
Animatic 76

Animation 46, 86, 123–127
Answer print 136
Appeals
  emotional 18, 20–21, 31, 46, 144
  rational 15–16, 20–21
Araldite 43
Art
  and advertising 1
  versus selling 9–11
Art department 82
Art director 37, 45, 63, 66, 80, 90, 129, 143–144, 152–153
ASA (Advertising Standards Authority) 25
ASA (American Standards Association) 101–102, 117
Aspect ratio 102–103
Assembly 130–131
Atmos track 134
A Typ I 159
Audi 146
Audio script 72–73
Avis 33

Baker, Jim 81
Bailey, David 148
Barrett, Freddie 41
Bartle Bogle Hegarty 57, 79
BBC 4, 126
BBDO 144
BCAP 27
Beatles 83–84
Beliefs 16, 31
Benson & Hedges 11, 54, 152

Benton & Bowles 9–10
Bernbach, Bill 32–33
Bernstein, David 3, 6, 22
Betacam 114, 137
B F Goodrich 33
Bids 88–90
Biro 23
   *see also* Parker Lady
Black & White whisky 30
Blanket 176, 179
Block(s) 175–177
BMW 150–151
Body copy 149, 157, 161, 168
Bogart, Humphrey 54
Bookbinder, Lester 11
Borg, Bjorn 35
Brand image 5, 18–21
Brand names 21–23, 158, 168
Braque 153–154
*Brideshead* 47
British Airways 86
British Caledonian 57–58
British Gas 58
British Telecom 54, 56
British Standard (BS 2961) 158–159
Broadcast TV systems 109–110
Bruno, Frank 146
BSF 83, 93–95
Budget/budgeting 80–95
Buffer shot 72
Bulmore, Jeremy 3
BVU 114

Cable TV 4
Cagney, James 54
Camera movements 67–69
Campari 28
Campbell's soup 115, 170, 185
Canada Dry 43–44
Candour 32–33, 155–156
Carlsberg 72
Cartoons 46, 123–124
Casting 82–83, 91–92
Cel 124–125
Celebrities 28, 34–36, 95, 155
Cell 181–182
Channel 4 94, 114, 126
Chaplin, Charlie 97
Chase 176
Chase, Lorraine 28, 36
Cinema 38–39, 42–43

Cinzano 28
Cleese, John 28, 91, 93
Coburn, James 72
Coca-Cola 40, 57, 170
Cognitive dissonance 31–32
Cold setting 171–172
Collett Dickenson & Pearce 76
Colley, Russell 12
Collins, Joan 28, 35, 67
Colour
   *see* Primary colours and Process colours
Colour correction (print) 96
Colour film 101
Colour grading and correcting (film) 115, 135–136
Colour reproduction 191–194
Colour TV 48, 108
Communicator, role of 33–36
*Company* 183
Computer animation 124–126
Copy clearance
   *see* ITCA script clearance
Copy language 149
Copy testing 11
Copywriter 37, 45, 63, 73–74, 80, 90, 129, 143–144, 155–156
Copywriting 144–149
Corporate image 5, 36
Courage 49
Crabbing 68
Craning 69
Creative awards 8–9, 11
Creative chemistry 63, 143
Creative grammar of TV 48–58
Creative strategy 8, 60–61, 143–144
*Crocodile Dundee* 42
Cromalin 195
Crompton, Alastair 145
Crosfield 193
Cypher 140

DAGMAR 12
Dai Nippon 193
da Vinci 115
DBS 4
Densitometer 194
DHL 1
Dichter, Ernst 22
Director 59, 66–68, 79, 91–92, 118, 120–123, 129

# Index 219

Dissolve 70–71
Distraction 26–28, 39
distribution 6, 119
Doctor blade 181
Dolly 68
Dot gain 194, 197
Double-head 60, 77, 131
*Double Indemnity*
  see Pirelli
Doyle Dane Bernbach 32
Drambuie 55
Dry offset 179–180
Dry proofing 195
Dubbing 132–134
Dulux 158
Dusenberry, Philip 144
Dylan, Bob 83

ECG 140, 172
Editing
  film 128–137
  video 137–142
Editorial ambience 38
Editorial style 27
Electronic colour separation 193–194
Electronic composition 172–173
Electronic Test Pattern 108
Em 162, 167
Emotion
  see Appeals
En 162
Entertainment 27
Equity 92–95
Eraser Mate 148
Esso 55, 145
Establishing shot 66, 72
EVT 137

Fade 70–71
Family of type 163
Fellini 79
Festinger, Leon 31
Fiat 57
Field 107, 110
Film
  formats 99–101
  grammar of 96–105
  production 120–123
  sound 103–105
  stocks 101–102
  versus video 116–119
Film text setting 172–173, 177
*Financial Times* 5, 29, 31, 97
Fine cut 132
Firm/fixed bid 88–90
Flexography 177–178
Foot Cone & Belding 81
Font 162
Forme 176
Formica 23
Frame rate (fps)
  film 97–98
  TV 98, 107, 117, 110
Freeze frame 73, 98, 118
FX 73

Gallahers 11
Galley proof 173
Germolene 152
*Gestalt* 29, 170
Grabber 48–49
Gravure 176, 181–183
Greer, Germaine 11
Gripping Stuff
  see Pirelli
Goodyear 34, 50, 93
Gordons 1
*Guardian* 38
Guinness 1
Gutenberg 170, 175

Halftones 175–177, 180, 182, 186–191, 194
Halifax Building Society 54
Hamlet 42, 56
Hand-held camera 69
Hard-sell 9, 50
Headlines 145–149, 170
Healthcrafts 148
Hedger Mitchell Stark 43
Hegarty, John 79
Heineken 11, 41, 76, 146
Helical scan recording 111–113
Hell 193
'Hidden persuaders' 39
Hofmeister 56
Hogan, Paul 42–43
Holsten Pils 54
Hoover 22

Horlicks 97
Hot metal 167, 171, 175
Hovis 57
Humour 28, 55, 57

IBA 25, 41, 48, 61, 63, 77–78, 136
IBM 171
ICI 36
IPA 9
Images
　see Brand image and Corporate image
Incompleteness 29–30, 45
Indirect letterpress 179–180
Innovation 9, 76
Innovation-prone 13, 37
Inoculation 32
Intaglio 181
Inter-character spacing 167–168, 173
Interline spacing 166–167
ITCA
　double-head approval 132
　pre-transmission clearance 136
　script clearance 60, 77–78, 81, 118
　script and technical requirements 73–74, 114

Jackson, Michael 84
Jaguar 149
JCB 23
Jingle 41
Johnny Walker Black Label 169
Justification 166, 174
JVC 111
J Walter Thompson 55

Keegan, Kevin 35
Kiam, Victor 51
Kit-Kat 152
Kleenex 23
Knocking copy 25–26, 32

Lanson 57
*Lawrence of Arabia* 48
Leading 166–167
Lee Lewis, Jerry 57
Legibility 158, 166–170

Lenses 68–69
Letterpress 171, 175–179
Lever Brothers 14
Levis 1, 128
Levitt, Theodore 34
Line length 166
Linotype 171
Lithography 176, 178–181
Live action 120–123
Location 81–82
Long copy 149
Loren, Sophia 21
Lowe, Frank 11, 76
LWT 126

McCann-Erickson 80
McCartney, Paul 83–84
Machine press production: common faults 196–197
McLuhan, Marshall 27
Magnetic sound track 103–105
Magritte, Rene 152
Mailer, Norman 3
Mark, Sir Robert 34, 50
Marketing mix 6–7
Marlboro 19–20
Mars 16
Martini 28, 38
Master negative cut 134–135
Match Print 195
Mechanical 180, 182
Media
　characteristics 40–44, 45–48
　expenditure 3–4
　role in persuasion 38–40
Message: effective approaches 26–33
Milk Tray 51
Milligan, Spike 54
Mirage 140–142
Misregister 197
Mix/mixing 70
Models 36
Modem 172
Monotype 171
Monroe, Marilyn 185
Murdoch, Rupert 178
Music 56–57, 83–84, 87, 90

*News of the World* 183
Night shooting 86, 117

# Index

Nike 84
Niven, David 35
Nixon, Richard 34
NTSC 110

*Observer* 183
Off-line editing 137–138
Offsetting 176, 179–180
Ogilvy, David 8, 10, 18–20, 28, 57, 63, 170
Olympus 148
Optical sound track 104–105
Opticals 71, 85, 118–119, 134, 136

Pack
 as advertisement 2
 design and USP 17
 shot(s) 36, 155
PAL 110
Pal dog food 16, 21
Pan/panning 69
Paper 176, 180–181, 183, 187, 197
Paradox 148
Parker Lady 33, 155–156
Pascal, Blaise 26
Pele 35
Persuasion 24–44
Peugeot 43
PG Tips 55, 133
Photo Typositor 173
Photo-composition 172–173, 177
Photographers 153
Pica 162
Picasso 153–155
Pirelli 49, 52–54
Pixel 141, 196
Planographic printing
 *see* Lithography
PMT (Page make-up terminal) 173
PMT (Photo-mechanical transfer) 173
Point size 161–164, 171
Post-production 122, 128–142
Post-syncing 122, 133–134
Posters 29, 43–44, 185
Pre-production 90–95
Presenters 50–51
Pre-transmission clearance 78, 136
Primary colours 101, 108, 191–193
Printing processes 175–185

Process colours 192–193
Proctor & Gamble 14
Production companies 79–81
Progressives 194
Promise 14–15
Proofing 182–183, 194–195
 *see also* Text proofing
Propaganda 24
Proportional spacing 168
Public Relations 2, 34–35, 157
Puns 28, 147, 149
Puzzles 29, 31

Quad 111, 114
Qualcast 148
Quantel
 Harry 139
 Mirage 140–142
 Paintbox 125–126

Radio 1, 39–42
Rawlings 29
Recipient 37
Red Star 54, 148
Reeves, Rosser 8, 14–18, 20, 47
Release prints 105, 136–137
Rembrandt 9
Repeat fees 83, 87, 92–95
Reproducing pictures 186–197
Retouching 187, 196
Reversing-out 160, 170, 180
Rhys-Jones, Griff 54
Rice Krispies 42
Rodgers, Everett 13
Rolling Stones 83, 126
Rolls Royce 20
Rolo 93
Rossini 57
Rossiter, Leonard 28
Rough cut 77, 131–132
Rushes 122, 130

Sainsburys 38
Salesman 2, 26, 37
Sales promotion 2, 8
Salience 49–50, 168
Salignac 153–155
Sans serif 158–161, 163, 167
Scanning 180, 182, 193–194
 *see also* Frame rate (TV) *and* Field
Scatter proofs 195

Schafline 187, 189–191
Schweppes 29, 146
Scitex 193
Scraperboard 191
Screen angle 192–193
Screen printing 176, 184–185
Screen size 187–191
Script layout and terms 62–63, 66–74
Scriptwriter
  see Copywriter
SECAM 110
Self-persuasion 26
Senefelder, Alois 179
Series of type 162
Serif 158–161, 163, 166, 183
Setting Room 158
Sex 28
SFX 73
Shah, Eddie 178
Sheraton 35
Shooting ratio 84–85
Shots
  classification of 67
  transitions between 70–72
Show-through 197
Silk Cut 29
Slice-of-life 50
Slow-motion 97
Slurring 197
Smirnoff 146, 148
Sony 5, 28, 93, 114
Sound 72–73, 103–105
Source effect 34–36, 38
Special effects 73, 86–87, 139–142
Springsteen, Bruce 83
Steenbeck 130
Stencilling 184
Stop-frame animation 123
Story appeal 20, 148, 150–151
Storyboard 61–66, 75
Stretch-printing 98
Strike frame 131
Strike-through 197
Strongbow 43
Studio versus location 81–82
Sub-heads 149
Subliminal use of media 39–40
*Sun* 38, 118
Super 49, 70, 74, 139–40
Sweeney, Pat 9

'Table top' 58
Teasers 29, 45
Ted Bates 8, 16–17
Telecine 115–116, 137
Teledata 47
Testimonials 55
Text proofing 173–174
Tilting 69
Time code 112–113, 137–139
Tints 191
Top-and-tailing 45
Toshiba 111
Tracking (camera) 67
Tracking (printing) 197
Transfer lettering 161, 173
Turner, Maurice 158
TV
  creative characteristics 45–48
  how it works 106–110
TV commercials
  approaches, techniques, forms 48–58
  pre-production and development of 75–95
  schematic evolution of 60
Typeface classification 158–161
Typesetting 170–174
Typesetting house(s) 157–158, 173
Type widths and weights 165
Typography 22–23, 145, 157–170

USP 14–21, 29, 144, 148, 153
U-Matic 114, 131, 137–139
Under colour removal 194

Vampire effect 28, 35
VHS 113–114
Video
  comparisons with film 115–119
  grammar of 106–114
Video camera 109, 194
Video effects generators 71
  see also Mirage
Video recording 110–114
Videotape formats/gauges 113–115
Vignettes 58
Visual puns 152
Visual transfer 41
Vladivar 43
Voice-over 72, 87, 133

# Index

Volkswagen 32–33, 147
Volvo 15
Vox, Maximilien 158

Waldie, Alan 128–129
Warhurst, Michael 80
Warhol, Andy 10, 185
Waterford 148
Weather insurance 88
Web-fed 176, 181, 197
Webster, Nicky 81
Welles, Orson 72

Wet-on-wet 196–197
White, Don 80
Wild track 134
Wilder, Billy 54
Wimpey Construction 55
Wipe 70–71, 118
Woolwich Building Society 93

x-height 161–162, 167

Ziessen, Meno 85
Zoom 67–68